FLOW STATE RUNNER

**Activate a
Powerful
Inner Coach's
Voice**

JEFF GRANT

Print Edition ISBN: 978-3-9524667-0-4
e-Book Edition ISBN: 978-3-9524667-1-1

Published in Switzerland by Hillseeker Publishing,
a division of Hillseeker Fitness GmbH.
Hillseekerpublishing.com

10 9 8 7 6 5 4 3 2
First Edition

Contents

For Mom and Dad

Thank you for supporting me every time I wanted to learn something new and for your endless love and encouragement.

Charity Support

Ten percent of the profits from the sale of *Flow State Runner* will go to support the Face-to-Face Project and non-profit organizations working to reduce the prevalence of childhood obesity.

The Face-to-Face Project provides impoverished communities with the tools and resources they need to break the cycle of poverty with a focus on permaculture and organic farming practices, health, and youth development. I've volunteered on site in Malawi and Cambodia with Face-to-Face and believe strongly in the positive impact of their approach.

For more information, including a link for donations, please visit the following link: http://flowstaterunner.com/charity/

Acknowledgements

"Alone we can do so little; together we can do so much."
— *Helen Keller*

<u>Starting to write</u> your first book is a major step, the culmination of years of thinking, "I should write a book one day," years of pondering topics, and years of doing other things instead of taking the plunge!

I started writing *Flow State Runner* about 24 years after my wife, Becky, said in response to a teenage note "you should be a writer" and 5 years after my long-time friend and college roommate Kevin Weathers started planting seeds for me to actually take that step by committing to write a book.

I am forever grateful of Becky's enduring support and love for nearly 30 years, especially during the 18 months this project took from start to finish, when she patiently listened over and over as I brainstormed, "thought out loud," and experienced a multitude of writer's high and low points. She once joked that she didn't need to listen to my podcast because she hears it <u>all the time</u>. Thank you for enduring that, Becky, and thank you for believing in me!

I am also thankful for all the runners I've coached over the years who encouraged me to organize my coaching guidance into a book. I appreciate your belief in my concepts and your persistence!

<u>Actually finishing</u> your first book: well, that turned into a huge endeavor that never would have reached the finish line were it not for a team of friends and supporters who stepped up at the right time with motivation, love, support, critical feedback, a reminder to play more, a reminder to work harder…you name it.

Thank you sincerely to all the runners and athletes who have entrusted me as your coach, especially those at the Hillseeker Training Center in Switzerland, from my online coaching practice, at SEALFIT and Unbeatable Mind, from my Wednesday night running group for several years in Zurich, and from my workshops at CrossFit gyms and fitness centers in Switzerland and the United States.

I would like to share a special thanks to the following friends, supporters, and sources of inspiration for their role in helping me develop and realize my vision with *Flow State Runner*.

Contributors and Interviewees: Thank you Charlie Baker, Sean Snyder, Michele Bierstadt, Mark Dowsett, Karen Meades, and Meg Lance.

Reviewers, Editors, Motivators: Thank you Becky Grant, Kiston Finney, Stephanie Hergenrader, Gwyneth Riebl, Eileen Pott, Karen Meades, Shane Gaherty, Leigh Pezzicara, Rachel Aarden, TJ Murphy, Peter Lewis, Danielle Gordon, Tara South, Jeff "Boomer" Alred, and Thomas & Christine Schlegel.

Cover and interior layout design: Thank you Oswald V. Cameron.

Teachers, Coaches and Mentors: Thank you Lisa Smith-Batchen, Nicholas Romanov, Guy Spier, Clay Cowdery, Cameron Shayne, Brad McLeod, Michael Ostrolenk, Matt Hart, Mark Divine, Catherine Divine, Joy & Ricardo, Rick Rushworth, Frank Hale, Doug Warner, Dr. Philip Jameson, Jamie Clarke and Dulce Aguilar, David Lertsin and Yuval Ayalon.

Authors and Thought Leaders: Thank you Mihaly Csikszentmihalyi, Steven Kotler, Jamie Wheal, Susan A. Jackson, and your colleagues in flow research, for lifetimes of passion and work in this domain.

Inspirations: Thank you Kevin Weathers, Glenn Wells, Bryon Powell (iRunfar.com), Dan Patitucci, Zach Even Esh, Mark Sisson, Robb Wolff, Kirk Parsley, M.D., Ray Zahab, Christopher McDougall, Dean Karnazes, Jeff Tucker, Tim Ferriss, Kelly Starrett, Ben Greenfield, Josh Trent, Sky and Tamara Christopherson, Joe Stumpf, Daniel Martin Eckhart, Tom Robbins, and Steven Pressfield.

Coaching Colleagues: Thank you to my coaching colleagues and friends in various countries, organizations, and events -- I greatly appreciate everything I've learned from you, as well as your friendship and inspiration. This includes Dave, Will, Lance, Shane, Dan, MJ, Derek, Rick, Faris, Chriss, Kyle, Pete, Charles, Danny, Sean, John, Mel, Tim, Noël, Gilles, Paul, and Wieland.

Friends: Thank you to my friends in Switzerland, who have become family and who have been wonderful listeners and supporters for all the years I dreamed of the book and started the project. That's you Spiess Family, Kat & Magnus, Thomas, Sylvain & Mathilde, Kate & Mark, Spike, Heather & Chris, Nick & Nicole, Fred, Bruno, Fowlds Family, Kathy & Carsten, Fiola, Nick, Stu, Nicolas & Janine, Mike, Ryan, Rahul, Chrigu & the BMB Family, Jayne, Howard & Fiona, Mike & Rachel, Naomi & Roli, Marco & Irena, Phil & Helen, Daniel & Jane, Birch Family, Debbie & Gurvinder, Rahel, Nadja, Robert & Stephanie, Simon & Lene, Moran & Simon, Andrew & Nadin, Abi, Kay, Emma, Paul, Christian, Jen, Rene, Ted, Marko, Matthias, Dana, Penny & Sean, Joe, Thomas & Louisa, Jan, Iris, Monson Family, Lynn, Tue & Jennifer, Stefan, Janosch, Lee, Santiago, Oscar, Kerri, Karen, Chris, Jonathan, Philippe, Barry & Michelle, Femi, and many others I'm sure to have accidentally overlooked, but appreciate no less.

Thank you as well to my dear yoga teacher friends around the world for your inspiration and counsel.

Thank you my friends in the US, Canada, UK, Netherlands, Germany, Thailand, Australia, New Zealand, Mexico, Chile and elsewhere who sent notes or posted messages of support during this project.

Family: Thank you to my parents, Garry and Shelia Grant, my parent-in-laws, Meg and Rick Lance, my sister, Jennifer Grant Dillard, and to Mark, Jessica, Mickey, Chris, Manisha, to my supportive and incredibly positive aunts and uncles, my grandmother, Mabel Harmon, my wife's grandmother, Inez Lance (1916-2001), and the rest of my family in the US — you have been an endless source of positivity and motivation!

Introduction

"A mentor is someone who sees more talent and ability within you, than you see in yourself, and helps bring it out of you."
— *Bob Proctor*

Thank you for the opportunity to coach you, to influence your running and to help bring out the best in you. It is an honor to be entrusted with the time you're spending reading and considering the concepts, lessons, and exercises in this book. Your confidence and curiosity inspire me to make a difference in your life — and that inspiration motivated me to write this book! During the pre-writing ritual I undertook every morning before penning these words, I visualized helping you make a difference in your running. This was incredibly inspiring. Thank you for the motivation! Let's jump right in to making that difference.

A harmonizing paradigm

There is no shortage of books offering running guidance. These span a wide range of topics, from training, fueling and performance to efficiency, speed, durability and injury prevention. Many of these works had a major role in my fulfillment as a runner and development as a coach.

While there is some excellent guidance out there, I am not satisfied with the full toolkit currently available for runners because there is a key element missing: it could be referred to as a harmonizing paradigm, an integrated model, or simply glue.

The existing knowledge blocks for runners are strong and powerful, but without glue, it is difficult to hold them together for consistent, practical application *on the run*. Specifically, I'm referring to a runner's ability to <u>package</u> the knowledge and <u>integrate</u> it into a regular and sustainable running practice.

The ability to remember and apply effective cues and actions is vital to increasing your performance and training awareness, especially when you are away from a coach or technique book, two and a half hours into a long run, in a rainstorm while running in the mountains, in the middle of soft sand sprints, intervals on a track, or your first 5K.

Being able to remember and integrate this knowledge, whether six months or six years after reading a book or attending a workshop is challenging. *Flow State Runner* offers a framework to consolidate and integrate key knowledge, and the tools to recall this framework as if a running coach is on your shoulder, appearing automatically to support you whenever needed.

The integrated Flow State Runner model combines physical technique, mental training, and spiritual connectedness. It is designed to be a "plug-and-play" model that is modular and harmonic.

In my coaching practice, the Flow State Runner model has worked well with a variety of running techniques, mobility practices, and in many ways, with life in general. It is a complement, rather than an alternative, to many effective running techniques. Its underlying driver is to develop and strengthen your Inner Coach's voice.

Aligning Mind and Body

Time and time again, I've seen runners develop one area of technical expertise, but fail to perform consistently with the efficiency, speed, or race readiness they desire. While runners may understand and practice various techniques, from mobilization to an effective foot pull, when the rubber meets the road (literally) something is missing. Many runners fail to realize the benefits they seek because they are unwittingly holding on to excessive tension and not effectively orienting their minds to overcome daily expectations and stress.

I see this general tendency often in the yoga students, business coaching clients, and athletes I work with, and as a coach this keeps me awake at night. These inspired people are so close to realizing their goals, yet are being held back. Without a harmonized view, integration of the best physical and mental techniques is not poised to happen on a consistent and sustainable basis. Likewise, when mind and body are not in alignment, reliably and consistently reaching flow and optimal performance is not going to happen.

Developing your Inner Coach

You may have already observed my repeated use of the word *integrate*. This is intentional and illustrative of my paradigm. I am an integrative learner and teacher, meaning that I study a broad range of topics and perspectives and then work to tie together key pieces, which often seem unrelated, at the right time for each individual to learn and advance themselves. My aim in this book is to teach you an important over-arching model that will support you while you practice your favorite running techniques, mobilizations, and training approaches. My mission is to help you develop an Inner Coach's Voice in your head — a voice that will integrate knowledge, will carry on long after you've finished reading this book, and will guide you toward long-term running efficiency, fitness, and enjoyment. I offer you the glue and guidance on where and how to apply it.

Managing Technology, Stress, and Overload

We live in a time of technological evolution when there is an app or platform for everything, yet we have a tendency to turn these potentially supportive tools into a torrent of overload. We turn more into less. From our self-imposed social media expectations and comparisons to overloaded inboxes and ever-growing communications options, we bring a lot to our minds, and then we turn to running to find relief and stillness from that overload.

Yet, technology is also pervasive in running, where our experiences run the risk of becoming increasingly detached from the moment as we focus primarily on tracking, sharing, and comparing rather than on experiencing running and life <u>in the moment</u>. The risk in our always-reachable, modern world is that we never reach our full potential because of how we approach a proliferating set of inputs, measures, messages, and "noise" in life.

In *Flow State Runner,* I will teach you a fresh perspective on technology and running, on yin and yang balance in your running practice, and on leveraging tools such as breathing, concentration, and visualization to help you thrive.

The Road to Flow

My aim is to help you advance your running practice in a sustainable manner that leads to higher performance and increased experiences of flow while on the road, trails, or in life in general. We'll dive into the world of flow, building a baseline understanding of the triple flow paradigms of neuroscience, sports psychology and spirituality, and learn how we can translate the flow cycle into running. I will teach you a way to integrate flow enablers into your running practice and to outsource handling of flow inhibitors to your Inner Coach. Thus, we'll work together to strengthen your Inner Coach, to expand your running playbook, and to quieten your Inner Critic.

My passion for coaching

I designed *Flow State Runner* to include a large amount of coaching input, from a super hero's utility belt of mind tools to guidance on training and workout design. I also dive into the topic of racing, where I provide pre- and post-race rituals and other valuable coaching insights.

This book is animated by what I've learned and developed on my 20-year quest to maximize fulfillment in my life, to pursue epic challenges, and to push past what I thought were my genetic limits. I'm not an elite runner — far from it. While I do have a collection of race medals across all distances — from my coveted first 5K to extreme ultra marathons and stage races — none are for podium finishes. Development as a runner was a challenge for me — nothing came easily, and I wouldn't have had it any other way. Overcoming this challenge yielded my special journey of learning and enabled me to become an effective coach.

Here's a look at how it unfolded:[1]

At 24-years old, I was seventy pounds (32kg) overweight and had been gaining weight steadily with each passing year. I led a sedentary lifestyle, firmly entrenched behind a desk in an IT job and on the sofa at home. My standard January ritual was to buy a new pair of running shoes with a commitment to "finally" start running. By the end of each year, those shoes were more at home in a fast food restaurant than on a running path. My wife would drag me out to the park with our spirited Cocker Spaniel puppy, and do her best to coax me into running just 400 meters. I never made it.

That all changed in 1996. I lost seventy pounds in nine months and finished my first Ironman, albeit with excruciating knee pain and a very ugly 6-hour limping marathon. I cried when I crossed the finish line, from the joy of making a dream a reality and also of finally wearing out a pair of New Year's resolution running shoes by actually <u>running</u> in them!

That year of training and the final exam of the Ironman was a transformational experience and launched me on a fulfilling and healthy path. That first Ironman finish came at a cost, leaving me with a long list of runner's injuries. I didn't have a clue what I was doing when it came to training or taking care of my body, but I was hooked and went on to finish numerous Ironman triathlons and ultra-marathons over the following years. I also set off on a path of building a strong knowledge base in endurance training and racing, originally to prevent my own injuries and improve my performance, and later to coach others.

My quest led me to work with many great coaches and mentors, including the infamous ultra-marathoner Lisa Smith-Batchen, endurance sports writer Matt Hart, founder of Pose Method® Dr. Nicholas Romanov, Kancho Cameron Shayne of Budokon® University, and retired US Navy SEAL Commander Mark Divine, founder of SEALFIT®. I am grateful to each of them for lessons that have supported me along the way and helped inspire those I coach each day.

Following years of training runners and triathletes as a second job, I began coaching full-time in 2010 and made building better runners and helping people improve their lives my full-time life pursuit. I have now taught thousands of runners directly and many more indirectly through workshops in Europe and the US, at the SEALFIT® Academy in Encinitas, California, and via online programs, such as Hillseeker®, Unbeatable Mind® and SEALFIT®.

My passion is coaching. It's the fire behind a rocket-fueled approach to life that leaves me buzzing with each opportunity to work in-person or virtually with runners, athletes, moms and dads, teens, executives, and anyone else who wants to learn a new paradigm and improve themselves. I've directed that passion into developing this resource to have a profound impact on your running.

Value of Running

Running has not only been transformational in my life, it has been a constant that I've relied on time and time again for establishing and maintaining health, fitness, and balance. Running has kept me balanced during years of intense work with an expat job in the finance industry. Running kept me fit while traveling to over forty countries. Running kept me healthy when faced with the distractions and temptations of our modern-day lifestyle. Running brought me new friendships, valuable on-the-move chats and priceless connections with others through training, racing and coaching. Running inspired me to experience amazing adventures and led me to experience moments that I'll never forget, from epic desert and mountain runs to simple but beautiful Sunday afternoon runs in the sun with my wife.

I hope running already is, or soon becomes, equally valuable to you. I want you to be a healthy, effective runner, to realize your dreams and goals, and to smile when you finish your first twenty-minute run, first 10K, first marathon, first ultra-marathon, or whenever you discover the joy of achieving even more than you thought possible.

Roadmap

Section 1 comprises Chapters 1-10. This section holds the philosophical underpinnings of the Flow State Runner coaching model. It offers a broad primer on flow, lays out a supporting model for reaching flow state more often in running, and teaches the reader how to develop a powerful and lasting Inner Coach's voice. Section 1 also covers physical running techniques, breathing, awareness and mind training, integrated learning and much more. It ends with a very insightful coaching FAQ. These chapters will flow best when read in order.

Section 2 comprises Chapters 11-15. This section is full of mental training tools, workouts, guidance for racing, insights on technology, and more. These chapters are resources that can be read in any order. You'll likely want to refer to these in the future when planning training and preparing for events.

Section 1

1. *Experiencing Flow State in Running*

*"Shibumi has come to denote those things that exhibit in paradox and
all at once the very best of everything and nothing:
Elegant simplicity. Effortless effectiveness.
Understated excellence. Beautiful imperfection."*
— *Matthew May, The Shibumi Strategy*

The Gift of Flow State at the Marathon des Sables, Morocco

With helicopters buzzing overhead, camels moving about and sand
blasting every exposed skin surface, today's stage of the race is off and
the first steps (well, the first few hours' worth of steps) feel, let's just
say, "very uncomfortable."

My strategy is to run in the lead pack up to the first big climb (at
the 4KM mark). The climb is so steep that a fixed line is installed near
the top. This section also contains loose rock and a narrow passage, so
the race organizers tell racers to expect delays. I want to avoid waiting
in a queue at all expense, so I know that I need to be in the top 10 or
so when the climb starts. I believe that once I'm on steep mountainous
terrain that my passion for hills will take over and I'll get up the incline
quickly on pure adrenaline. Once over the big climb, I plan to run 9
minutes hard and walk 1 minute fast — over and over until I reach the
finish line 8 or more hours later.

I repack my front pack several times to ensure that I can locate
everything quickly, by feel. My compass is the most handy — just in

case I need to navigate through a maze of sand dunes (assuming that I am in one of the leading groups). I also have quick access to anti-inflammatory meds, salt tablets, and food. I don't plan to stop for any breaks, so all my nutrition will be on the run or during walk breaks. I will unscrew my water bottle tops during the final 10 meters leading in to each aid station and stop only long enough to fill the bottles with water. I will speed-walk all the steep inclines and run the downhills all out — even if rocky or sandy. I will ignore the knee pain, and if that proves impossible, I'll focus on the pain and turn it into its own energy source.

I don't know how I can race an 80KM/50-mile stage in the week-long Marathon des Sables with legs that are already trashed and a knee that hurts so much I had to limp to the start line today, but I intend to do anything and everything possible to make today the best racing experience of my life. If supernatural is possible, I want today to be the day I experience it. Formerly overweight, sedentary and with a background that included Husky-sized jeans more so than athletic genes, today's stage is more about proving to myself that transformation is possible and that there is an athlete hiding somewhere under my skin, waiting to be revealed at the perfect time.

Grandmothers & Village Girls

I know that I need all the mental and spiritual help I can get today. Drawing on the power of visualization and dedication, I decide to dedicate the first three sections of today's stage to my grandmothers. In turn, each section brings its own gift — which I felt were gifts from them. My dad's mother brings me surprise winds at my back during the first hour (which served to lighten my heavy legs); my mom's mother brings me inner strength and a palm-tree laden oasis during the second half of the race when the heat is at its maximum and terrain is very challenging; and my wife's grandmother brings me a special experience that I'll share in a bit more detail below. It is a special time spent thinking about each of these important, warm, and loving women in my life and this helps me in many, many ways to make it through today's stage.

During the segment I've dedicated to my late grandmother-in-law, I exit a particularly lonely stretch of desert and approach a village. The heat, lack of sufficient calories, and general state of my body (wrecked) is creating a struggle. I'm relegated to willing myself to make every step. As the village comes into view, two little girls run out from under the shade of a tree. They grab my hands and start running with me. They're not wearing shoes and we are now on a surface with rocks scattered about, but the rocks do not concern them. No more than seven years old, these girls pull me through the sand for nearly a kilometer. They beam with huge smiles and continue to look up at me and giggle — all the while running fast enough to pull me across the undulating terrain. They finally let go of my hands and turn for their village. I am touched and elated and decide that this was clearly positive energy from my grandmother-in-law. Divine? Coincidence? Imagination? It doesn't matter. These little girls helped me through a tough spot at a time I was focusing my thoughts on someone special in my life. It is a wonderful connection and it elevates my spirits in a huge way.

A visualized peloton of friends

As I enter the final 11 kilometers, after 8 hours of desert running, I feel utterly exhausted. The strength of my grandmothers has powered me through most of today's stage, but with temperatures that have topped 120F/52C, I am running on fumes. During this last stretch, the winds intensify — HOT headwinds. I need help. I need support. I need to take control to make something special happen, to control my own destiny.

I begin to envision my friends appearing across the desert. They approach in two large groups, coming from both sides. They swoop in front and beside me, forming a peloton to shield me from the wind. As if we're all cycling now, they take turns pulling and each drops back to ride right in front of me — offering an encouraging word along the way. I see their faces and hear them shout "stay on my wheel Jeff, stay on my wheel!" They are working hard and taking this very seriously — sacrificing themselves to take the wind for me. They are putting in a maximum effort to pull me through the most challenging of moments. I can see them suffering — riding at their limits and working as a team to aid me at what is nearly my breaking point. The strength I feel from this visualization is surreal. Whenever my mind starts to wander and starts to think about the pain, the lack of a visible finish line in the distance, the headwind, the heat, the hills — I refocus on my peloton of friends and my energy level surges.

I approach a large section of sand dunes, steep and with very soft sand. Rather than dig into the sand, losing ground with each step, I float on top of it. Each step is quick, light and effortless. My gaze is soft, yet intent and focused. Other adversities seem to melt away. No longer am I thinking of the wind, heat, or pain in my feet.

The surreal feeling when perceived limits are exceeded

An hour passes and the finish line finally comes into view. The peloton quietly peels off to the side and disappears into the desert, leaving me to finish alone. I launch myself across the last kilometer of the desert sand to the finish line at top speed. I cross the line and break down in tears. I'm always emotional at finish lines, but it hits me hard today. Today's performance is far, far beyond previous estimations of my capabilities. The race organizers pull me aside for a gear inspection, to ensure that I hadn't cut weight by omitting mandatory equipment. I am stunned by a situation I find utterly surreal in the moment. I tell them that there must be a mistake in my position in the stage. I am in disbelief -- surely 200 runners have already crossed the finish line. They assure me that only one runner crossed the finish line before me at that point, so there was no mistake. (Naturally, I passed the inspection.)

Aside from survival, I accomplished my goal that day to maintain a high position in the overall standings. More importantly, I experienced the desert's magic and shared some wonderful mental energy and heart-warming thoughts with friends, family, and even Moroccan children. I experienced flow state.

Flow State Illustrated

This is what it is like to enter the world of flow. In Japanese, Shibumi or Shibusa is roughly translated as effortless perfection. Diving deeper into the meaning, we learn that it represents both an overarching appearance of simplicity, with an underlying impressive level of detail, texture or complexity. What appears to be a simple object or action is revealed to be full of meaning, deep beauty and seemingly effortless connections, meanings and details. Shibumi applied to running means integrating myriad details and complexities in such a way that it is easily, smoothly, and effortlessly implemented when needed. It means entering your flow state and becoming a Flow State Runner.

When one enters flow, everything trivial, everything non-essential to performance melts away. This is the state that Olympians aspire to reach in their critical moment of athletic performance. This is the state a musician experiences when performing a flawless performance in a large concert hall, or even alone when practicing his or her art and fully connecting mind and body. In flow, everything simply "clicks."

When I reached this state in the Marathon des Sables, the pain from my knee injury and from 3 prior days of desert ultra running disappeared. I was able to hold a pace I couldn't fathom. My legs were light and free. I was happy, joyfully fulfilled, and I performed at the peak of my capacity.

Reaching flow state is a powerful experience. It's a secret weapon that transcends physical techniques and mental tricks. It's the integral result — the coming together of all key building blocks of mind, body, and spirit — and the unleashing of one's greatest potential. Perhaps you get there in a BIG way (like in an epic race) or a small way (like a lunch run on a stressful day, where you re-enter your office completely transformed and finishing a day's work in two hours). It is an equally beautiful experience either way. What's important is that you recognize the existence of flow and organize the building blocks in this book to enable yourself to enter the flow state. To be clear, you MAKE this happen. Flow rarely shows up uninvited.

Inspiring you to experience flow state and teaching you to use it to improve your running technique and performance in both training and racing is a key aim in this book. If it transfers over to other areas of your life, even better. I cover flow from many angles and offer a series of exercises to help you on your own journey. I also offer additional resources for those interested in making a deep dive into this fascinating realm.

What is your motivator?

Consistently experiencing flow in running comes with an important prerequisite: you need to define what is the most important to you — in your running, at this time. In other words, what is your <u>motivator</u>? And I'm not talking about a loose definition like "I want to be a better runner." You need a clear driver.

Strong, clear goals are worded like *I <u>want</u> to do X* or *I <u>must</u> experience Y or I strive to <u>be</u> or <u>feel</u> Z*. Weak goals are a) undefined, b) vague, c) unrealistic. Set your sights on identifying clear and strong motivators in your running.

By the way, audacious goals are powerful motivators, but carefully consider what is audacity in a powerful, effective sense (*I will finish my first marathon*) and what is unrealistic in your current situation, for example targeting an Olympic record time as a new runner.

For some, the core running motivator is the same as what is the most important in their life at a given time. This was the case for me for much of the past 20 years, especially around peak endurance events, but it has varied from year-to-year and through different periods of my life.

For others, it's just a small piece in the puzzle of life. It could be as simple as "I want to run injury-free and lose 10 pounds" or as all-encompassing as "I want to run a marathon on every continent in 7 days."

It could also be intensely personal, such as honoring a relative or living a life to celebrate health or recovery from a life-threatening sickness.

Here are some examples from my experiences as well as others who have been kind enough to share:

My motivators over the years

At most given moments, I know what's the most important to me as a runner — what my chief motivator is. During my first 5K, it was to prove to myself that I had secured a transformation and *deserved* a place as a fit and healthy person. Once I proved that I deserved that place myself, I realized that everyone who wants to be a fit and healthy person deserves it. Later it was about discovery (*I want to know what it is like to finish a 10K*), quantifiable performance (*I want to see if I can break 3 hours in a marathon and 6 minutes for a mile*), exploring limits (*I will run 100 miles in the mountains to see what that journey is all about*), teamwork (*I want to be tested as a leader after being exhausted and not sleeping for 3 days*), and even entertainment (*I want to run a race where my entire focus is on making others laugh by carrying a 10-foot long alphorn and giving concerts along the way*). Sometimes these reasons started as questions (*is it possible for me to do x?*), and then became missions or mantras. At times my motivators have been so strong that I would have taken great risks to achieve my goal. At other times, they were merely drivers to offset intense workloads or optimize my performance.

My earliest motivator as a runner was "I am a new person and will never return to my couch potato days!". My mission for the Ultra Trail du Mont Blanc ultra marathon was "You must finish this race," with a simple mantra I repeated a thousand times of "courage," which I'll revisit in a later chapter.

Over the past few years, my motivation is simply to serve others, with a mission that has evolved to the following, which I'm able to articulate clearly:

> To help others improve their lives through my strong positive energy and passion, smile and humor, and commitment to self-mastery. To maximize the use of my unique experiences, lessons from mentors, and personality to inspire others and make a difference in the world via coaching, giving talks, and writing.

While helping you find the meaning of life would bring us both lots of joy (I imagine!), it's quite a bit out of the realm of this book. That said, to reach Flow State as a runner, it's extremely important for you to have some sense of what is important to you right now in your running world. What is your motivator? Is it to run more efficiently so that you can finish an ultra marathon? Run faster in a local 5K? Run with less impact so that you don't injure yourself? Become a better CrossFit athlete? Honor your grandmother/father, your community, your school?

It's going the change and that's OK — it SHOULD change, morph, evolve, zigzag, just as our journeys through life do.

In their own words

Next, a group of five runners share in their own words their insightful experiences with motivators.

Karen

For me, it is about being 90 years old — sitting in a rocking chair — telling a story. It is a story of my life — and it rocks! It is a story of love, adventure and taking risks. My external motivator was my mother who did nothing other than complain throughout my childhood. She didn't like her husband, her job, her life, she was afraid of everything — AND did nothing about it. My mother and I had some amazing conversations as I got older and was able to tell her she was my motivation to live life as large as I live it — she was the one I didn't want to be.

She told me she simply, humbly, she had no idea how I accomplished the things I did! In the end she was proud of me and I had an amazing understanding of how you could end up like her.

Sean

I've always maintained a lifestyle focus as my primarily motivator. My initial motivator was to get healthier and lose weight. That was a powerful motivator in my late 20s. I lost a lot of weight, shifted my motivator to keeping the weight off, and then again shifted it to completing races, both for the adventure and for the power of having a time-boxed goal to seek. I started with 5Ks and gradually grew the goals to half marathons, marathons and ultras.

In between times when I was race-focused, I always went back to the healthy lifestyle focus. Running is easy and one of the cheapest forms of exercise. All I need is a pair of shoes... or sometimes no shoes at all — so it has been very portable, which fits my job where I have to travel at times, as well as my lifestyle as a father of a young child.

Running is also good for mental health, allowing me to spend time thinking, solving problems, planning or just creating stillness in my mind. In recent years though, it's the adventure that motivates me. While I enjoy having a familiar route at times, what really excites me is going out and making it up as I go, jumping over things as I run, running through water, dodging things, varying the terrain, running sideways/backwards. This keeps it fresh, adds a refreshing jolt of energy to my day and makes me want to come back for more.

I remember how running was used in football practice as a punishment. Miss a tackle and the coach sends you on 2 laps, don't show enough energy or get caught talking and your sentence is 4 laps. Now I see it as a reward, my play time, and I just want to stay healthy and fit enough to enjoy this reward whenever I want!

Mark

I am definitely not a natural athlete. I enjoyed most sports as a kid, without displaying any particular ability at any of them. Oh, and I hated running!

Things changed in my late twenties when I had cause to move between several countries within 12 months. Running became a way for me to keep fit and discover my new homes. Over time, I came to enjoy running longer and when I stumbled across the classic challenge of a local half marathon, I took it on, got the t-shirt, and the bug for racing.

The next few years involved chasing personal bests and greater challenges: full marathons, trail races, and then the exotic world of adventure racing and ultra marathons, culminating in the 95k CCC (Courmayeur Champex Chamonix) race around Mont Blanc.

Then came the crash. After 7 years of planning, training and racing ever bigger races and successfully completing the foothills of my 'Everest' goal — the CCC being the little brother of the renowned UTMB (Ultra Trail du Mont Blanc) - I no longer had any desire to race. I had no injuries and other than a massive storm, the race had gone as much to plan as 20 hours of mountain running can. Nonetheless, suddenly I had no interest in either the UTMB or any other race.

Although I continued to run, it took almost 2 years and dozens of books to find my motivation again. As he does in so many things, Dan John gave me the most clarity: firstly, to 'Keep the Goal the Goal' and secondly in his distinction between Health and Fitness. In this context, I realized that the thing that inspired me most was my friend's father skiing with us in his 70's! The ability to move well as we get older is the most impressive thing I can imagine, as it demonstrates the outcome of a lifelong pursuit of Health, which is accessible to us all.

Consequently, I realized that my greatest motivation as the father of 2 young children is not only to teach them to move well, but to train myself with the goal of being able to mountain bike and snowboard with my grandchildren!

Michele

My motivation has certainly changed during my running "career." It's hardly a career, but I don't know what else to call it. When I first started running, my motivation was best described as obligation. I had just been accepted to West Point, and you have to run 2 miles during a physical fitness test in the Army, so I trained to run 2 miles — that's it, I wasn't planning to do any more than that. Then, my next motivation to run longer was boredom. I was stationed in Guantanamo Bay after college, and we worked 6 days a week. There was NOTHING else to do except drink at the officer's club, or run on the 10-mile stretch of land on the base. I chose to run with a fellow officer, and that's what we did every day when we weren't working. That's when I first realized how good it felt to run, and how it cleared my mind and took away the stress of my day. I actually started to feel comfortable as I started to go longer, and I became hooked.

As I started to run more, I entered short races and started improving quickly. It is easy to improve when you are doing something new and begin to work hard at it! Out of this rapid improvement phase grew motivation to compete and constantly challenge myself. I stayed in this mode for many years and began to pick harder and harder races and distances. I moved from 10Ks to marathons and then the 50-mile and 100-mile distance, always looking for more of a challenge and trying to continue pushing myself to go longer or get faster. When I trained, my motivation for getting out the door was to prepare for a specific race I had signed up for.

I have a family now, and a young daughter, and I find that my motivation is changing yet again. I no longer want to race, and I feel like I've done enough 100-milers and have no desire to put in the training to do more. Instead, my motivation has moved to peace of mind and adventure seeking. I have no races on my calendar this year, nor do I feel a need to do one. Instead, I run every morning with my dog because it is the best way to start my day. I can think clearly during my runs, I feel close to God, and my stress seems to melt away during a long run because it is so peaceful. I have seen so many things on the trails that I wouldn't be able to see otherwise, and I have learned to really appreciate being able to do so. I ran the Grand Canyon a couple years ago with a friend, and just got back from a weekend running across Bryce Canyon with twenty-nine other ultra-runners. It wasn't a race, just a run with some people that share my passion and were there to push their limits while enjoying nature at the same time. Just like my adventure run at the Marathon des Sables many years ago, the things I took away from this Bryce Canyon run were appreciation for my health, our amazing gift of nature, and the friendships I built for a lifetime with people I knew for only 2 weeks. That is my motivation now, to experience new things and get to know myself better, and share experiences with others whom I connect with on a level that words can't express. That's quite a progression over time, I think.

Charlie Baker

Running has meant a lot to me. It has kept me in good shape and kept my mind on my objective. I love racing. You need to work on it though. There is a certain amount of training which you have to do, but I absolutely love it. Had I not been in the Senior Olympics I probably would have already died.

Author's note: Charlie Baker is a role model of mine. At 87, he has earned a collection of medals, many of them Gold, in the National Senior Olympics Games in the United States. He shares perhaps the most powerful motivator I have ever heard: <u>life</u>. We'll revisit Mr. Baker's remarkable story in a bit.

Extraordinary learning

Retired US Navy SEAL Commander, Author and Coach Mark Divine, founder of Unbeatable Mind and SEALFIT, teaches that warriors strive to do "both ordinary and extraordinary things extraordinarily well." As the physical act of running is indeed "ordinary," this is exactly the aim of runners seeking a higher level of performance. By doing ordinary running extraordinarily well, we enable ourselves to do extraordinary running (long distances, obstacle course races, running under load), extraordinarily well.

First though, we must practice the art of extraordinary learning, a journey that we can accelerate by identifying uncommon, exceptional performance in others, including those in vastly different activities, and then mapping their key performance traits to our activities. This approach takes many learners *out of the box*, as it involves imitation both within and outside of a targeted discipline. It is the cross-application of knowledge. Simply put, I'm indeed suggesting something along the lines of studying piano to improve your running skills and studying swimming to improve your knife-sharpening skills!

When teaching runners, I frequently use the term transference — in other words, experiencing something vividly and then transferring that experience and applying it to another area. It is a valuable tool in any type of learning process. When we broaden it to running and then think outside the box of mirroring what other runners do, we open ourselves up to an infinite world from which to learn. With this expansive view, there is a much greater chance of finding a connection and resonance with lessons that *click and stick*.

Here's a very simple example to illustrate:

Skip several steps normally and then tense your feet, ankles and lower legs. Hold that tension and now skip again. It's likely the most awkward skipping you've ever attempted, right? Immediately after attempting tense skipping, skip normally again and notice how relaxed your lower legs, ankles, and feet feel. Now alternate between this type of gentle skipping and running, and try to make your lower limbs feel just as supple when running as when skipping. Notice a difference? That's transference, in this case, of a feeling and perception.

<u>And here's a more complex example:</u>

Lift an arm and stare at your hand. Now lower your hand. Pull out your smartphone or any type of stopwatch. Lift your arm again and start a 1-minute countdown timer. Stare at your fingertips as you take the entire minute to lower your hand as smoothly as possible and in constant motion. Focus intently for maximum smoothness. Try it one more time, but envision that you are in a medieval castle entertaining the King and your livelihood and perhaps even your life depends on your ability to execute this movement flawlessly without the slightest pause, jitter or hesitation. Are you ready? 3, 2, 1 Go!

One minute later: Did you remember to breathe for that minute? I hope so, but it is common to hold your breath when tasked with something of this nature. I also hope you experienced a moment of deep focus and concentration. Now, remember what that focus felt like, capture the feeling completely, and go have a conversation with someone, transferring that same level of focus to your listening skills. You may be surprised at what you hear or perhaps at how difficult it is to listen with the same level of focus. It is a great practice in active listening and building awareness and also serves a good example of the concept of transferring an experience from one activity to another vastly different activity.

Learning from others

Below is a series of stories from vastly different perspectives. Each contains something special about flow state performance that we can examine, mirror and transfer into our running.

Kids

There is much to learn from kids about efficient running and it's simple: don't try, simply play. Watch kids run and you'll quickly notice that running is in most cases their secondary focus. Their primary focus is to tag a playmate, kick a ball, or in a giggly trot, not let Mom or Dad catch them. So, what happens when running is the secondary focus, or actually, not even a focus at all? Its natural efficiency surfaces. In kids, the key elements of efficient running technique occur naturally with no thought or special effort from the runner. Much of what adult runners break in terms of their running technique, kids do right because they are not thinking about it and they are in play mode (something adults are very good at forgetting). Kids are exceptional at finding and keeping flow when running and we can learn a lot by mirroring their approach. I used this approach in a mountain trail marathon race once to snap myself out of a negative attitude that was about to consume me and derail my race. On a short descent, I simply started running nearly out of control with arms flailing and a big stupid grin, channeling my inner 5-year old. It made me laugh and quit taking things so seriously. It also loosened me up and that made a huge difference in rebounding mentally as well as physically.

Key takeaways:

- Playfulness of running / smile & laugh
- Feet <u>reacting</u> to keep up with a falling body, as if running itself is a surprise and may only be stopped by bumping into another object (hopefully soft!)
- Low tension level throughout the body, as evidenced by frequently falling out of the run or simply sitting down (for the little ones)

Musicians

Music has always been an important part of my life, and I spent my youth and university days pursuing mastery of the trombone. This is a tricky instrument to play because the notes are produced with a combination of air speed, lip tension, and the length of the piping the musician selects for each note. The trombonist selects this by allowing the slide to pause at the exact right place for a given note and then synchronizing air, lip buzzing and articulation. It gets really challenging when there are many different notes, tightly packed together at a fast tempo. To novice trombonists it seems impossible to move the slide quickly enough to reach all the notes and to do so with the accuracy required for the music to be in tune and pleasant to the listener's ears.

I learned a valuable lesson from Dr. Philip Jameson, my music professor at the University of Georgia. He taught me that when faced with a technically demanding section of music, to practice without making sounds, just visualizing playing the right notes while moving the slide back and forth as smoothly as possible and with as little tension as possible. Once those neural pathways were greased for low tension, high speed movement, the sounds and notes could be added in gradually and only as long as the same movement pattern persisted. The concept was to metaphorically *crawl* with low tension and high speed. Then walk. Then run. And most importantly, greet the technical passage with relaxation and confidence, rather than tension and insecurity. This approach worked very well in my budding musicianship and offered broader applications when faced with complexity in life. I learned quite a bit about how to tackle complexity through these studies.

What does a musician's approach to performing challenging musical sections have to do with running? Think about what happens when you approach a steep hill or the final 200m of an 800m interval and you will likely find the answer. Your ability to be a virtuoso as a runner is linked very closely to a musician's virtuosic abilities, which must be practiced and refined over time, but rarely simply ever just happen.

Key takeaways:

- General tension level must be at its minimum to execute technical movements or face adversity and challenges.
- Developing musicians must master the concept of thinking and playing <u>through</u> a passage of notes instead of experiencing overload by becoming affixed on each individual note. The same applies to running in technical terrain.
- An intrinsic, passionate connection to an activity is where the magic of flow happens, as the activity goes beyond execution of the physical to expression of the integral.

Desert runners

As I raced the Marathon des Sables, I noticed how effortlessly the Moroccan runners moved over the soft sand in the dunes sections. As each runner must carry food and survival gear for a week, runners are not light on the dunes, but the Moroccan runners appeared weightless. I watched them time and time again seemingly float on top of the sand, while I (and many of my compatriots) would punch through the sand with every labored step, often losing 1 step for every 2 we took.

At first I was frustrated watching the master desert runners in the dunes, often from an increasingly growing gap behind them. I quickly changed my paradigm and switched to learning-mode, a much healthier place than jealousy-mode. Immersed in a more beneficial paradigm, I unwittingly began my journey into unlocking efficient running technique for myself by simply observing and mirroring these hyper-efficient runners. While my initial focus was on their zero gravity foot strike, I later shifted the focus to their body language, overall body positioning, and even their faces and carried the lessons into how I coach running. To this day I mirror their running approach every time I'm fortunate enough to run on soft sand.

Key takeaways:

- Adapt to your environment
- Light, quick steps with a floating landing
- Low body tension, especially on the softest, steepest terrain or other adversities

Dogs

I am often greeted when I arrive at my training center by an enthusiastic dog, a lab named Daisy. She'll sprint up to me, receive her welcome head scratch, sprint into a field, sprint to get her Frisbee, dash back for another quick visit, trot over to her owner, dart side to side with unbridled enthusiasm to go — somewhere — anywhere. Maybe back into the field again, or up the hill, or down the hill. Who cares? "I just wanna RUN," her body language says!

Daisy had a massive hip operation a year ago, so it's even more amazing how well she has returned to running. When I watch her run, I always think about how well dogs embrace running for the joy of play and of movement. They are also very agile, with the ability to go from running in circles chasing their tails to quick direction changes while chasing Frisbees and balls. And when they see a bird or squirrel, an instinctual focus takes over and the On/Off switch for speed is simply turned ON.

Run like Daisy!

Key takeaways:

- Speed is always a simple on-off option. Enter into it with minimal tension (especially in shoulders and neck) and with a chaser's mindset.
- Keep it playful. Run for the joy of the movement with the same unconditional love approach of a dog.

- Incorporate agility moves and fluid direction changes running to improve virtuosity.

Yogis

Yoga is a fascinating art and ancient science. Watch a trained yogi simply breathe and move and you will see an impressive level of kinesthetic awareness. You may also observe an outer stillness (low tension level) that leads to an inner stillness (calm, quiet mind). Lastly, you will see respect: respect for self, for others, for the practice and movement, and for the training space.

I started practicing yoga 20 years ago, as I trained for my first Ironman triathlon. Its impact on my daily life as well as on my endurance sports performance and recovery, motivated me to become a yoga teacher and to find great joy in sharing it with others. Try yoga yourself and you will be opening a new world that can positively influence your mind, body and spirit.

If you already practice yoga regularly, then reflect on what aspects of yoga could be transferred into your running.

Key takeaways:

- Body awareness and connection to breath
- Patience and self-respect of our unique bodies and physiology
- Calm face, relaxed jaw and shoulders

Blind Runners

For non-marathoner readers, have you ever considered what it would be like to run 42KM (26.2 miles)? Imagine the average number of steps taken in a marathon run. For most, it's in the range of 45,000-55,000. For each of those steps, assuming you have vision, imagine what you see with each step: the runners all around you, the colors, the obstacles, distance marker signs, aid stations, your hands, your legs, your torso, the sky, trees, buildings, hills, bridges, etc. Now consider for a moment that you see nothing — pure darkness. For many, the initial reaction could be frightening. With sight turned off, turn to your other senses. What do you hear? The sounds of feet, of your breath and others, street music, the wind, an airplane, vehicles, birds, water. What do you smell? The bakery you just ran past. Coffee. Other runners. What do you feel? Tension. Relaxation. Busy mind. Still mind. Positive. Negative.

When one sense is turned off, by choice or life, others often flourish, as if their individual volume knob has been turned up. When these senses are awakened or highlighted, we receive new inputs, which we can use to refine our mind/body/spirit approach to running.

I frequently use eyes-closed exercises when coaching runners, and the results always make a big impression.

Key takeaways:

- Awareness, connectedness and appreciation for non-visual inputs and how your body and mind function
- Trust of your body and non-visual perceptions
- Joy for the movement (sounds, air, smells, etc.)

Soldiers and Law Enforcement Officers ("LEO")

I am very fortunate to coach a wide mix of athlete groups, including current and aspiring military and law enforcement professionals in Europe and the United States. I love working with these men and women. I honor their work and commitment, and I believe that their ability to run efficiently has great potential to optimize their tactical effectiveness and perhaps even preserve lives.

Soldiers and LEO have many difficult tasks to perform in their daily work, tasks that are rarely solely running, but that may be influenced by their ability to run efficiently. Think of it in these terms: Run like your life and your teammate's lives depend on not only the run, but what you must do when you arrive at the destination. If these professionals run inefficiently, they risk creating a liability for themselves and their team and diminishing the scope of success for their task at hand. Running is one of many tools they seek to develop, for conditioning benefits as well as tactical performance.

Key takeaways:

- Running as a tool where economy results in an optimized ability to perform a core job
- Running style must be adaptable and reproducible throughout a variety of changing environments and variables, including adverse terrain and running under load, carrying gear and wearing awkward footwear, clothing, and body armor.
- Awareness requirements are high (threat assessment, situational awareness, obstacles, mission), thus flow is imperative.

Adaptive Athletes

As I started my lecture on efficient running at a SEALFIT Academy the autumn of 2013, I noticed that a front row participant was wearing a blade prosthetic leg. I asked him about it and learned that while serving as a US Marine in Afghanistan, he sacrificed his leg from the knee down in a bomb attack. Yet, here he was about to tackle a week of intensive physical training followed by a 50-hour non-stop, no-sleep physical and mental toughness crucible known as Kokoro Camp (where the athletes cover far more than a marathon on foot and complete an exhausting array of other audacious physical challenges). It was an honor to meet him, thank him for his service, and be influenced with his incredible positive energy. As I lectured though, I was wondering "how do I teach him efficient running?"

I hadn't previously worked with adaptive athletes and wasn't quite sure how to approach it. I went with honesty: "I want to help you, but

I have no idea if what I'm about to teach will work for you. Keep what does and let's work together to find a better way for whatever doesn't. First, tell me exactly what you do to make that blade work."

This approach worked great for him. We learned from each other: he learned about running and I learned about heart. He finished the grueling 50-Hour Kokoro Camp. He later became a SEALFIT coach and founded American Military Leaders of Tomorrow (AMLOT).

Key takeaways:

- No excuses. There is no room for self-pity, jealousy, or complaining. Work with what you have.
- Heart conquers many mental barriers and physical obstacles.
- Run with joy for the movement.
- Move what you need to move where you need to move it with the minimum amount of effort required to move it. Don't overcomplicate it.

Japanese Tea Ceremony

Have you ever watched a Japanese Tea Ceremony? If not, please visit YouTube and have a look. It's a beautiful art, combining meticulously performed micro actions with flowing movement. The art of the performance is so special it has its own name in Japanese. The entire ceremony is delivered with incredible respect and focus. It is a shining example of flow. The fluidity of motion is mesmerizing and creates an instant feeling of relaxation. No motion is wasted or performed without extreme care. This includes how the fingers clasp a bowl (chawan) or fold the linen cloth (chakin). Movements are deliberate and never rushed. They follow in a well-rehearsed manner, but do not feel blocky or overly structured. No shortcuts are taken. When watching, one feels immersed in the moment; that nothing is more important to the host than honoring tradition and her guests.

Think back to the last time you drank a cup of tea or any warm beverage, including a pricey treat from your local Starbucks. Would you have viewed it differently had you been served the drink in a ceremony like this?

Recall your last run. Were there any elements of a Japanese Tea Ceremony present? If not, try to incorporate one on the next run.

Key takeaways:

- Respect for movement leads to respectful, smooth movements. Take the first step of every run as if it were the first movement of a Japanese Tea Ceremony and you'll be setting a much different feel for the rest of the run.
- Structure is required for flow, but the movement doesn't need to appear disjointed or choppy. Practice technique until the mechanical, structured aspects of it flow smoothly under an overarching air of calmness.
- Breathe like you want to move. Notice the calm, relaxed breathing of a Chanoyu host and the resulting motions in the body. This would not be possible any other way.

Senior Olympics Runners

As I mentioned earlier in this chapter, Charlie Baker is an inspiring role model as a Senior Olympian. He started competing in track and field events in his mid-60s. That's right, he decided in his mid-60s to take up the sport of sprinting, throwing and jumping. He lives across the street from my wife's parents, and each time we visit home, I have a few precious moments to catch up with him. The time feels selfish in a way, as I draw profound inspiration from each talk. I am utterly amazed with each conversation at his vitality and enthusiasm for not only lacing up his shoes to run, but to **compete**! In a May 2008 interview, Mr. Baker offered this simple, but valuable insight, "We don't quit playing because we get old, we get old because we quit playing."[2]

Mr. Baker enthusiastically shared his story for this book, speaking with a great sense of humility and focus on how his love for running and discovery of it later in life could perhaps inspire others. His huge collection of medals, many of them Gold, and his commitment to training are astonishing. Mr. Baker's insights spanned the practical to the motivational, with nuggets such as, "Do your exercise first, then sit and drink coffee. So many people do it backwards."

Speaking on his own experiences with flow, he offered, "I have had times when things are *right*. You will always feel good when things just feel *right* and you are doing the things you like to do." His true competitive nature shines through as well, with him sharing, "I do not like to lose in a real race. I always try to win — even in a practice run. Once you feel good about your fitness and form, stay close to the front so that you can pass others when the finish line is in sight."

Key takeaways:

- It is never too late to start your journey as a runner. Your running career starts when you decide it starts.
- Flow happens when you spend time doing the things you like to do.
- In Mr. Baker's words: "When you get into a new sport, get to know people in the sport and slowly build your base fitness and knowledge base. Don't rush out and buy all the equipment first and don't try to kill yourself on the first race, as you'll end up broken both physically and financially!"
- If negativity creeps while training or racing, escape the feeling with thoughts of winning. Just "hang on, keep your stride and just do the best you can. Forget about other competitors."

The above lessons influenced the development of my model of coaching, which you will see in various lessons and exercises throughout the book. The above is merely a sampling — we could consider many others. I encourage you to be on a constant quest for other flow state performers and to consider the possibilities for transferring their lessons to your art and pursuits.

Now, with a wide range of flow experiences and images in your mind, let's go for a virtual run together deeper into the world of flow.

2. Flow State Primer: 3 Lenses on Flow

"Learning is an ornament in prosperity,
a refuge in adversity, and a provision in old age."
— *Aristotle*

"The beautiful thing about learning
is that nobody can take it away from you."
— *B.B. King*

Dr. Mihaly Csikszentmihalyi pioneered research on flow. In *Flow: The Psychology of Optimal Experience*, he defines flow as "being completely involved in an activity for its own sake. The ego falls away. Time flies. Every action, movement and thought inevitably follows from the previous one, like playing jazz. Your whole being is involved, and you're using your skills to the utmost."

Dr. Csikszentmihalyi describes flow as an optimal state of consciousness, one with total absorption, where time both slows down and speeds up. Further, he offers that the happiest people in life cultivate the most flow — *cultivate* meaning that they work for it. Flow doesn't simply show up for the lazy and uninspired.

Flow is often described as that place where we feel our best and perform at our highest levels, perhaps even significantly exceeding our perceived limits.

We see this when figure skaters and gymnasts produce remarkable performances, full of complexity, yet executed flawlessly with grace.

We see this when a long distance runner and ski mountaineer like Kilian Jornet or Swiss climber Ueli Steck seemingly float up mountains, harnessing incredible athletic prowess and grit over extreme obstacles, yet with precision and what appears to be tranquility. As described astutely in an outstanding NY Times Bestseller book on flow, *The Rise of Superman: Decoding the Science of Ultimate Human Performance* by Steven Kotler, flow is astonishingly present in a modern adventure and extreme sports, from big wave surfing to MegaRamp skateboarding and wing suit skydiving.

We see flow as well when watching marathoners like the legendary 1984 Olympic Marathon Champion Joan (Benoit) Samuelson continue to connect together decades of incredible performances, including a 2:47:50 finish at the Chicago Marathon in 2010, the fastest-ever performance by a woman over 52, or video footage of Heather Dorniden's astonishing recovery from a fall in the final heat in the 600M race at the Big Ten Indoor Championships in March of 2008.

Seeing Flow in Ourselves

The previous examples are flow state expressed on grand stages. These get our attention and prompt our heads to nod, "Yes, amazing, that's flow all right." While we can learn a tremendous amount by studying these performances, they do not however represent what flow state may or may not be in our lives, in our running — in *your* running. To shift ourselves toward more Flow State Running experiences, I encourage you to start on your own small stage in your daily life, and then work up to *your* grand stages.

For some, their small stage is running marathons and their grand stage is a sub-24 hour 100-mile ultra marathon finish. For others, their small stage is running 20 minutes without stopping and their grand stage is finishing their first 5K race. The subjective *"grandness"* of your stages doesn't matter — what matters is that you are able to identify flow at its most modest presence in your own activities and then work to expand this progressively to more challenges and greater frequency.

I recall my first experience with flow state on *my* small stage of daily life, as an overweight 14-year old trying to earn a place on my junior high school wrestling team. In popular 1980s wrestling training attire, with the belief that I'd sweat my way to weight loss in just a few runs, and (let's be honest) in hopes of attracting my first girlfriend, I set out on a run through my neighborhood wearing thick sweatpants, multiple layers of shirts and two plastic garbage sack *jackets* intended to seal the heat in. The plan was to run for 20 minutes, but I ran for an hour and didn't want to stop, despite being massively over-heated, slightly dehydrated, and completely unfit.

Every moment of that run was beautiful, so much so that I still remember it thirty years later. I remember the hills, the trees, and the feeling of being in the zone for the first time. My legs were light and my pace was faster than I'd ever run. I felt confident, something unique for the overweight, 14-year old me. I felt so alive and free when running, and it was a vastly different experience from the runs I'd been forced to do in football practice, in gym class, and in a failed attempt to earn a spot on the track and field team. This was my first experience drinking from the well of flow and experiencing a special mind space for the first time. In a fleeting moment though, it was gone. I had created it momentarily, but did not yet have the knowledge to consistently replicate it and integrate it into my life.

My aim — ensure you understand the flow basics that underpin the model, drills and exercises

My aim in this chapter is to offer you a primer on flow — a primer that provides a foundational understanding of the ingredients for flow state experiences. This base comprehension will help you better understand the models, drills, and exercises I offer, as they have been informed or inspired by the existing body of flow research work and have proven consistently effective in my coaching practice. This primer is also designed to help you further develop your Inner Coach mindset and capacity to guide yourself through a continued evolution of self-coaching, training, and development, including the capacity to design your own drills and exercises.

To be very clear, *Flow State Runner* is a practical guide for cultivating flow in running and developing your Inner Coach — it is not meant to be a rich guide into flow in general. While research and documentation on flow goes back to the 1880s, most research was documented in the 1970s-90s, with another resurgence in recent years. For those interested in studying the science, sports psychology and other aspects of flow at a deeper level, please refer to the many excellent resources in the Appendix, including the recent work and programs from the Flow Genome Project (FGP), cofounded by Steven Kotler (author of *The Rise of Superman*) and human performance expert Jamie Wheal. In addition to offering courses and access to the latest research and knowledge on flow, the FGP seeks to map the flow genome by 2020, to bring it back to solid scientific footing in terms of brain neurology, and to progress our knowledge base of flow.

In this chapter I introduce and summarize some key flow knowledge areas for you, and then segue into explaining my paradigm that translates this knowledge into a model for runners and specific mind tricks, workouts, and race tactics that runners will benefit from.

Next, I offer a summarized view of the key aspects of flow knowledge that relates to our task at hand: your performance and fulfillment as a runner.

Flow State Defined

Many runners may have a good sense qualitatively of what flow is, have likely seen it in professional athletes, and hopefully have experienced it at least once. Most runners are also familiar with some commonly known, anecdotal references (in the zone, switched on, totally absorbed, on auto-pilot, Runner's High, etc.). While these terms and their associated feelings are recognizable to us as runners, there is a much deeper view of flow: one that we can see through several different lenses experienced at varying degrees of quantitatively measurable and qualitatively reported phenomena. These lenses or perspectives include:

- Neuroscience: Brain Waves and Neurotransmitters
- Sports Psychology
- Spiritual

My belief is that all three are inter-connected and valuable for runners to explore and consider. Let's get a high level feel for what each involves.

Neuroscience

Scientists have long since identified specific changes in brain waves and secretion of hormones related to sports and human performance and patterns related to flow state experiences. With advancements in technology such as wearable tracking devices and other sophisticated measurement tools, including devices that can be swallowed, attached to or even embedded under the skin, there is exciting potential for research into the neuroscience of flow.

Brain Waves

Brain imaging and EEG (electroencephalography) brain activity measurement offer insights into electrical frequencies and patterns as well as areas of the brain actively engaged. This allows scientists to study how the brain is operating on an electrical level when athletes perform. It is in this domain that we hear flow-related terms such as "transient hypofrontality," and can consider the impact of our predominant brain wave activity at a given time.

Our brain operates in key measurable frequencies or waves, with one pattern or wave predominant at any given moment and each wave well-suited for a certain type of mental functioning, such as decision making, creativity or restoration. Listed in order from highest to lowest frequency, these waves include gamma, beta, alpha, theta, and delta.

Beta is where most adults spend our waking hours. It is a state of high frequency brain wave activity focused on powering the prefrontal cortex (PFC), which is the brain region in charge of cognitive processing. The PFC is our thinking brain — where we evaluate, plan, analyze, feel self-conscious, compare, judge, second guess, critique and worry, often ad nauseam to our detriment — but also to focus, think and get things done and marked off of our to-do lists.

Beta is a powerful brain wave associated with the brain's micro-managing, cognitive command center, but it is one that is expensive (requires a lot of energy), moderately slow in its processing speed, and not best suited for creativity, rapid automatic pilot execution of patterns, uninhibited expression, and thus ultimately, flow state experiences.

Got it. So, beta waves and prefrontal cortex isn't where I want to be for flow. Where is it then?

First, let's take a quick look at the other brain waves. Gamma, the fastest of our brain wave frequencies, is associated with forming ideas, learning, and perception. Alpha is associated with implicit action, in-the-now presence, calmness, and relaxation. Theta is associated with daydreaming and light sleep, as well as emotional connection, vivid imagery, processing new stimuli, and creativity. Delta, the slowest frequency, is associated with deep, dreamless, restorative sleep and rejuvenation.

A useful synopsis as explained in Steven Kotler's *The Rise of Superman* is that peak flow performances occur when athletes are predominantly experiencing alpha and theta brain wave patterns, with spikes of gamma activity, and with an associated down-powering of significant activity in the dorsolateral PFC. Flow is thus a special brain wave state between being awake and asleep, where we escape the grasp of self-consciousness and self-judgment and excel with the execution of successful patterns and individual expression.

So, as runners seeking flow we simply need to find a way to chill out, escape beta, and turn our brains off, right?

Yes and no.

In running terms, anecdotally speaking, it is important first to understand that the default for many runners is predominantly in a beta wave state. Why? It is because we are thinking about work or school, emails, social media, relationships, news, pace, heart rate zones, opportunities for a good photo to share, our weight, the terrain, the route, the upcoming hill, technique, our next race, our last race, etc. We're thinking, thinking, thinking. This is frustrating and ironic, given that many of us run simply to find stillness against this barrage of noise, not to amplify the noise. On *good* runs, we may break free of this thinking mode at some point, perhaps experiencing stillness or even flow. On other runs, this may prove elusive or happen quite late in the run, in the final moments before returning to the next item on our to-do list.

So, yes, as a general goal toward more Flow State Running experiences we want to chill out and mute our beta activity. We want to become totally absorbed and lose ourselves, without our brain spending so much energy distracting us with comparisons, judgments, and critiques. We want to shift from our explicit (conscious) system that micro-manages our actions to our implicit (subconscious) system, where we are guided fluidly by intuition. We want our run to help us "get out of our heads" or turn our brains and Inner Critic off. We want to enter alpha and theta states where our running shifts to effortless auto-pilot, allowing us to look around, enjoy nature, forget our worries and run free.

It may come as a surprise to some, but to get to the flow state we seek, we must not to strive to strengthen the brain, but instead to weaken it — to power down parts of the dorsolateral prefrontal cortex, while keeping the medial prefrontal cortex engaged for creativity and individual expression, and shifting the rest to autopilot mode, relying on patterns we've ingrained through training and can ultimately repeat from intuition.

Incidentally, we want to do this *chill and escape beta* process even when running intervals and pushing ourselves to the limits, especially when doing so! This is a theme I will revisit again in future chapters.

And here is the NO part of the answer to the question "*do we simply chill and escape beta for peak flow experiences?*" In the next chapter, I introduce the flow cycle, and the key part of the cycle is a Struggle phase. In this phase, we actually need some beta brain wave activity to set up the conditions for flow. We also need it in situations where we have not developed and ingrained response patterns, such as when facing technically challenging course conditions and other adversities. So, it is less about chilling and escaping beta than it is about minimizing this activity to the smallest amount required to get the job done. Our tendency is to have more beta and more dorsolateral PFC activity than we need, and this blocks flow.

This is why I emphasize to the runners I coach to train with adversity checklists and to ensure that they've completed sufficient training in a wide variety of adverse conditions to develop patterns, which their implicit system can later recall instead of requiring new processing and evaluation of the explicit system when the new situation arises. For example, if an ultra runner experiences nighttime fog and they've rarely if ever trained in that condition, their dorsolateral PFC will block flow and require a lot of energy to process this new condition, to project future outcomes because of it, to compare it to times when there was no fog, to fixate on changing the setting on their headlamp, etc. If the runner has trained in this condition, it is much more likely that they will revert to autopilot mode as their implicit system recognizes a pattern it knows and simply plays the associated script to address this pattern. I'll expand on this further into the book.

Bringing my yes and no answers together, in Flow State Running we seek an experience where we're on automatic pilot, totally absorbed and running at our highest potential of technical, mental, muscular, and cardiovascular potential regardless of the adversities we encounter. This means recognizing our propensity for beta wave activities, even when running, and taking actions both before and during our runs to tap into beta when needed, but primarily to shift to alpha and theta states. This means developing and recalling adversity response patterns that we've ingrained. This means training ourselves to dial down our thinking brain and dial up our pattern-response brain.

So how do we accomplish this yes and no together?

In later chapters, I approach this from a variety of angles, including breathing exercises, music, visualization, pre-workout rituals, and more. I also teach you to incorporate it into workout design and race strategy. Continuing, let's looking at the body's fascinating messaging platform.

Neurotransmitters

A neurotransmitter is a chemical messenger used by the brain to rapidly transmit signals between neurons. Neurotransmitters can excite, inhibit or cause a mix of actions in the destination neuron. In simpler terms, this means that a reaction in one part of our body can chemically fire up or dampen a response in another part of the body, including the mind.

When runners think of the neurochemistry associated with running, the first thought is usually endorphin release and the feel-good sensation of Runner's High. Endorphins, short for endogenous morphine, are natural pain killers, or rather pain signal blockers, produced by our bodies in response to stress, including strenuous exercise. There's been some debate the past two decades in the scientific community about the specific connection between endorphin release and <u>euphoria</u> (the feeling most commonly linked to Runner's High), but for the purposes of this primer, it's important to know simply that endorphins are one of many neurotransmitters associated with flow and that our scientific understanding in this area is still evolving.

In addition to endorphins, recent research highlights the role of endocannabinoids, notably anandamide, in exercise-induced euphoria, as well as the role of the fat hormone leptin.[3] Anandamide is linked to inhibiting fear, among many other effects, including similarities with marijuana-related effects of expansiveness and empathy.

And then there's the hormone leptin. According to a recent Canadian study, "The euphoric feeling that gives runners a motivational boost in the middle of their workout is in part modulated by the satiety hormone leptin." This research suggests that, "falling leptin levels send a hunger signal to the brain's pleasure center to generate the rewarding effects of running".[4] This is of interest to us as Flow State Runners as changes in leptin levels have been linked to body fat, fasting, sleep, and exercise, thus connecting each via lifestyle choices to our ability to set ourselves up for Flow State Running experiences.[5]

The neurochemistry story is more complex than *run for a while, endorphins are released and you feel good*, isn't it! Let's take a step back now and look at the basic players. Relative to flow, in addition to endorphins and anandamide, the hormone leptin, other neurotransmitters involved include dopamine (arousal and engagement), norepinephrine (energy and focus), and serotonin (after glow). In addition, stress hormones adrenaline and cortisol have a role in the cycle. It's a fascinating part of human anatomy how this actually works, but I'll save that exploration for you with the many resources listed in the Appendix.

Steven Kotler's synopsis of dopamine's role in pattern recognition in *The Rise of Superman* is well worth a read, not to mention his in-depth look at the associated neurotransmitters and page-turning stories from extreme adventure athletes.

Neuroscience and the future of Flow research

To close out this brief overview of neuroscience and flow, keep in mind that it is in this area that we'll likely see the most advancement in the coming years, with the Flow Genome Project's efforts, as well as the rapid advancement of sensors and technology to measure and amass data from myriad new devices and sensors. This will be very interesting to runners because we're by default in the group of early adopters for measurement devices, including those that track heart rate, steps, distance, speed, pace, and more recently wattage, stride, impact, and more. I'm excited about what the future holds in this area. I also share more on these topics in Chapter 14, which focuses on Technology.

So, what does the neuroscience view on flow mean for us as aspiring Flow State Runners?

The following key takeaways are here as a summary for you. They are drivers for the *Flow State Runner* concepts, models, drills and tips.

- We need to become adept at slipping into alpha and theta states while running, even though our default is likely high-thinking, self-critical beta.
- To avoid reverting back to beta wave functioning, practice adversity patterns to reduce the need for overthinking those situations.
- If you build it, flow will come: When the right mix of neurochemicals and brain waves are in place, there is high likeliness that conditions for flow are being met, thus we need to actively pursue and train toward that mix in our running.
- Stress and diet impact flow, both positively and negatively, so their use and management must be factored into our mindset, training, and racing from a flow perspective, in addition to the obvious performance and recovery perspectives.
- We can benefit from following modern flow research, as the insights gained from rapid technological advancements is poised

to move our collective knowledge a major step forward.

- If you want more flow state experiences, avoid overloading your running experiences with attention placed in real-time on technology (devices, apps, social media) that inherently will keep your thinking brain engaged (PFC) and your brain predominantly in beta. Consider using devices and apps in the background instead of ones that require your attention during the run.

Sports Psychology

There is an entire view on flow that we can take through sports psychology alone, spanning a wide range of topics, including emotions and mindset while running and training; how runners approach competition; stress management and overload; motivation; self-coaching; emotional maturity; and processing fear, uncertainty, and doubt.

There exists a veritable plethora of books in this area. These include Susan A. Jackson and Mihaly Csikszentmihalyi's *Flow in Sports* and other classics, such as *Inner Game of Tennis* by W. Timothy Gallwey, Terry Oarlock's *In Pursuit of Excellence,* and Gary Mack's *Mind Gym: An Athlete's Guide to Inner Excellence.* There are also the recent works from Mark Divine, *Unbeatable Mind* and *Way of the SEAL.*

From these resources and more, we can study how thought leaders in this space describe peak performance, how extreme adventure athletes accomplish the seemingly impossible with their bodies and machines, how mountaineers tap into a special mind space to deal with life-threatening ordeals, and how US Navy SEALs function as a high performance team under extreme stress. The keys to the metaphorical *flow car* are readily available in this body of knowledge, from Jackson and Csikszentmihalyi's flow fundamentals and templates to Divine's Five Mountains model that integrates the perspectives and development across physical, mental, emotional, intuitional, and spiritual aspects.

In a massively simplified take on sports psychology, we can consider how to suppress, ride, exploit, influence, detect, and redirect. We can journal, review, visualize, frame and reframe, self-motivate, perform rituals, use lucky charms, honor superstitions, let go of things, hold on to things, close our minds, open our minds, go deep or stay aloft, use mantras, watch motivational videos, examine our past, work with therapists, listen to music, float, meditate, laugh, and even chant. We can do some or all of those to perhaps phenomenal effect on our capacity to perform at peak potential or simply to be happy.

For most runners, the challenge isn't a lack of sports psychology insights. It is a matter of overload.

It boils down to simple questions: for a given run, race or race preparation, which approach do I rely on? What do I think about? What do I do to get my mind in the right space? Simply put, what do I remember from reading X books, and am I able to recall it when I need it most?

I encourage you to adopt a mindset where your aim is not to know it all, but to know what works for you, to keep evolving that self-knowledge, and to maintain a burning curiosity to try new things. This means being your own scientist and relentlessly experimenting on yourself, pushing your boundaries of knowledge forward. Don't just try concepts and exercises that you immediately feel comfortable with. Try the unusual, the uncomfortable, even the bizarre. Vary not only the concepts and exercises you apply, but also the settings you apply them to (e.g., weather conditions, day/night, solo/group, training/racing, season, etc.).

In *Flow State Runner* I share with you exercises, workouts, and concepts that have proven effective for me and for those I've coached. Aspects of sports psychology come into play in the inhibitors and enablers section next, as well as in many aspects of my Flow State Runner model and the associated exercises, workouts and concepts.

So, what does the Sports Psychology view on flow mean for us as aspiring Flow State Runners?

- Read, listen, learn, share, try, explore. Go deep when you discover approaches, authors and coaches that resonate with you. Consider new, unusual, and uncomfortable ideas. Self-experiment.
- Include psychological aspects in your running model, workouts, training plan, racing, and recovery. Don't just read about them and then go back to business as usual. Train these aspects with as much planning and journaling as a typical marathon runner does with the kilometers they cover each day.

Spiritual

The spiritual lens may also be applied to flow to better understand how to set optimal conditions, experience powerful moments of presence, and acknowledge those moments with gratitude and not judgment. Years ago at the onset of my journey as a runner, I never would have envisioned that spirituality would play an important role in my future running and coaching practice. At the time, I considered myself far from spiritual.

Growing up in a religiously conservative community, my relentless curiosity and openness wasn't a good fit for many of the "religious" mindsets I was exposed to, so I had grown to find little personal appeal in organized religion. This led me to enter adulthood suspicious of any approach that felt religious, cultish or remotely dogmatic, and thus to throw out spirituality or spiritual-feeling practices as the idiomatic *baby with the bathwater*. I eventually reframed my view of "spiritual" and found elements of spirituality that served me quite well as a runner. While I'll set aside integration of religious paradigms or practices into running for individual exploration, I will share the impact of two powerful spiritual-associated tools I've experienced both as a runner and a coach: yoga and music.

Yoga

Yoga was my first repeatable path to stillness, and stillness was my first path to repeatable Flow State Running experiences.

I attended my first yoga class 20 years ago as an injured triathlete looking for some relief from Iliotibial Band Syndrome and low back pain. This was back when we'd find local businesses in the Yellow Pages — a large printed book of business phone numbers, so I looked up "yoga" and selected the nearest studio. That was the extent of my research.

I walked into that first class dressed to run, with no mat and no clue what was about to happen. I was the only man in a class full of women more than twice my age. The style was introduced as Hatha Yoga.

I was quite intimidated at first — for several reasons. The first was my self-imposed spirituality shield at the time. I hoped yoga would help with my back, but didn't want the spiritual stuff, especially if it even hinted of religion. The second was admittedly the coolness factor. At the time, there were no hot yoga classes, yoga set to hip hop or heavy metal music, yoga for athletes, etc. My triathlete friends were out training on their bikes and at the swimming pool, and in my mind, I was inside a comfortable yoga studio surrounded by grandmothers, bolsters, and lavender-scented eye shades. The last reason was that the class members seemed to know what they were doing, knew fancy Sanskrit names for a host of poses, and could go into positions far beyond the realm of what I believed my body could ever do.

I kept showing up though, dressed each time in my 1990s runner's tank top and shorts with hamstrings so tight I could barely touch my knees, much less my toes; I was there every Monday evening. While I found the physical relief I was looking for, eventually solved the IT Band problem, and made massive improvements in my mobility, I also discovered a hidden prize: an incredible calming effect after each session. This calming effect did wonders for my stressed out IT Project Manager's state of being. I'd walk in the door after a stressful day at the office and an even more stressful commute, worrying about every project, every email, every detail — and walk out feeling calm, centered and at peace. It happened every time, and every time I'd react with surprise and wonder. All the items I had identified as intimidators proved non-issues. I found that I enjoyed the light elements of spirituality, that triathletes in general benefited more from training mental stillness than overtraining the body — thus mind training was indeed cool, and that yoga was about an individual's journey, not about anyone else in the room.

I eventually found myself excited about joining a yoga class for the mental relief more so than for the physical benefits. I also began to run after yoga sessions and I was surprised at how I instantly fell into a state that used to take most of my run to reach, especially after very stressful work days. For me, yoga quickly proved a major contributor to my happy quality of life, as well as my productivity and performance in both sports and career.

Yoga as a complete system

Yoga means "to yoke" or to join together. While it is often used in the West with a view toward stretching or even working out, the practice originated in India as a means to reach stillness of the mind, tying together mind, body and spirit into oneness. As a complete system, yoga is a powerhouse generator of flow experiences, with a connection to numerous scientifically validated aspects of flow, including presence, breath and focused concentration, struggle and release, deep relaxation and more. I would argue that a holistic yoga practice is a one-stop shop to flow.

While there are many different forms of yoga, what resonates with me as a runner is a variety of Ashtanga-rooted practices that link movements and breath. For my personal practice, these include Budokon, Rocket, Kokoro Yoga, Ashtanga Primary Series, and in general, Vinyasa Flow. These practices are a challenging moving meditation, which I'm able to transfer into my running. I've also found tremendous benefit in Yin Yoga, as a path to stillness and recovery, which is a crucial aspect of repeated flow experiences.

Yoga had such a profound impact on my life that I eventually pursued and completed 500+ hours of teacher training and receive a lot of joy from teaching others yoga. For 20 years I've incorporated yoga into my daily routine as well as into pre-race rituals.

There are 8 aspects of the traditional system of yoga. While these extend beyond the scope of this book, four to note are breathing, concentration, meditation, and physical poses. Breath is so important to Flow State Running that I gave it a full chapter. Concentration, one of the key ingredients identified by Professor Csikszentmihalyi's work, and meditation practice are also key contributors, and I cover them in Chapter 5 on the Dome of Awareness.

Eastern Practices

Moving even deeper into Eastern philosophy, we can also look to chakras, or the energetic centers of our bodies, as well as Chinese Medicine (meridians, acupuncture, acupressure) and the associated practices of Tai Chi and Qigong for insights and techniques that may contribute to our flow state experiences while running. This is in harmony with the direction taken by Danny Dreyer in *ChiRunning* as he merged his experiences practicing Tai Chi with his passion for running. I've experienced positive results with the integration of Qigong breath and movement practice as preparation for long runs, as well as powerful chakra meditation sessions, energy that I was able to transfer into excellent running experiences.

Music

Perhaps a surprising practice to introduce in a section on spirituality and flow, African drumming and percussion music in general offer a unique gateway into cultivating flow. While I grew up playing brass musical instruments, I gravitated to percussion as a side music hobby as a teen and later began to collect and play African drums and other interesting percussion instruments, such as steel handpans. Drumming, particularly in a group setting or drum circle, opens the door to creative and spiritual expression, while serving for many as a meditation practice.

Drums are the ultimate primal instrument, with fossil records indicating their existence for at least 6,000 years. For many cultures, drums play a major role in ceremonies, rituals, dancing, and community. One of the highlights of my life and a major flow moment was playing a dirt-covered and roughly constructed Djembe in a drum and dance circle in an impoverished village in Malawi, surrounded by villagers who danced and drummed full of smiles and joy that one wouldn't think possible while living under such harsh conditions. Yet they drummed, danced, and sang like they had everything in the world, fully alive *in the now*. Time ceased to exist for me in that moment, and I felt an incredible community, humankind and universal connection. To this day, I incorporate music and drumming into my baseline personal practices, as well as my coaching.

While playing any musical instrument or immersed into listening to music offers similar benefits that can be transferred into your running experiences, a basic African drum offers a very low entry barrier for non-musicians to explore as their first instrument. Inexpensive drums are typically readily available and the only skill involved to begin your journey is to strike it! It won't take long before your inner child or primal roots kick in. As I was taught in Malawi, you begin to play by matching your heart beat, and expand from there to match whatever you feel.

Spirituality, Meditation and Science

When speaking of spiritual practices, it is easy to appear distanced from the quantitatively measured world of neuroscience and psychology, and thus more in the domain of what is termed pseudo-science. That said, while meditation was once seen as a hippy activity found solely in the spiritual realm, an increasing amount of scientific data is backing meditation's impact on changing not only our health, emotions, and performance, but also quite literally, our brain. Emma Seppala, Ph.D., Associate Director at the Center for Compassion and Altruism Research and Education (CCARE) at Stanford University, summarizes meditation's scientific validations across 20 improvement areas in an insightful September 2013 article for *Psychology Today*.[6]

As technology evolves and we're able to measure more, it will not be surprising to see greater quantification of the impacts of spiritual practices on our minds and bodies. What matters in your life though is what makes a difference for YOU. So, experiment on yourself!

So, what does the Spiritual view on flow mean for us as aspiring Flow State Runners?

- We can take a spiritual path toward flow, through yoga, meditation or prayer, through music, art, or many other pursuits that tap into our unique spiritual triggers.
- There is value in seeking development areas OUTSIDE of the common. Had I kept myself ring-fenced with other triathletes in my area, I never would have experienced the massive growth and fulfillment I have through yoga. Cross over the tracks and be open to vastly different ideas, where hidden gems abound!
- Read, listen, learn, share, try, explore in the spiritual realm. Go deep when you discover approaches, authors, and coaches that resonate with you. Consider new, unusual, and uncomfortable ideas. Self-experiment. Drop preconceived notions and ignore any dogma that doesn't serve you.
- Don't underestimate the power of breath training and meditation in flow and for life in general.
- Seek opportunities to develop your spiritual side, ranging from your warrior spirit (with endurance races, epic adventures in nature, and transformative events such as SEALFIT Kokoro and 20X) to your inner spirit (meditation retreats like Vipassana or

religious activities that resonate with you), and activities that are off the beaten path of many athletes (music, dancing, art).

- Include spiritual aspects in your running model, workouts, training plan, racing, and recovery. It doesn't have to be a 90-minute yoga practice each day; it can be as simple as a few poses at the right time, simple Sun Salutations in the morning, or just reading about the yoga system. It doesn't have to be taking drum lessons, but can simply be playing make-shift drums with your 3-year old niece. It doesn't have to be 10 days at a silent meditation retreat, but can be simply sitting alone in a nearby forest for 10 minutes and observing your thoughts. To reiterate a point I made earlier, as it is very important: don't just read about these practices and then go back to business as usual. Pick something to try and train these aspects with as much planning and journaling as a typical marathon runner does with the kilometers they cover each day.
- Lastly, don't worry about what others think of your spiritual practices — if a practice serves you, own it proudly!

The intersection of all Neuroscience, Sports Psychology and Spiritual Views

As I mentioned earlier, my position is that all three views are inter-connected, valuable for runners to understand, and worth considering in your approach to running. It is absolutely possible for you to experience flow in your running without understanding the neuroscience, psychology or spirituality that on some levels are connected to it. I provided this high-level look to give a simple basis for content I share later in the book and also to spark the interest of anyone who wants to go deeper in any of the perspectives. Please consider it also an invitation to further explore and experiment with views that may offer a new paradigm for you.

Chapter closing

This primer chapter is an attempt to summarize a massive body of work and a key set of my philosophical underpinnings in coaching into a brief overview that sets the stage for the Flow State Runner model and associated exercises and workouts. For those inspired to make a deep dive into the scientific underpinnings, case studies, and latest research on flow, I've included a list in the Appendix of many relevant works in this domain. Dive in, it's a fascinating world!

Now, my coaching mission is to take you deeper into its practical application for running.

3. The Flow Cycle, Stress and Cultivating Yin

*"Anyone can make the simple complicated.
Creativity is making the complicated simple."*
—Charles Mingus

Flow occurs in a cycle

Flow occurs in a cycle, not via an on-off switch, ejection seat handle, or rocket launch button. If it were simply binary (Flow On - Flow Off), it would be wonderful as we'd likely already have smartphone and smartwatch apps to instantly activate it! Maybe someday we'll have an app or smart pill for flow activation, but for now we have to set the conditions and make it happen, and according to Mihaly Csikzentmi-halyi, it happens in this cycle:

1. Struggle
2. Release
3. Flow
4. Recovery

While the flow phase itself may be considered the Holy Grail, it's the one phase that requires a roll-up-your-sleeves effort to orchestrate. Once you're in it, you're in it. The bulk of the work in setting up the conditions for flow takes place in Struggle and Recovery, with Release also requiring a modicum of elbow grease.

The struggle is real

Flow doesn't happen without a Struggle phase. During Struggle, beta brain waves are active, the dorsolateral PFC is switched on, and the body is releasing cortisol and norepinephrine to keep us focused and alert. The key to this Struggle phase is getting right what Csikzentmihalyi terms as our challenge-skills (CS) balance. Jackson and Csikzentmihalyi write in *Flow in Sports*, "The CS balance is a golden rule of flow." Explaining that it is linked to our subjective perceptions the authors state, "It is not so much what the objective challenges or skills are in a situation that determines the quality of experience, but what a person thinks of the available opportunities and her capacity to act." Drawing on their research, they offer an insightful CS model, illustrating the quadrants of anxiety, apathy, boredom, and flow, and an extensive, useful guide to developing an effective CS balance in athletes from a wide variety of sports.

In short, we need to be sufficiently challenged to prompt activation of certain neurotransmitters and brain wave patterns, but not overloaded with a challenge that is so far over our heads that we freeze in fear and overly activate our minds in coming up with endless failure scenarios and other inner criticisms, thus undermining our flow.

Kotler examines extreme adventure athletes in *The Rise of Superman*, making a strong case for flow occurring when we push our limits and highlighting flow drivers when the struggle is so real that the athlete is putting their life at risk. This is certainly struggle on a grand stage and one can certainly imagine scenarios of "give me flow or give me death," as there is no option but to be in flow to pull off such awesome feats.

As a runner, you don't need to surf a 60-foot wave or leap off a cliff to get your struggle on (unless that's your passion as well), so mapping this to the smaller stages of your daily running environment, you need to include an element of struggle in any run where you seek flow, and that element of struggle needs to be sufficiently challenging for you to bring you out of your comfort zone, but not so much so that you freeze in a state of anxiety. I term these *micro challenges*, as they need not be the focus of the run, but rather they are brief enough struggles to serve as a trigger to launch your flow cycle.

You can achieve micro challenges in running in many ways: speed, duration, terrain, environment/weather, weight, tasks, practicing a new technique, uncertainty, etc. I offer ideas and specific guidance for these and more in Section 2. This is important — the sooner you bring these micro challenges into a given run, the better you've set the stage for a follow-on flow experience. When you are in the micro challenge, put all of your focus on that effort, not on your expectation of flow's arrival.

I can actually hear the voice of overweight 22-year old me saying, *"But getting off the couch to run IS a struggle on its own. Isn't that enough?"*

At the beginning, perhaps it is, especially if there's sufficient anxiety about the prospect of running that your system is flooded with stress hormones. But as fitness and skill improve, including your subjective perception of your skill and your confidence, the challenge needs to be appropriately elevated. So, my fear of not being able to keep up with my wife during my early days of running was a sufficient struggle for a while, but once my fitness improved, I had to up the challenge, which I did at first with moving to trail running and technical terrain. She still makes me work hard to chase her on hills though!

A popular motivational slogan often echoed by Commander Mark Divine at SEALFIT is *Embrace the Suck*. Borrowing from this, I say *Embrace the Struggle*, as it's the ticket to play in the world of flow!

Just let go already

If you get stuck in Struggle, flow will never happen, so now that you've set up a good struggle, it is time to break from it. The Release phase marks a shift from beta to alpha brain waves, the initial down-power-ing of parts of the PFC and the release of hormones to extinguish the fire set by the Struggle's release of adrenaline and cortisol. This is the moment to shift the brain's activity from micro-management and focus on all physical, mental, and emotional aspects of what you're doing into

FLOW STATE RUNNER

a brief moment of letting go. It is a required bridge to cross over into flow, but you can make it a short and fun bridge.

In runner's terms, this could mean simply a spontaneous hill sprint (the Struggle), followed by a few minutes of quick backwards walking, allowing your concentration to drift and sense of focus to fade. For many, an effective Release requires going off-script, that is, doing things that you normally do not do in a run. You now have not only coaching permission, but encouragement to go off-script. Embrace these brief off-script moments for the sense of adventure and fun introduced into your run and knowledge that it's a key component of the flow cycle.

Here's a practical running workout example:
Your workout plan is to run 6 hill sprints, each a 1-minute interval followed by 1 minute of rest. To set the conditions for a flow state experience, add a pre-interval early in the run. Make it 30 seconds and do it when you're not quite warmed up enough to be mentally prepared (assuming you have the health and fitness for this). After this interval, complete a task completely out of the ordinary for your runs.

For example, skip, run backwards, hold in plank position, do some somersaults down a grass hill, slide down a playground slide, etc. This activity can be very brief. Then return to your run, and when the time is right, complete the interval series.

While there is never a guarantee you'll have a flow experience in those intervals, you will have set yourself up with optimal seed conditions, and you can begin to tweak the variables to discover what ratios will unlock your flow experiences. What we're looking for is a set of Release Triggers that work for you. You may also find that it unlocks for you after the run, once you've moved on to another activity.

Humor is another path to Release, and it is something that you can do even in a race setting where you are pushing the pace. There's a style of yoga called Laughter Yoga where the intention is, you guessed it, to use laughter to reach a state of mind-body-spirit connection. Laughter is an excellent release mechanism, one that helped me through a particularly

62

rough moment of Ironman Hawaii, where I averted a near meltdown on the bike course by getting myself started with small chuckles at how *stupid* it was to bike through the lava fields in high heat, high humidity, and strong winds that were always in your face, and to do that BEFORE running a marathon. I ended up on the side of the road at mile 85 of the bike in tears as those small chuckles turned into roaring solo laughter. And while I looked crazy, that little fit of laughter had a massive effect on averting the meltdown and having a great finish to the bike course.

You can use *play* as well for Release, and I highly recommend it! I've stopped mid-run to swing on playground toys, hop from log to log in the forest, splash through streams, and play fetch with a friendly dog. I've even carried musical instruments on runs and paused for a few minutes here and there to play. And no excuses with this one, the instrument I like to carry on mountain runs is a 10 foot / 3.3-meter-long Swiss Alphorn! But remember, the size of your instrument is not what's important, it's that you recognize the value of play in triggering a shift in brain wave activity and as a trigger into flow. You can always just howl at the moon, high five a race volunteer or complete stranger, skip a rock, hurdle over some kids playing in the creek, or do whatever your primal mind yearns for to create a moment when you Release and forget about your running.

Here's a metaphor on Struggle and Release that may help. When I turned 30, I developed an interest in gourmet cooking. I took some cooking classes and learned how to blanch green beans. In short, the process is to boil them for only a minute or two, just long enough to bring them to al dente and stimulate their bright color, but not so long to make them soft or dull. Then you immediately dump them in ice water, which stops the cooking process abruptly. You finish them in a pan with garlic and olive oil. Perfect color, perfect texture. So nice!

Struggle and Release are like blanching. Struggle is the rapid boil and Release is the immersion into ice water. And building on this, flow is the final dish, with its nice aroma of garlic and lemon zest!

Go with the flow

Following Release, we enter Flow, where we figuratively ride the wave. In Flow, we stop trying, stop thinking so consciously, and allow time to feel altered. We're in a low alpha, high theta brain wave state, operating on auto-pilot as we execute patterns, while remaining open to expressions of creativity as new patterns are formed.

Recovery

Coming out of Flow is Recovery, and this is where many runners get it wrong, constantly push for more mileage, faster times, sleeping less, and living a fast-paced beta-driven life, with little time devoted to mind training, meditation, relaxation, healthy nutrition, and proper sleep. The Recovery phase is mandatory if you want to continue to have flow experiences.

This restorative phase involves the obvious physical recovery from our running. In addition, this phase is where we find (and require) delta brain wave activity during deep, restful sleep. It involves emotional rejuvenation in the form of recognizing and expressing gratitude for the flow moments, even the brief ones, as well as checking in on our goals and expectations, including what we see as our big picture (fulfillment, quality of life, journey).

Key takeaway for runners on the flow cycle:

- Seize adversity as a moment to spawn Flow. Think, "This is the exact Struggle I need for flow. Thank goodness it's here!"
- Ensure that every run includes at least one micro challenge early on, even if it's just the blanching equivalent of 1-minute green beans in boiling water. Adjust your micro challenges as skills and technique improve.
- PLAY! Every run needs a moment of Release built into it. If you're not good at using play for release, plan for it and fake it

'til you make it.
- Plan and honor your Recovery efforts, including mindset, sleep, and nutrition.

In Section 2 of this book, I include templates, ideas, workouts and more to help you organize Struggle, Release, and Recovery, and integrate these phases into your training and racing approach. With a base understanding of the flow cycle, we'll now look at flow pre-requisites, enablers and inhibitors.

Flow prerequisites and enablers

From baseline practices that you do regularly to spot drills, there are many practices and mindsets available for you to tap into to increase and improve your flow experiences in running. Some of these are tied to the research of Csikzentmihalyi and colleagues in sports psychology and flow research. Others link to anecdotal experiences in my coaching practice. All of these will appear later in this book in the form of drills, exercises, workouts, and other suggestions for experimentation.

The first group are a subset of flow prerequisites identified by Csikzentmihalyi:

- Clearly defined goals
- Focused Concentration
- Belief in yourself and your sense of control, loss of self-consciousness
- Instant and Unambiguous Feedback
- Presence, mindfulness, in the now mentality

Next are enablers generally and anecdotally associated with flow that have proven themselves to be successful in my coaching practice:

- Breath Training
- Yoga
- Time in nature
- Artistic expression
- Mindsets and paradigms: gratitude and abundance
- Play & Primal connection
- Technology (can serve both an enabler and inhibitor in my experience)

Flow inhibitors: What gets in the way of flow?

Flow is good that you would think we'd simply leave the flow tap turned on 24x7. Unfortunately, we are very good at getting in our own way, at blocking ourselves. Here are the top flow inhibitors I've encountered while coaching runners, each of which I approach in this book to help you overcome them with greater frequency and quality in your running.

- Inner Critic
- Stress, overload and burnout
- Lack of focus, scattered thinking
- Emotions
- Fear, uncertainty, and doubt
- Negativity and scarcity mindset
- Technology

Integration and outsourcing

My aim is to teach you a way to integrate flow prerequisites and enablers into your running practice and to outsource handling of the inhibitors to your Inner Coach. Thus we're working together to strengthen your Inner Coach, to expand your running playbook, and to quieten your Inner Critic.

Stress & Burnout: I'm too stressed for flow, but I want flow to get unstressed!

Trying to pursue flow in a life that is packed to the brim with high stress is akin to trying to discern the subtleties of a fine wine after eating a mouthful of a spicy, sugary candy. Just as you'd ideally have a clean pallet to savor the wine, you also need a *clean, moderately reasonable* stress foundation in life, upon which to cultivate flow experiences.

I can feel the anxiety from some readers already with this, and can envision hearing the reaction: "This is impossible. I have kids, a stressful job, a house under renovation, four email accounts — all with full inboxes, more to-do lists than I can keep track of, etc. My running is a break from all of that stress. It is the only place I really have control and don't have stress. How am I supposed to lower my stress to improve my running experiences when my running experiences are what lowers my stress!"

I get that — I've been there, in a high stress life, one that I tried to balance by adding more goals and activities, which inadvertently added more stress and increasingly higher expectations across all my focus areas. If you want more flow though, you have got to make a change in your daily life equation to bring down your overall stress level.

I worked in the field of IT Project Management and Vendor Management for 18 years. During the last 6 years of that career, I moved abroad, traveled extensively for work, and worked very long hours. The balance was shifted far toward work and I was feeling the stress, in terms of weight gain and an increasing desire for a nightly cocktail to "take the edge off" my day.

Rather than move too far down the path of "solving" the problem by artificial means, I turned to ultra endurance sports. I figured that the best way to balance my work pressures and time commitments was to occupy my personal time with endurance training and racing. As my work felt extreme, I sought extreme challenges, such as ultra marathons. I began to train 15-20 hours a week for ultra marathons, often sacrificing sleep to honor my training commitment. I did late night 3-hour runs after work in the winter, 6-hour runs on the weekend, running commutes to and from work, and 5-6 high intensity CrossFit workouts per week.

On the positive side, I completed races, had a great time, made new friends, and met my performance goals. On the negative side, I still found frustration with body composition. I was still in a constant state of stress. My sleep wasn't good, and taking sleep meds wasn't helping. In the end, I wasn't performing at my most optimal, in sport or at work. I was also quick to snap at others out of frustration. My tipping point was during a running commute home after 12 hours at the office. I fell while jumping to avoid a group on a narrow sidewalk and tore ligaments in my ankle. I refused to let that situation or late night of work "steal my run," so I suffered through a brutal 10 kilometers, and ultimately a hobbling, excruciating walk to get home. I did a lot of additional damage to my ankle on that ego-fueled trip home, and I was out of running for nearly 6 months. Following that, I reevaluated. In an attempt to do it all, I had fallen into an unsustainable stress routine — that ankle injury was my wake-up call.

Yin and Yang Balance

In Chinese philosophy, yin and yang describes how opposite or contrary forces are actually complementary, interconnected, and interdependent in the natural world, and how they give rise to each other as they inter-relate to one another. Many tangible dualities (such as light and dark, fire and water, expanding and contracting) are thought of as physical manifestations of the duality symbolized by yin and yang.[7]

Borrowing from Chinese Yin and Yang philosophy, I teach a paradigm that we live our lives with a mix of yin and yang activities, which if we don't balance, will eventually balance themselves for us in an uncomfortable manner. In this model, yin activities can be seen as representing water — flow, quiet minds, listening, experiencing, receiving, being, connecting with our authentic self, connecting with nature, and connecting with others. Yang activities can be seen as our fire — expecting, desiring, pressures, busy mind, striving, speaking and doing.

Returning to my story, I could easily place in the yang category my job, my travel schedule, my lifestyle expectations, my sleep routine, my physically demanding yoga practice, and my cross-training approach. At its extreme, yang puts us in the red zone, a zone I know all too well. Too much yang without a corollary yin component is not sustainable. It puts us into chronic stress mode, where we not only miss out on flow state experiences, we will eventually break.

As runners, athletes, and people in modern cultures, we are very good at stress. We try to squeeze it all in: always connected, always reachable via multiple mediums both personally and professionally, daily workouts that we post on social media and track via myriad devices and apps, endless expectations of our time and attention in-person and virtually, striving for personal records and race medals, chasing likes and Strava attention, email overload, WiFi-enabled bodyweight and body fat scales, constantly scanning news feeds, online reputations to manage, working long hours, limited sleep, long commutes, and on and on.

Even our cross-training approach, easily illustrated with the popularity of CrossFit, often brings another set of high intensity efforts, quantification, and comparison. While this approach to training is quite effective at building fitness and community, it is yet another aspect of our hectic lives that adds yang pressure (workouts for time, as fast as possible, as many reps as possible, push to compare your numbers and continuously beat them). There's nothing wrong with this per se, but it is yet another yang card stacked on what is all too often a house of yang cards that will eventually collapse without a yin counterbalance.

In *The Primal Blueprint* Mark Sisson describes a great contrast of families, starring Grok — a primal role model, and his modern antithesis — an average over-stressed man, Mr. Korg. Sisson's description of the fictional Korg family is painful to ponder because it is so real and relevant to modern society. Even with fitness, which could be a yin force in our lives, we often twist it into a yang role, by solely focusing on metrics and pressure, and not giving ourselves a yin complement.

Got yin? If so, is it enough to serve as a sustainable complement to the yang in your life?

But what's the solution? What's the yin component we need to create enough balance? Does this mean not working hard and not setting challenging training goals?

We can fight fire with fire, fight it with water, or fight it with a creative mix of fire, water and tools. If we fight it just with fire, we risk burning even more of that which we do not wish to burn. If we fight it with just water, we may not have enough water, especially as the fire builds in intensity. If we employ a creative mix though, perhaps creating fire breaks, lighting back burns, working with weather conditions, and using a mix of chemicals and water, we can eventually put the fire out. Even better if we also do fire prevention activities like clearing brush and other combustibles and educating people on fire prevention. Sure, lightning can still strike, but we've stacked the odds more in our favor.

Just as lighting more forest on fire without using fire breaks won't put a fire out until it burns everything in its path, adding yang to yang will not help us reach our running goals in the long-term and will ultimately burn us out. Also, our goal isn't to put out a fire, it is to use the fire to burn what it needs to burn (burning through adversities and training to strengthen us toward our goals) while protecting what we want to protect (our mental health and quality of life) in a manner that is sustainable (our yin and yang balance). Our lesson as runners is to create a yin and yang balance, with yin as the ingredient most of us need to emphasize and with a variety of approaches for that emphasis.

Let's start with running. Running attracts us with its ability to help us escape, find calmness and stimulate creativity. We can make running yin or yang, based largely on our expectations and conscious decision before and during a run.

Yang Run

For example, a classic yang run typically looks like the following:

- Heart rate monitor on, target zone set for Zone 4 (anaerobic threshold training), low range beep alert set at Zone 3. Workout mode set on smartwatch and recording started to track route and other data. Issue encountered with GPS reception at start — runner spends 5 minutes dealing with it.
- Social media performance tracking app on with real-time feedback enabled to compare to prior efforts and other runners, aim to get King of the Mountain (KOM) back on favorite climb. This app posts automatically at the run's conclusion, and cross-posts to Twitter and Facebook.
- Two stops to take photos to post on social media, which will synch to the to the social media performance tracking app. Short video filmed as well, showing feet splashing through stream. Three takes to get the video just right.
- Music app with run mode on, music set to 190 beats per minute. Signal lost in forest — runner stops to deal with it.
- Power meter on shoe to track cadence and wattage — will review post-run. Power app started before social media performance tracking app.
- Focus is to win KOM on the climb, stay in Zone 4 for at least 70% of the run, and not expressed, but felt, get likes and attention from the social media posts.

Yin Run

And a yin run looks more like this:

- All intrusive technology left at home
- Focus is primarily to listen to and identify nature sounds and notice as many instances and variations of the color green as possible.
- On the climb, focus all thoughts on the power of the stream you can hear
- Get as many people to smile at you on this run as possible
- Go dark, off-the-grid: no social media related to this run. No photos, no tweets — just presence and memories.

Notice I didn't say anything about pace, intensity, or duration? That is because it doesn't matter. Either run could be slow or fast. Either run could be short or long. Either run could include a few, many or no intervals. Yin in my model does not mean physically quiet, low intensity, or slow. It means an experience with a level of mental stillness that is complementary to the noise and expectations in the rest of our lives.

I am also not saying that all of your runs should be yin runs. I'm simply offering a tool, a structured way to approach running to allow it to serve a yin role when you want it to, or a yang role when you want that. Some readers will want all of their runs to be yin runs. Others will perhaps target one run a week as a yin run. And the rest may love the aspects of their yang running so much that they seek yin experiences elsewhere. As long as balance is achieved, as a coach I'm happy for you.

You can do the same with cross-training, maintaining your strength and/or conditioning aims, but shifting away from the yang pressure and expectations that rule our lives to a more yin approach. In my experience, MovNat® approaches this very well with combos, or combinations of movements, performed with more of a play, adventure or primal mindset.

Outside of running, options for adding more yin in your life could include the obvious, like yoga, particularly yin yoga, but also activities such as hiking, stand-up paddling, and many other sports, as long as the sessions are with a yin approach. Outside of sports activities, good yin options include playing music, reading, painting, cooking, wood-working, knitting, meditation, and an unlimited amount of simple activities done with a focus on mindfulness. There's also sleeping more, vacation time, and pure Rest & Relaxation.

Yin seeking & the choices we make

Finding yin is more about awareness and the decisions we make than the particular activity selected. It is about recognizing the increasing tendency toward a technology-fueled focus on a quantifiable, data-driven life, dialing back some of it, and then adding sufficient qualitative experiences in life and in training to serve as a counterbalance. It is about shifting your focus to the simple things, moments of human interaction, relationships and experiences, and to true in-the-moment presence. Your decisions on how and when to use technology and the expectations you set before running, workouts, and other life activities will have a major impact on what is yin or yang in your life.

Going back to the basic idea of yin and yang, of complementary yet interdependent forces, if you want or need a high level of yang to suit your lifestyle and general life situations, it is only sustainable if you add more yin. Else, nature will find the balance for you, and these course correction moments are often expensive and shocking. It is much better to build the balance yourself than to have it established for you!

Stressed out endurance athletes, please receive this message: yin is a necessary and integral component of your training. Give yourself permission to incorporate yin activities into your routine not only without guilt, but with pride that you are wise and disciplined enough to commit to a balanced and sustainable approach to your passion, performance, and longevity.

Returning to my stress story, nature indeed found balance for me, sidelining me from running for a very frustrating half-year. Had it not been an ankle injury, it would have been something else. I had built myself a forest full of dry tinder, waiting for a spark to set off a large wildfire. What I would have done differently with a Yin and Yang mindset is add at least one yin run a week, include some yin races in my calendar (substituting them for yang races, a topic I cover in Chapter 13), swap out a couple Bikram and Ashtanga yoga sessions each week for Yin Yoga, spend a little more time with my musical instruments, and get out of the office more just to take a walk. None of these would have been major changes in my life at the time, but in their totality would have made a major impact on my balance, flow experiences, and overall quality of life.

Bridging flow experiences

A beautiful thing about flow is that once we cultivate it in one area, we often are able to bridge this to another. We can bridge flow in running to flow at work (just think of that lunch run where you were lost in the zone and followed it up by crushing it at work in the afternoon with a stream of ideas to solve a problem you'd been stuck on for days). We can bridge flow across experiences in our runs, from running to other activities, and from other activities into running. I often use playing musical instruments to stimulate flow before a run, and the flow from that run to stimulate flow in my writing after the run. It is interconnected and each experience is richer because of this connection. I encourage you to build an awareness of flow experiences in different areas of your life and then experiment with bridging across them and building new bridges between flow. And let's not overcomplicate the bridging process. It is experiential and more about awareness and intention than a calculated set of steps to make it happen. That said, following the general guidance in this chapter and the specific guidance I offer on running will hopefully help you in your journey. Recognize also that sometimes the flow you are cultivating via your running shows up after the run and fuels an outstanding moment of creativity or productivity for you.

Flow Burnout

The downside of bridging flow experiences and actively seeking a lot of flow has to do with expectations. If you're aiming for high achievement across too many areas all once — job promotion, first ultra marathon, long triathlon a month later, online university program, baby on the way, moving across county or continents, etc. — you're poised to bridge your drive and energy across all of them to positive effect, but also at risk of creating an overload and burning out across all of these tracks. This can happen at a macro level (bad year, burnout) or micro level (bad day, non-productive and stressed).

Again, we go back to awareness and expectations. Plan your high performance, yang-focused targets wisely and with consideration of the need for yin complements. This could translate into building in yin recovery windows (e.g., two months with no structured training), or taking on only 2-3 big challenges across life at once (ultra marathon and online program now, then a period of non-structured play-oriented training while focusing on the stressful job project and the move).

Summary guidance on stress, burnout & yin-yang balance

1. Recognize and do something about your hidden stress contributors.

- Seek and destroy self-created stress that stems from unreasonable or un-useful expectations you set or allow others to set for you.
- Resist the culture of always being reachable and expected to respond to every instant message, email, phone call, voice mail and social media post immediately.
- Simplify your life: Leo Babauta's ZenHabits.net is an excellent resource for lifestyle guidance on simplifying your life. Check it out.
- Reduce the noise: Mark Divine teaches a news blackout in the

Unbeatable Mind program, as it's easy to create a lot of stress just by constantly tuning in to a 24x7 news cycle. Dial back your need to constantly check news and social media, especially during times when you seek more flow experiences and higher performance.

- Make yourself a priority: Whether you are leading a business, managing the needs of a large family, or both, if you do not take the time to focus on yourself (your health, fueling, recovery and stress management), you will not only miss out on optimal personal performance, you will find it increasingly difficult to support others. Be there for yourself to be there fully for others.

2. Consider your yin-yang balance with an eye toward your sustainable mind-body-spirit. For most, this means adding more yin to the equation. Invest more in recovery time, in powering down and consciously choosing activities that support this. Approach it with as much attention and discipline as you do physical conditioning.

3. Leverage flow in one area to generate flow in another. When you are "switched on" in one area, recognize the potential for bridging that flow to another area in your life. Also recognize that you may have to power some areas down from time to time, that is, regulate your expectations up or down to maximize your performance across multiple areas of your life without burning yourself out trying to seek peak flow experiences at home, work, and on the trail all at once, all the time, in all facets.

4. Quality over quantity: Instead of getting swept up in technology's push for a more quantified life, aim for balancing those innovations and constant stream of insights with a more qualified life, full of quality moments of communication, presence, and experience.

Chapter closing

Now that you are equipped with knowledge of the key flow topics and a set of important coaching insights into flow enablers and inhibitors, we're ready to move on to the integrated Flow State Runner model.

4. Integrated Flow State Runner Model

"It is not hard to compose, but what is fabulously hard
is to leave the superfluous notes under the table."
— Johannes Brahms

"The constant dilemma of the information age is that our ability to
gather a sea of data greatly exceeds the tools and techniques available
to sort, extract, and apply the information we've collected."
— Jeff Davidson

How do we consider, sort and apply so many lessons and insights from various technique books, workshops, articles, blogs, YouTube videos and our own trial and error? How do we then expand that to consider out-of-the-box ideas? Further, how do we integrate this knowledge in a manner that we can consistently call upon in peak states of intensity, fatigue and adversity? How do we get ourselves quickly into a mindset to accept the most helpful inputs when needed?

This is the *raison d'être* of the integrated Flow State Runner model. The short answer is that we place the knowledge into a simple and easily recallable framework and train ourselves to operate within that framework. The longer answer is the entirety of this book, but we begin with a study of this model.

As mentioned in the Introduction chapter, the integrated Flow State Runner model combines physical technique, mental training, and spiritual connectedness. It is designed to be a "plug-and-play" model that is modular and harmonic. In my coaching practice, the Flow State Runner model has worked well with the Pose Method®, ChiRunning®, mobility practices, and in many ways, with life in general. It is a complement, rather than an alternative, to many effective running techniques. Its underlying driver is to develop and strengthen your Inner Coach's voice.

Inner Coach

In the Introduction, I stated that the ability to remember and apply effective cues and actions is vital to increasing your performance, especially when you are away from a coach or technique book, two and a half hours into a long run, in a rainstorm while running through a city, or during full-speed soft sand sprints, intervals on a track or your first 5K. This "ability to remember" is your Inner Coach, the coach on your shoulder, and the coach you hear in your ear.

Your Inner Coach will guide you to focus on the most effective thing at the optimal time. Six months from now, you may not remember specific text on these pages, but if you plant the seeds of considering and practicing this model, those seeds will grow into oak trees of knowledge that you will likely never forget. You will benefit from your Inner Coach's voice, and it will grow stronger over time. It will speak up during your training runs and races, help you recall effective performance cues, and help you stay focused on what matters the most for the situation at hand. Your Inner Coach is not to be confused with normal mind chatter, where the subconscious mind attempts to steal the show from life in the present moment and provide you with non-stop dialogue, thoughts, worries, etc. No, your Inner Coach is there to serve you and guide you toward your goals as a runner. Its cultivated presence alone will aid in muting mind chatter while guiding you to Flow State Running moments.

Visual Models

The start to developing your Inner Coach's powers is to study, understand and ultimately internalize a clear visual model. A model is merely a representation of things or concepts. We're all familiar with models for cars, buildings and the planets in our solar system — these models are relatively easy to grasp; however, when we dive into conceptual models, things sometimes get foggy. To see through the fog, it helps to map conceptual models onto tangible things. That's what I provide you with in my model for reaching flow state by integrating your running technique priorities into your performance.

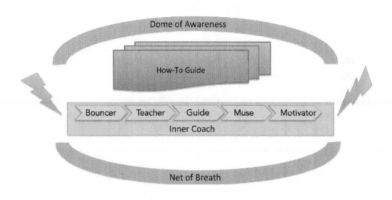

Image: Flow State Runner Model

Flow State Runner Orb

Think of the Flow State Runner model as an orb or a floating circular ecosystem. One of the best images I've found for this is the electric plasma globe from the 1980s. If you're too young to recall this, here is a picture, followed by a description.

Image: Plasma Globe.

The electric plasma globe was a glass sphere resting on a pedestal with an attached electrical cable. One could plug in the Plasma globe, touch the glass and a magical world of colors and electrical arcs appeared. Release it and not much happened. Touch it and it arced to life. Consider that image and then take a step deeper into this conceptual model.

Dome of Awareness

Covering the top is a dome of our model orb that I call the Dome of Awareness. The Dome sees all, hears all and feels all. It operates as an objective, yet interdependent entity. The Dome scans for the health of the runner it monitors, assesses situations, and sends out alerts.

Net of Breath

Supporting the bottom is the Net of Breath. The Net is made of a very strong mesh, that enables not only air to pass through, but also provides a supporting structure, without which the orb's ecosystem will not thrive. Simply put, the Net of Breath allows oxygen to feed the fire while providing an earthquake-proof foundation.

Bolts of Energy

When connected to an electrical source, there are Lightning Bolts arcing back and forth from the edges through the center. These are the sparks of energy, the spirit that charges and recharges the ecosystem. They are also the moments of adversity that arise to challenge you and create the struggle required to break into a flow state.

Nucleus of Knowledge

In the middle is a nucleus — in our case a Body of knowledge or How-To Guide containing techniques, cues, tips, pointers and experiences. The nucleus may be small and dense or large and loosely connected. Either way, it is a necessary but insufficient condition for the health of the ecosystem.

Inner Coach and Its Five Roles

Lastly, there's your Inner Coach and its virtuoso ability to play various roles when you need them the most. Your Inner Coach is a Bouncer, Teacher, Guide, Muse, and Motivator. Your Inner Coach is there to deal with your Inner Critic, to remind you of cues, to keep you focused, to inspire you, and to fire you up with a shot of adrenaline.

When attempting to improve your approach to anything, the quickest path to failure is to focus on multiple things at once, or worse, the contents of an entire How-To manual at once. Solving this challenge falls in the domain of a well-rounded and practiced Inner Coach mindset.

Tying it all together

Think about what makes organizations and ecosystems thrive: homeostasis. Each member of the ecosystem contributes, and the particular combination of members defines the ecosystem and its sustainability. Reaching flow in running requires a well-balanced integration of physical techniques, the dome, the net and sparks — with a targeted Inner Coach's voice broadcasting on a single frequency.

Before moving on, please take a moment to commit the basic Flow State Runner model to your memory. Envision the orb, the Dome overseeing all, the Net under it and bolts of energy zapping the orb. In the middle, see a glowing ball, representing the How-To of a particular physical activity, and tuning in to the voice of a coach offering only clear guidance. When you touch the orb, energy zaps through it, the Dome watches and guides, the Net keeps the structure supported and intact — the combination of which allows the inner part to glow.

The Burpee Flow Experience

Now, before we place running into this model, let's sharpen our understanding of it by taking it for a couple test drives with a simple bodyweight exercise: the burpee. For readers who have never tried a burpee, it's a challenging exercise that uses all the joints in the body and can easily chew up even the fittest athletes.

With our burpee selection, in the middle of the model we'll place a How-To Guide on performing the physical movement. The How-To Guide looks like this:

- **Step 1.** From a standing position, bend the knees and place both hands on the ground.
- **Step 2.** Jump the legs back to arrive at the top position of a push-up.
- **Step 3.** Lower to the ground until your chest touches.
- **Step 4.** Jump the feet forward, lift the hands from the ground and land with wide feet, heels contacting the ground, just like the bottom of a squat.
- **Step 5.** Stand up, jump and clap your hands over your head.

Burpee Example - Test Drive 1

For our first test drive, the task is *Do 5 burpees*. We follow the How-To Guide and repeat Steps 1-5 for a total of 5 burpees. For a single rep or a small number of reps, the How-To guide is sufficient instruction to successfully perform the job.

If we intensify the task, let's say to: *Perform 100 burpees in less than 6 minutes*, we will find that most people reach the limits of the basic How-To physical instruction. Fitness will certainly play a large role in the completion of this task; however, so will attitude, spirit, breathing, resilience and other factors. Relying on the How-To Guide is necessary but insufficient to achieve our performance goals in this more challenging task. How-To only gets us so far. Let's run this task through the Flow State Runner model to structure our Inner Coach's voice to guide us through the challenge of integrating the physical, mental and spiritual characteristics demanded by the task.

Burpee Example - Test Drive 2

Envision that you have completed the first few burpees of 100, aiming to finish in less than 6 minutes. The **Dome** is the observer and as such, runs a body scan and notices a super tense body during the first 10 reps and a negative inner dialog starting. The **Dome** flags each issue and calls **Inner Coach** into action.

Dome of Awareness

Inner Coach kicks in as a Guide, linking the **Dome's** scan with practiced, successful patterns in the **How-To** Guide and then delivering a single cue at a time. The first cue is *light like a feather*. **The Guide** calls for that cue over and over until the **Dome** calls for another one. For the purposes of this example, I've included the cues I use often for burpees. The cues coming from **Inner Coach** is a subject covered in detail relative to running in Chapter 9.

The **Net of Breath** engages with two deep belly breaths after every 10 burpees, with a focus on full exhalations. Later, the **Dome** calls for the **Net** to link *courage* to each inhale and *relax* to each exhale.

Net of Breath

The Energy Bolts strike soon under the adversity of this challenge — this releases adrenaline, cortisol and norepinephrine — all of which heighten your state of awareness and presence. At the 50 and 75-rep marks, the bolts strike again and call for a shout of "I've got this. Do it! You rock!" You visualize seeing the electrical charge building, feel the static build up and feel the POP each time the bolts hit. This supercharges your adrenaline release!

Other cues are ready if needed and represent the physical instructions: feet sweep to squat, hips lead, float down, float up. **Inner Coach** manages the selection and single use of cues, one at a time, ultimately leading you to a successful finish.

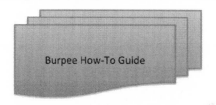

Burpee How-To Guide

98, 99, 100 in a time of 5:56!

A Model of Coherence

As a living, breathing ecosystem, the model delivers an optimized performance, which in this example is reaching a challenging time goal.

With an initial Plasma Globe image and our simple and slightly more complex burpee examples as test drives to understand the model, let's now move on to mind training and our study of the Dome of Awareness, without which flow state is but a wish.

By the way, this is a great point in the book to pause for 1-100 burpees (reader's choice) to immediately apply this model. Set your timer, and go!

5. *The Dome of Awareness: Training the Mind*

*"What is necessary to change a person
is to change his awareness of himself."*
—Abraham Maslow

Under the Dome in my first ultra

Finally! Finally, my turnaround point is in view. I strain my eyes to be sure … yes, that's it. The pain in my right side is killing me. Just stay with it. Don't give up. Stay with it. You can do this. The self-affirmations continue and I put one foot in front of the other. Just keep going.

Can I do this? Yes. What about the side pain? Ignore it. Are you sure you are strong enough for this? No, but don't stop now. I push onward with a laser-beam focus on the turnaround point. Get there. Get there! The drill sergeant in my head screams at me to keep moving. Get there, Jeff!

I make it. Reaching the turnaround is a huge joy, but I know the worst is yet to come. I'm in new territory now, never having run this far. The side pain won't go away. My breathing is heavy — I just can't seem to get in enough air. Breathe deep Jeff. You've got this. You will finish.

One foot in front of the other, that's all I can do. Why are you doing this, Jeff? Because I have to. I promised myself. My stride is shortening, my feet moving only at a shuffle. I shuffle onward, refusing to walk. DO NOT WALK! DO NOT WALK! I tell myself over and over. Shuffle, shuffle, shuffle — just keeping moving! It hurts — I want to walk. I want to stop. Why am I doing this? Am I causing long-term damage?

You know why you're doing this Jeff. Keep moving! My lower back is aching now. My knees hurt too. Nothing feels good. I'm moving so slowly. The sun has set and it's getting darker by the minute. Do not walk! You must finish.

Relentless forward progress — I remember this slogan and repeat it over and over. Think of your wife and your family. Do it for them. This is your moment to shine, to realize a dream. Now run!

After what seems like an eternity, I see the finish line. My pace quickens and my heartbeat jumps into high gear. I want this. I can do this. I will do this! My shuffle upgrades to a full-on run. I feel no pain in my feet, no pain in my side. I run hard for the finish blowing past another runner and almost into the path of a car. I give it my very best effort, and my run turns into a sprint. I'm out of my body now — bolting for the finish. I feel chill bumps on my arms and see a grand finish stage, full of bright lights and screaming fans.

In complete silence, I cross the finish line. No one is there to cheer. The only fanfare is in my head. I am overcome with emotion and drop to one knee. I feel a sick at my stomach and need some water. I now feel my aching feet and knees and back. Moments later I smile. I have accomplished something amazing — for *me*. I have accomplished something no one would have imagined even 1 week ago. I've run 5 kilometers without stopping. That's right, 5KM. It took me, in my 32kg /70lbs. overweight body, nearly 40 minutes, but I didn't walk once. I had just finished my first "ultra" run — at least it was ultra to me, and I was unbelievably happy.

Nothing like the first time

This was my first taste of the Dome of Awareness and of hearing my Inner Coach's voice. I remember it vividly; it symbolized a commitment to a physical transformation as well as an immersion into the world of removing myself from the physical and "seeing" myself from the outside. As if I had an eagle's eye view flying above, I watched myself running, noticed issues that needed to be addressed and prioritized them. And as if a coach were running beside me, I "heard" an Inner Coach's voice speaking to me and offering guidance and motivation. This may sound to some like a hallucination, but it is far from it.

No, when harnessed, this voice (and the perspective from which it speaks) is a game changer. In this first-time experience, I made it happen, gave it life and even gave it a commanding accent. Fortunately, in this pivotal running experience, the voice was positive and led me toward my desired outcome. Later, especially in ultra marathons, I would be visited by a negative voice, which I created, and which I call the Inner Critic. It is a dangerous, devious voice, expert at unraveling your mind and body. We'll talk more about Inner Coach and Inner Critic in Chapter 9.

To each her own ... gym, that is.

There is a captivating world of empirical, experiential and ancient knowledge around training the mind, with resources spanning books, camps, silent meditation and yoga retreats and more. Western culture embraces the concept of physical training in a major way, as evidenced by countless gyms, exercise equipment, workout clothes and training gadgets. As a simple example, imagine a scenario with several business people finishing a day at a conference. They briefly chat in the hotel lobby about their plans before meeting for dinner:

Jessica: I'm going to hit the hotel gym for a killer Burpees, Thrusters & Kettle Bell Swings workout my CrossFit box is doing today.

John: It's almost race season and I need speed, so I'm going out for an interval run.

Alexis: With my marathon in a month and our final pitch to the client tomorrow, I'm going to my mind gym to work on stillness.

John: To your what?

Alexis: My mind gym.

Jessica: *Where* is that?

Alexis: Right here (points to head) and here (points to heart) and all throughout actually.

Jessica: What will you *do* when you're *there*?

Alexis: Deep breathing, a visualization exercise, a positivity practice and a brief meditation.

John: So you're going to take a nap?

Alexis: Funny, Mr. Fartlek. No nap time in today's session, but alpha waves do leave me feeling refreshed.

Jessica: Sounds a little too new age for me. It's Burpee time!

John: Me too, gotta run. Have a nice nap!

Not far-fetched, is it? The Western world, and perhaps parts of the modern Eastern world as well, is not (yet) comfortable in the mainstream with the concept of mental training, at least not in the same accepted manner as physical training. Some see it as new age spirituality. (I'd suggest that this "some" may not so readily find themselves engaging in flow experiences.) What is strange about this misperception is its lack of alignment with history: notably the ancient, noble warrior traditions of the Orient. The training of the Samurai and Ninja, for example, was built on mastering the mind, the mental and spiritual, before mastering physical movements. We see this in the martial arts practice today, where a major emphasis is placed on breathing, visualization, and mental stillness. The mind gym concept is not a new fad to optimize performance, it is the original foundation.

In *Unbeatable Mind*, Mark Divine offers, "The discipline of the warrior is to train for full-spectrum integration, ready to respond to any challenge with a virtuosity born of a clear heart and mind." Clearing the heart and mind takes place in a mental training space like the mind gym. That's how the Dome of Awareness and Inner Coach grow more powerful every day.

Spring-boarding to the practical

While I introduce a wide range of knowledge areas to inform your running practice, my central aim is to integrate high-impact concepts and skills and to help you to channel them into practical application. The next step to this end is a discussion of the practical application of mind training. The resources in the Appendix will assist those interested in further exploration of mental, emotional, and spiritual training. These books offer a much deeper look at the "why" behind the guidance I offer. Let's move now to the practical.

Most running technique approaches start with the physical — where to put the body, how to move the arms and legs, and how to synchronize movements. After working with countless runners in technique workshops, I know that when the mind is in the wrong place, it doesn't matter how the body is organized, the runner will not reach an optimized flow state of performance. Even if a runner momentarily reaches it, it is doubtful that she'll be able to sustain and repeat it. Reaching flow state requires a foundation designed to support flow state's high speed processing and high bandwidth data transfer, to borrow the language of technology. So, instead of starting with the physical and putting frosting on the cake with the application of mental techniques at the end, we're starting with the mental, and we'll build from there.

Floating at the Top

If you recall from Chapter 4, the Dome of Awareness floats at the top of the Flow State Runner model.

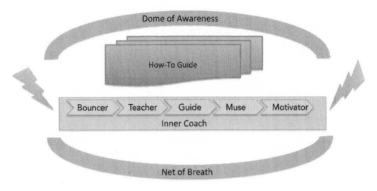

Image: Flow State Runner Model

The Dome is the master of senses with the ability to see all, hear all and feel all. It operates as an objective party, dependent on the body, but operating at a different, higher level. The Dome handles 3 important functions.

1. **Scans**: for the health of the ecosystem in its domain, notably your physical body and your inner dialogue
2. **Assesses**: evaluates observations against your practiced patterns, your goals and How-To knowledge
3. **Calls to action**: selects coaching cues and calls for Inner Coach

Building the Dome's Foundation

The Dome of Awareness is a critical concept to understand, practice and internalize. I'll teach you how to operate the Dome in the next chapter using a simplified acronym: "SPA," for Scan-Pick-Act. Before we get there, we need to ensure that a strong foundation is in place and maintained. There are four main Dome baseline practices to immerse yourself in and ultimately master.

- Prime the Mind
- Practice Body Awareness
- Assess Tension and Strive for the Minimum Effective Dose (MED)
- Build and Train in your Visualization Run-Simulator

With these in place and growing over time, you'll be poised to engage the Dome in every run. Now, let's study each in detail.

1) Prime the Mind

I envision that even if you're not reading these words right now on a gadget (tablet, smartphone, e-reader, etc.), that you've likely used one within the past couple of hours, if not the past few minutes. They've reached ubiquity in our daily lives. If you were to pry open the nearest tech device (*don't try this at home!*), you would find high performance microprocessors, memory, and other supporting features (antennas, sensors, battery, etc.) all resting on a silicon foundation. None of these high performance parts can contribute to the device's delivery of book pages to your eyes or a myriad of other dazzling features without their connection to one another via a high performance bus, which is the superhighway of circuitry connecting the specialty components. The most powerful microprocessor is useless unless it is connected to a superhighway capable of sending it input and receiving its output as fast as it can handle the workload, and the most powerful, sensitive sensor is useless unless it is connected to something that can pass along what it senses.

Thus, in terms related to Flow State Running, we must have a daily mind training practice that effectively greases the neural pathways, or in the technology example, lays down and clears traffic on the connecting circuitry in our minds. With that in place, we can run high performance tasks through our "computer" and get the output to our bodies.

Using another visual example, think of various highways connecting specialty processing centers in your brain, as well as memory banks and sensors. These highways sometimes get clogged with traffic and often that traffic has nothing to do with the task you are focused on. We need a traffic clearing system, and that happens through regular mind training practice.

Have you ever been on a long road trip that required driving through a major city en route to your destination and you just happened to be passing through that city at rush hour? Whenever that happens, instead of spending a short time driving past the city, you are now caught up in its inhabitants' daily commute, where you may spend hours just to move 20KM.

"No!" you cry. "I'm not part of this — I'm not going where you are going. I'm just passing through!" In those situations, what you want is a Police escort that you can call upon to immediately clear your lane and lead you on your way unimpeded! In your mind space, you can make that happen — you can create the ability to summon a Police escort whenever traffic appears and clogs the highways of your mind. The more your practice summoning and using that Police escort, the easier and more quickly it will come, and this will have an immediate impact on your running.

To prime the mind to operate in Dome of Awareness mode, embark on a daily mind training practice of at least five minutes. I list three practices below as starters and include references in the Appendix to more. Your dedication to completing these exercises and practices consistently will directly translate into your ability to interact with the Dome of Awareness in your running. If you have a meditation practice already and/or spend more than five minutes on these types of mind training activities, you're doing the right thing — so keep at it and incorporate the rest of the Dome exercises into your practices.

For each of these exercises, set a five minute count-down timer and perform the task. Eventually this may feel like it's not enough time, especially as your training and experience progresses and your still mind opens benefits to you that leave you seeking more stillness. Thus, it is always OK to lengthen the exercise and dive deeper into concentration and meditation practices. If you are just starting out though, I suggest keeping it simple and aiming for completion of just five minutes a day.

Mind Primer 1:

Concentration in Movement: Think of yourself as a robot, requiring an instruction for each tiny micro-movement to perform a task. To move any part of your robot body, you must issue a command, specifying which muscles to flex or relax to yield a movement, as well as how much tension to apply and when to stop and start the movements. Keep it simple, such as opening and closing your hand from a fist to lying flat on a surface. Take 2.5 minutes to open it and another 2.5 minutes to make a fist, issuing instructions in your mind for the movement of each digit at each joint while you stare intently at the movement. Other movement patterns include taking one or a few steps, moving into our out of a yoga pose, or doing a smooth dance.

When I studied orchestral conducting briefly in university, I would often set a count-down timer for 5-10min and just walk around the house conducting at different tempos with one hand and picking up objects smoothly with the other. The objective was to train my myself to move one hand smoothly to deliver an expression while the other moved rhythmically. It was an extremely effective exercise and also proved to be a meditative practice. Try it the next time you're moved by music for some air-conducting!

Mind Primer 2:

Hyper-focused listening: This exercise works best in nature, but it is possible in any environment. You job is to listen to ambient sounds intently for the full five minutes, while allowing your ears to tune in to as many different sounds as possible, one at a time. In nature, this may start as hearing the sound of some nearby birds, but grow more deeply as you tune it to the sound of wind in the trees, a dog barking in the distance, a rooster crowing, running water, and more. In an urban environment, it will be different types of vehicles, conversations and accents, the hum of a light, an airplane, etc. Even in a sensory deprivation or *floating* tank, which is an excellent relaxation and mind training tool, you can tune into the sounds of your heart beat, breathing, and the water.

Mind Primer 3:
Color-Absorption: Have a look around you and focus on the first color that grabs your attention. Bring all of your powers of focus to that color. Think it, feel it, absorb it. Observe other senses that this color activates. Does it bring back a memory of a time in life? An experience? A smell? Does it make you feel warm or cold? Does it make you happy, sad, energized, calm or some combination? Notice any shadows you see on the surface with this color. Any variations, where it's lighter or darker. Allow your focus to soften and blur and notice any changes in your observations. Then, bring your focus to a very sharp level, almost looking through the color. Notice any new thoughts that arise.
Notice the next closest color and repeat the exercise.

Additional mind primers include yoga, playing a musical instrument or composing music, cooking, breath training, observing birds and insects, forest walks, and for some, smooth movement sports such as swimming, carving skiing, XC classic or skate skiing, rock climbing, etc. If you notice a connection between mind primers and yin-contributing, flow-enabling activities that I discussed in Chapter 3, you're making the right association.

2) Practice Body Awareness
To place our bodies in the most efficient positions for running and most importantly, to then keep them there when faced with all of the adversities runners face (weather, fatigue, terrain, etc.), we need strong

proprioception, that is, a strong sense of where our bodies are in space in time. While much of proprioception is handled on automatic pilot by the brain (e.g., Someone tosses you a ball as a surprise and your hand instantly moves into place to catch it), it is possible to train and strengthen your mind's ability to recognize inputs and connect them to exact body position and tension. This is a very important area to develop in your quest for more Flow State Running experiences.

Body Awareness Primer 1

Stand up and close your eyes. Reach your arms up in the air, from the side of your body to outstretched overhead. Lower one arm to any height and position your wish (halfway down, 3/4 of the way down with elbow at 90°, etc.). Lower the other arm as you lift the opposite arm, reaching to a different place either out or up. Continue this opposite lifting and lowering pattern, bending at the elbow and arriving at different starting and finishing positions with each movement. After a series of raises and lowers, freeze and guess where your hands are in relation to your body. Draw a mental image of the exact position of your arms, the angle at your elbows, the specific direction each hand faces, the nearest point on your body from your index fingers and the exact separation of your fingers. Open your eyes and test yourself. Were you able to sense precisely the ending position, in all of its detail?

Body Awareness Primer 2

Repeat Body Awareness Primer 1, but this time after a series of alternating arm up-down movements, attempt to stop with the arms level, palms facing and separated by the width of two fists, thumbs up. Open your eyes and see how you did. If you struggle with either of these exercises, keep practicing them. It gets better! If you find them easy, then increase the challenge by first turning in circles and jumping up and down (eyes remain closed). Then move your arms, attempt to stop with them level and open your eyes to check your results.

Body Awareness Primer 3

Film yourself running. This works best with a friend who films you from the side, with the camera panning with you as you run past. Review the video frame by frame and notice how you strike the ground, the positioning and movement of your arms, the angle of your head, the angle of your foot and any other body positioning factors that catch your eye. Experiment with making a change and re-filming. Notice how it feels to you in comparison to how it looks on the video.

This approach often works best using an exaggeration method: try exaggerating where on your foot you contact the ground, filming one video with a significant heel strike and another video where you land as far forward on the feet as possible. Remember, this exercise is about developing greater body awareness, particularly in areas where you haven't practiced a high level of awareness. That is why the exaggeration method is so effective. You are emphasizing both ends of the spectrum of body positioning and movement. By doing so, you will program the mind to understand how it feels throughout all of the spectrum and how to engage your body effectively to operate exactly where you want it to in the spectrum. To that end, it is important for the mind and body to collect and process a large number of inputs.

Speaking of video, some coaches, myself included, offer remote video analysis services. This is a good way to bring expert eyes and guidance to filming. There's nothing like seeing yourself on film! I've filmed countless runners who are 100% certain that they (insert action: are forefoot runners, never heel strike, have a fast cadence, have a relaxed upper body, etc.), and who learn upon reviewing their video with me that what they perceive about their body's positioning and movement is opposite of what it is actually doing!

If you have access to a local coach, then you can't beat the combination of reviewing yourself on film and then working with a coach in-person.

Body Awareness Primer 4

Go for an adventure run, that is, a run full of variation and play. Vary the terrain and incorporate features in the environment such as stairs, grassy hills, parks, puddles and roots to jump over, etc. Occasionally freeze while moving on or near these features. Close your eyes and memorize how your body feels in its positioning and alignment. Think anatomically: where are your feet in relation to your hips? How high or low are your knees and what is their relative difference? Where are your arms in relation to one another and your feet? Which way are you looking and what is the angle of your neck? Open your eyes and check your awareness powers. Reinforce where you got it right and learn from where you struggled to sense your body's real position. Memorize the position and try to repeat it later on a different obstacle or simply mid-run.

Blind running is also an excellent awareness teacher. Run across a large grassy field free of obstacles. Close your eyes for as long as you feel comfortable. Running without your sense of vision will immediately open your other senses, which in turn will teach you more about how your body feels in various positions.

3) Assess Tension and Strive for Minimum Effective Dose (MED)

As I mentioned in the Introduction, runners often fail to realize the benefits they seek because they are unconsciously keeping too much tension in the body. They may understand the mechanics of efficient running technique and strive to put their body in the right place at the right time, yet it feels awkward, forced and far from efficient. The underlying issue is tension, excessive muscular tension to be precise.

Consider a runner out on a lunchtime run, stressed from a busy morning of work and worried about a series of meetings in the afternoon. During her run, she holds that stress first in the form of a clenched left fist. That tension carries itself upstream to her left shoulder and across the body to her belly and right hip. On top of this physical tension, she adds to her normal work worries the self-pressure to run with perfect technique and at a specific pace, thus introduces more layers of tension. During the run, despite her best efforts, she never reached flow state and worse, felt tight, slow and mechanical throughout. Her breathing never felt smooth and easy and now her left knee is hurting again. Argh!

The difference between a Flow State Run that leaves her smiling and a frustrating run that leaves her with new layers of stress is her awareness and management of tension. By holding on to too much tension, she blocked her body's ability to move smoothly, lightly and in accordance with the physical technique she's pursuing. Even worse, the tension traveled to other areas of her body, increasing its negative impact with each foot strike and creating a target rich environment for injury.

When the tension is released and reduced to its lowest level needed for the task at hand, the mind will follow, and the body will be freed to move where it needs to be and when it needs to be there. Tim Ferriss drew from a pharmacology term to make an excellent point in his bestseller *The 4-Hour Body,* and it's a term I'll further borrow as it perfectly describes the desired state of muscular tension we seek while running: Minimum Effective Dose or MED. Ignore excessive tension at your own peril. Scan, find and release it to reach arrive at MED and ultimately Flow State.

While there is no Silver Bullet to immediately cease tension and dissolve stress, the aforementioned mind training and awareness primers will help you build a strong foundation upon which to employ assessment and MED tools. These mental tools allow you to detect different levels of tension in the body, understand upstream and downstream tension, including your mind, and to adjust the tension to appropriate levels. Lastly, it is important to remember to regularly repeat the scan, as tension is a restless beast, waiting to pounce the moment a new adversity enters your run.

It helps as well to consider our default state. As humans with active minds capable of imagining, perceiving, worrying and doing countless other tasks simultaneously, we're very good at bringing too much tension to the table. We typically and intrinsically find ourselves defaulting to states of stress, rather than calmness, distraction rather than focus, and worry rather than confidence. Thus, it is likely that your assessment of tension will result in a need to dial it back, rather than increase your tension, especially in running.

It may help to think of tension and MED in terms of a mixing board used by sound engineers or DJs. Imagine you have a console containing many sliding buttons, known as faders or sliders, to adjust the tension in various parts of your body from Level 0 (no tension whatsoever) to Level 10, max tension. Slider 1 is feet, Slider 2 is hamstrings, Slider 3 is upper back, and so forth. You are the engineer controlling this tension mixing board each time you run. It is your choice if you want to set all sliders to Level 3, all to Level 8 or use a mix that suits your practical and artistic needs. It is also your choice if you want to set it and leave it in place for the entire run or constantly monitor and adjust based on the evolution of your run, the change in terrain, the change in your goal or plan, etc.

What is our natural tendency for tension in running? Too often, especially when faced with an adversity such as a steep hill or fast interval, it is to hurriedly smother the mixing board with our hands and mindlessly slam all of the faders up to their max setting. This is the quick *fix-everything-including-the-kitchen-sink* approach of immediately dialing up the tension levels in our body. I'll borrow a term from *Spinal Tap* fame to describe this default response, and refer to it as *Turning it all up to 11.*

Image: example sound mixing board

Just as the result of sliding all mixing board faders to their max setting in a music concert is an unpleasant distortion of sound that drowns out the nuances and subtleties of music, the result in our bodies when running is that we lock ourselves down and prevent efficient technique execution, as well as our ability to reach flow. The next time you encounter a hill or start an interval run, ask yourself if you are moving all tension sliders "to 11." If so, pull them back to zero and employ the artistry of a sound engineer to increase only the faders that are absolutely necessary up to the level where they produce the sound you are looking for, but nothing more.

Assessing excess tension is best illustrated with two simple exercises.

Tension Assessment Exercise - Standing
Stand up and scan your body simply noticing tension levels and rating your muscular tension on a scale of 1 to 10, with 1 complete and total relaxation and 10 as maximum tension (all muscles engaged strongly). When you notice different tension levels, rate whatever tension level fits a given area. It is normal to have a range of perceived tension levels in the body, even when simply standing. Now bring all of various tension levels to Level 5 evenly spread across your entire body. Don't forget your neck, jaw, tongue, fingers, belly and toes.

Gradually raise the tension level to 6, 7 and 8, holding each for several seconds. Recover at Level 3 for ten seconds. Then return to level 8 and on to 9. Recover at Level 2 for ten seconds. Lastly, move to Level 10, a true Level 10, where every muscle in your body is at maximum tension. Hold this for ten seconds, then relax. Practice cueing yourself to reach a certain level throughout your entire body, and then instantly arriving there.

Tension Assessment Exercise - Running

Repeat the standing tension awareness exercise while running. First, observe and asses your natural tension level, overall as well as in different areas of your body. Do you normally run at a 3? Or perhaps a 7? Or are your legs at a 3 and shoulders at a 9?

Wherever you are naturally, experiment with running at Level 3, Level 7 and Level 10. The objective in this exercise isn't to arrive at the perfect tension level, but to develop your awareness of muscular tension in your body while running. Try the assessment at different paces and different types of terrain. What happens when you encounter a hill or run an interval? Are you able to maintain a specific level or does it immediately jump to 10? Are you able to sprint at a 3? How about sprinting with the legs at 8 and rest of the body at 2? Try it!

Awareness of how muscular tension feels in different parts of your body and at differing levels of tension or contraction is the first skill to build, first stationary, and then in movement. With this concept in place, let's move on to determining your Minimum Effective Dosage (MED).

As mentioned before, MED is all about setting the muscular tension to its lowest level needed for the task at hand. When placed in an adversity, such as trying to learn and hone a new technique or running up a hill, runners tend to ramp up the tension level throughout the body to a level much higher than needed. The Dome offers you a goal (MED) and an Inner Coach's voice to remind you to keep assessing and adjusting your tension to reach it. Let's learn and practice MED first.

MED Exercise - Standing

Return to standing at Level 10 and hold it for ten seconds, and then relax. How long do you think you could stand in a true Level 10? 30 seconds? 1 minute? 10 minutes? For most, after just a minute or two, either we'd subconsciously reduce the tension or we'd pass out! If the challenge were simply to stand still for one hour, we'd never choose Level 10 as our tension level for standing. We'd want to choose as low of a number as possible.

Next, pick your tension level for a 1-hour stand and set yourself at that level for a 30-second stand. After 30 seconds, stay in position and complete the following:

- Soften your knees
- Relax your belly
- Relax your tongue
- Allow your shoulders to sink lower
- Soften the space between your eyes
- Exhale slowly and release any lingering tension

The quest we are on is to find your MED for standing and you may have thought you found it before you started the 30-second test. One or more of these additional cues likely helped you relax more deeply, thus more closely approaching your true MED for standing. This illustrates that our perception of relaxation of muscular tension often doesn't meet reality. It requires practicing our awareness and assessment skills until they are finely tuned habits. Plus, the only way to really know MED is to go below the lower limit. In the case of standing, this would mean relaxing so much that we fall and then standing again right at that limit before falling.

MED Exercise - Running

Go on a run and after you've assessed your average tension level, experiment with systematically releasing tension throughout the main tension-holding areas of your body (hands, shoulders, neck, jaw, belly, hips, legs). Run at an easy pace and see how low you can go. Then increase the pace and try to maintain the lowest possible MED. Remember, MED is the minimum amount of tension required for the task at hand. Just because you're running fast doesn't mean that tension is instantly high. Instead of taking a top-down approach, where you turn all muscles up to 8 or even 10, take a bottom-up approach, where you only turn on just enough tension for the muscles that need it, with the others left on idle at the lowest possible tension level. Try this exercise in challenging terrain as well, always striving to reduce tension to arrive at your MED.

In Chapter 7, I share techniques for quickly releasing tension, which I term tension-dumping. The key takeaway at this stage is to regularly pay attention to tension in the body — how to identify it, how to measure it and how to bring it to the minimum amount needed for any given task.

Let's return to our lunchtime runner. Imagine that if 5 minutes into the run, she scans her body and notices the tight left fist. Her Inner Coach speaks up, cuing her to dump tension. She opens her left hand, shakes it and moves her arms in circles. She takes a few deep breaths and brings her awareness to releasing as much tension as possible in her body, starting with her left arm and traveling throughout. This stream of tension release travels all the way through her shoulders and neck and down to her belly and hips. She immediately feels lighter and smoother, at which point the mechanics of good form are enabled and seem natural. Her pace increases and she feels like she's floating. Enter flow state.

4) Build and Train in your Visualization Run-Simulator

Visualization is the practice of creating an image or movie in your mind and using your contemplation of that image as a simulator, to train and acclimate your mind for being there in the physical world at a later time. The more time you spend in the simulator reinforcing the desired outcomes, the more enabled you will be to realize the outcomes in real life. It is an investment in the future you wish to create for yourself.

Visualization can be used to see yourself in an end-state, accomplishing a goal, such as your arrival at the Finish Line at a race. It can also be used to rehearse an action, feeling or movement, such as seeing yourself floating effortlessly through the last 10KM of a marathon or running a challenging mountain pass at night 150KM into an ultra marathon. Visualization may also be used to shift your mind's paradigm to trick it into removing self-imposed limits. For example, in the opening chapter, I shared a powerful, personal Flow State experience of racing in the Sahara and visualizing a peloton of friends shielding me from the heat and wind. Alone in a sparse lead group, I needed support, so I created a virtual world to surround me in that scorching, desolate desert. This visualization immersion immediately triggered a flow state experience, which quietened my mind's resistance to holding on to what seemed like an impossible pace under the conditions. The result was a performance far above what I believed was possible, aided greatly by a visualized scene and the energy it delivered.

You may have noticed professional athletes practicing visualization in the moments before competition, with their eyes closed and perhaps arms and shoulders offering a glimpse of the choreographed moves being played on a film in their mind. It is commonly seen in skiers, bob sled racers, Formula 1 drivers, platform divers and gymnasts, and is used across a range of sports, arts and technical disciplines. Visualization training propels you toward flow in running by providing a simulated environment where your mind controls your effortless, light execution of your efficient movement. By logging time in this simulator, like a pilot does to develop their skill and practice for a variety of scenarios, you will accelerate your experience development and more quickly acclimate mind and body to what flow state feels like and how to return to it with less effort.

Building your Simulator - Visualization Fundamentals
Follow the Crawl-Walk-Run approach to build your own simulator for Flow State Running.

Crawl first by sitting with your eyes closed and creating a static scene in your mind. The power and the beauty of a visualization is in the details, and those details are very important in creating an effective mind training experience and building your baseline for more Flow State Running experiences. The more detail you add, the more profound visualization experiences you will build. From nature, to artificial structures, to the weather, become a master at painting mental images. If you are visualizing a running track upon which you will later place a high performance image of yourself, see the color and texture of the running surface, see the infield, the long jump pit and the pole vault area. If you are visualizing a trail, see the trees, roots and rocks. See a lake, mountains and birds flying. See the width of the trail, as well as subtle changes, such as areas that are wet or muddy.

Become an expert at visualizing in as much detail as possible, and stretch beyond images to visualize with your other senses to include sounds, smells, temperature, wind, and emotions. Build a library of detailed, pre-built simulator scenes that you can call upon in the future: track, trail, mountain, desert, urban, rain, night, sleep-deprived, etc. Try to think of any condition that you may ever encounter in your running and prepare a scene to store in your visualization library.

Walk next, by making the visualized scene not only detailed, but also dynamic. Consider commercial flight simulators, which meticulously incorporate detail (video, computer graphics, physical controls) and hydraulically driven movement to offer the pilot as realistic as possible simulated experience in response to input controls and various scenarios (weather, equipment failures, etc.). The scripted scenarios offer a critical opportunity to learn from prior experiences and to practice in a safe environment. For example, a flight simulator may include a scripted scenario for a rainy night-time landing at Amsterdam Schiphol Airport on runway 18R with a strong, gusty westerly wind. With the script set, the pilot practices his actions in response to the script and thus safely explores, tests, learns and reinforces desired actions and outcomes to best fit the scenario. Let's transfer that to simulators for running and build your dynamic simulator by thinking through and then visualizing various scripts you expect or you wish to encounter in your running. This could include your desired response to challenging weather conditions or extreme fatigue, or simply an effortless run on a beautiful day. I encourage you to invest time in building scripts that emphasize positive patterns and overcoming adversities. The more vast your library is and more time you spend reviewing these mental films, the more likely it is that your mind and body will return to these "known" states when you are running.

In my research for *Flow State Runner,* I completed a Superbike Motorcycle Racing course. Before each track session, I would visualize driving my rented Ducati through each corner on the race track. In my eyes-closed visualization, I would work the controls of the bike, shifting gears, applying the throttle, leaning and looking through the corner to my exit point. I would visualize the feel of gravity in the lean, the pressure of my leg on the gas tank, a relaxed grip and a calm breath and the feel of acceleration as I confidently carved the bike out of the corner. When I experienced high speed cornering on the track, I felt like I had been there before and felt much more confident than prior to the visualizations when I felt intimated by the bike and the course.

Lastly, *Run* by creating and experiencing a detailed, dynamic visualization on the go — while under movement, either in training or in a race. In my visualization in the Sahara, I built a strong foundation by regularly practicing visualization prior to the race. I had routine mind-training sessions, where I saw myself running across sand dunes in my full desert racing gear, covered in a layer of sand and feeling the intense heat. In those visualizations I saw myself focused, but with an ever present smile. I visualized feeling light, free and happy to race in such a beautiful landscape, regardless of the adversities it offered. This is exactly how I felt when encountering the race in real life, so my run-simulator proved very effective, allowing me to train in a virtual Sahara during a snowy winter in Zurich.

While I was well-practiced in visualization training, I had however never visualized a supporting peloton of friends pulling me through the final section of the long stage. That visualization opened itself to me in the moment, in-flight, as I was in desperate need of something extra to achieve the goal I was chasing. I started this visualization while running by focusing on the details of each of my friend's faces. I saw that they were suffering in the heat, but were fully passionate about getting me to the finish line. The look of my closest friend experiencing pain to help me achieve a goal sent a jolt of lightning and adrenaline into my system, as I felt driven to honor his effort by giving all of myself. I saw that look in his eyes — a look of emotion and fatigue — and I visualized it in great detail. I saw my friends running in front of and beside me. I zoomed out, and viewed myself and supporting friends from overhead, as if from the race helicopter. I viewed our entourage as a powerful and unstoppable wave rolling across the desert, hell-bent on rolling right across the finish line with more energy every second.

There is immense power in an ability to create the energy you need *in-flight*, in response to whatever situation you encounter. Start simple on your next run by visualizing someone special running at your side. Take time to see the details of his or her face and expressions. Perhaps you simply bask in the warmth of running with a loved one, or perhaps you hear them offer words of encouragement. You can expand on this by linking people to scenarios where you would benefit the most from their support. For example, in my visualization library, I can call upon my late grandfather to appear running at my side to offer me confidence early in an ultra marathon, when the end is a seemingly impossible 24 hours away, and my late Cocker Spaniel "Brandy" to remind me to keep it playful in the mountains, as she would constantly sprint ahead, turn and smile at me, wag her tail like crazy and sprint ahead again.

We will revisit Visualization in Section 2, as it is a very important tool in training and racing.

Building a strong foundation

To review, the Dome performs three core functions: Scans, Assess and Calls to Action. The Dome's ability to perform these functions at an optimal level is linked to your practice of mind primers, body awareness activities, MED and visualization. With each of these baseline practices established, you will be well on your way to building a strong and enduring Dome foundation.

Now let's shift to activating the Dome!

6. *Operating Your Dome of Awareness*

"We become what we behold.
We shape our tools and then our tools shape us."
— Marshall McLuhan

SPA

To help you remember the Dome's functions, we can use the simple acronym "SPA" to indicate the three Dome steps of Scan-Pick-Act.

Scan	Pick	Act!
Perform Body Scan	Select ONE observation	Take immediate action!

Step 1 — Perform a Body Scan

The first function of the Dome of Awareness is to scan for the health of the ecosystem in its domain — you. This is performed with a body scan, which in practice is a scan of both mind and body. The body scan is a conceptual practice that can be associated in the physical world with any type of diagnostics machine that scans our bones and soft tissue. I like to think of it in sci-fi terms like a futuristic scanner that can "see" not only the physical, but also our tension level and thoughts.

Developing an ability to scan your body and mind in a consistent manner is a key fundament to development of a strong Inner Coach mindset. This is important, because we are very good at self-diagnosing the symptom of a problem, not the cause of it. When we spend too much time and energy on dealing with the symptom, we can become mired in a negativity spiral and miss an opportunity to address the underlying cause. When you remove the immediate need for a solution and start with an objective scan of your systems, you open yourself to more quickly identifying the root cause, which you can then deal with using your Inner Coach's voice.

Here's a story to illustrate:

A few hours after landing in Southern California following twenty-two hours of travel from Zurich, I went out for a planned 2-hour jet lag-shaker run that turned into a 5-hour adventure that taught me a lesson and illustrated the value of the Inner Coach mindset and body scans. During this run, which was somewhat playful and easy for the first few hours, I abruptly hit the wall and spent an hour in an ever-slowing slog, mired in negative thoughts. Noticing that my pace had significantly slowed and that I was no longer enjoying the experience, I immediately diagnosed "the problem" as my mindset. I told myself to toughen up, set a good example and pick up the pace. I continued to hammer away at mindset and attitude, raking myself over the coals with self-talk and getting slower by the minute.

It finally occurred to me to hit the stop button on my problem-solving approach and visualize a coach simply watching me run, looking inside my mind at my thoughts and giving me some guidance. I saw this coach operating a scanner starting at my head and working down. When the scanner reached my lower torso, it noticed that I was bent over, folded at the waist well beyond the guidelines of proper technique. The scanner also picked up that I was distracted with an overload of thoughts and problem-solving instructions, that my breathing was labored and that my right knee was in pain. I allowed the scanner to complete its journey from head to toes and then I selected just one of the areas it identified as a concern. I selected posture and made the simple adjustment of standing up taller and opening my diaphragm.

Within minutes, I noticed a change in my breathing, followed by a return to a feeling of lightness. As I returned to an efficient position, my pace increased and I once again began to notice the beauty of the surrounding area. My negative self-dialogue simply vanished, not via the brute force approach I had been applying, but via a simple body scan and posture correction. On my post-run review, I traced the root cause further up-stream and determined that I had been under-focusing on my core training and it was a relative weakness in my core that led to my slow slide to a rounded, bent position. I made sure that my body scan checklist for future runs included a check for this slight forward bend and I devoted much more time to core training!

Instructions for performing a Body Scan

- Start at your head and work down to your feet with a visualized review of the key physical and mental aspects you wish to monitor.
- Spend only as much time in each area as you require to observe what is happening in the moment.
- Observe the body:
  » posture
  » tension level
  » movement patterns
  » sounds
  » pain
  » breathing
  » rhythms: pace of movement
- Observe the mind:
  » thought patterns (positive-negative, encouraging-discouraging, critical-supportive, fear-confidence, past vs. present vs. future)
  » traffic: the amount of thoughts flowing through your mind,

> including simultaneous instructions and cues you are feeing
> yourself related to technique
>> emotions

- Be objective — separate your scanning function from yourself.
  See it as a 3rd party, a coach or a robotic scanner. View the
  scanner as a search for any findings that are an anomaly from
  your most-optimized version of yourself in a given activity.
- Don't rush to jump to assessment or action. Scan, identify, mentally note, and move on.
- Repeat the scan regularly and especially when conditions change,
  such as terrain, weather and required intensity. Scan whenever
  you notice negative thoughts. Scan when you feel an ache or
  pain. Scan if your pace falls off or if your heart rate increases
  and pace stays the same. Scan before you require an increase in
  intensity, such as preparing for intervals or a sprint finish. Scan
  if you feel like you're not enjoying your run or simply feel your
  mind is too busy.

Below is an example of body scan questions. I encourage you to
develop your own scanning checklist, based on your unique needs. As
you build experience running with a heightened sense of awareness,
your knowledge base of *things to pay attention to* will grow. Be structured in how you document and recall this, so that the recall happens
automatically with that coach on your shoulder, or your Inner Coach.

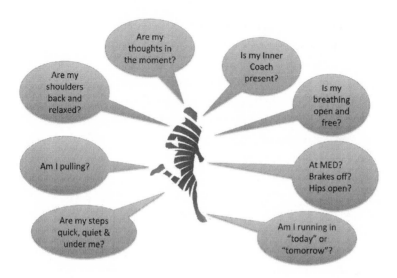

Image: Body Scan

Technology & Body Scans

We are in the age of an Internet of Things, where devices are ubiquitous, connected, and while not (yet) omnipotent, certainly aware of a tremendous amount of what we communicate, what we do and what our bodies do. In Chapter 14, I offer a look into the use of technology for scanning, measuring, and guiding Flow State Running. The challenge is less about finding a solution via technology than it is about reducing the overload from an overwhelming and constantly growing number of options, devices, and quantitative measures. From power meters that measure your wattage while running to numerous sensors that measure heart rate, blood pressure and other biometrics to at-home devices that measure brain activity during meditation, there is no shortage of scanning options! I'll discuss in Chapter 14 ways to reduce the overload and take advantage of technology in a way that brings stillness and flow, rather than a hyper-active mind that is so occupied with data and measurement that it never quietens enough to allow flow to occur.

Step 2 — Assess and Select

With the scan completed and observation data collected, the Dome shifts to an assessment and selection phase. Like a scientist reviewing experiments in a set of Petri dishes, your task is to evaluate your observations, consider them against your practiced patterns, your goals and How-To knowledge, and then prioritize your findings.

Ultimately your aim is to identify a single top priority observation to address, a selection you will make in the *Call to Action* phase. Sometimes this selection will be obvious. When this occurs, grab onto it and address it with by giving yourself *One Cue Only*. When it is less obvious, review your observations with an eye on patterns. These patterns will come from your knowledge base and from your in-flight observation of new patterns that have formed.

You may ask yourself "What if I don't observe anything?" That's OK! Just mentally note this occurrence, as it is an excellent baseline performance measure for you, and continue your run.

Pattern Recognition

Become a master at recognizing mind-body patterns that occur in your running. These patterns offer you insights into how your mind and body functions. They also offer multiple angles of attack when issues arise that decrease your likelihood of entering flow. To "see" these detracting patterns, think up-stream and down-stream from where your scan detects an anomaly. And note that up-stream and down-stream often includes emotions, thoughts, feelings and other creations of the mind. Below are some example patterns. The arrows indicate a tracing up-stream or down-stream of the likely root cause or effect.

- Right knee pain —> left hip tightness —> stressed about a project at work
- Heavy legs —> tight back —> not enough sleep last night
- Sluggish —> breath labored —> shoulders rounded
- Unmotivated —> left shoulder tense —> cadence is slow

- Not at MED —> hands in clenched fists —> abs overly engaged

While there are some common patterns of inefficiency found in groups of runners, your patterns are unique to you and it is your job to discover, unravel and replace them. The only way to become an expert at pattern recognition is to document your experiences. Keep a journal, paper or electronic, and note anomalies and issues that occur together. Don't overthink it — just briefly note what you experience in your runs. Also note what action you took to address the pattern and the results of that action. Be a meticulous scientist in your quest to experiment (on yourself) and to document your findings.

Final selection
Taking care to avoid analysis-paralysis and an overload of inputs, quickly narrow your findings down to 2-3 primary concerns using your intuition. With these noted, keep it very simple and evaluate them against two criteria to make a final selection:

1. **Injury and Health**: Which has the greatest impact on my health or is associated with the most pain?
2. **Motivators and Goals:** Which is most closely linked to my motivator (quantitative goals, qualitative goals, experiential goals, etc.)?

Step 3 — Take Action on ONE observation
The last function of the Dome of Awareness to call for your Inner Coach to take care of it. With your selection in hand, allow your Inner Coach to speak up, using *One Cue Only* to coach you toward an action to address the selection. Allow some time for the coaching and the change to take effect and then repeat the Dome's lifecycle of scan-assess-select. Once the desired change is observed, if your scans still detect anomalies, make a new assessment and selection and continue the lifecycle.

Processing Speed

It may seem to you that this whole scanning, assessment and selection process could take as long as your entire run, but that's not the case. With consistent practice and a shift in your mindset to think it terms of scan-assess-select, you'll find that it is possible to complete the process in minutes or even seconds. The brain is an incredibly powerful organ, especially when it comes to pattern recognition. Keep practicing and maintaining awareness and thinking in terms of patterns and you'll be able to reduce the time and energy required for the Dome's activities until it essentially happens on automatic pilot.

Running Under the Dome

I encourage you to develop a ritual of engaging the Dome of Awareness every time you run. Find a creative approach to hitting the Dome's "on" switch, an approach that is memorable and resonates with your style.

The approach I use is to take three deep breaths, with each of the three long exhalations feeding the power supply of what I visualize as a transparent dome hovering above me. After the third breath, I begin my run. During the run, I visualize the Dome as ever-present, gently guiding the SPA process (scan-pick-act) and continually learning from Dome's reception of new inputs and realization of new patterns. I don't view the Dome as my thoughts or my voice, but as my Inner Coach, objectively observing and guiding me through whatever I encounter along the way.

You will notice when you reach flow that the Dome becomes a very passive observer, perhaps not even indicating its awareness until flow begins to fade or new variables are introduced. Your consistent practice of the Dome concept will ensure that it idles while you're in flow, and that it is ready and waiting to step up the instant your flow state experience begins to fade.

Once your run is completed, take a moment to review the Dome's logs, which are your recollection of the Dome's observations and selections and your feedback on the response of your mind and body. This is critical information for your system of continual learning and growth. It is worth the time to document it in a journal, electronic note, or voice memo to yourself.

Let's move on to a discussion on How-To Guides and the integration of physical techniques for running.

7. How-To Guide: Organizing the Body

"We could all use a little coaching.
When you're playing the game, it's hard to think of everything."
— *Jim Rohn*

Run like a Kang'oma girl

Standing under the rustically fashioned goal, the young Malawian girl eyes the goal and takes the shot, tossing a soccer ball up to a rusty hoop perched atop a small tree trunk driven into the dusty soil. She misses the first time. Her teammate recovers the ball and passes it back to her. One more shot…she makes it! One hundred women and girls erupt in cheers, rush the dirt netball court, and sing as they run in a group all around the village. I watch mesmerized and completely lost in sensory overload. It is one of the most exciting sports moments I have ever experienced!

I'm in the Kang'oma Village, near Lilongwe, in one of the poorest nations in Africa, Malawi. Several years ago I launched a series of 24-hour workouts as fundraisers for a project from Face-to-Face[8] to improve lives in Malawi. Now I am in Malawi for the first time, with a chance to make new friends and learn firsthand what life is like in this impoverished land. This netball game is part of a tournament our charity organized to bring several villages together to learn from our sponsored, model village about their progress on health and agriculture projects.

What we don't know in the moment is that this is the first time in nearly three decades that the women and girls had played a sport

125

with an audience. The young girls are just having fun, while the elder women are blissful with nostalgia and beaming with hope. I cheer along with the women, and with my multiple cameras bouncing around my body, I run after the group to film them. The group of fans ranges from 6-year olds to villagers in their 60s. I film the celebration from many angles and eventually find myself drawn to their running style. It is effortless. Running barefoot, and with many of them carrying babies in sarongs tightly attached to their bodies, they float across terrain that frequently trips me up. They run with a quick cadence and beautiful upright body position. They are so smooth — it is as if they are floating. Their smiles say it all and radiate not only joy, but a complete lack of unnecessary tension in their running bodies. They are not *running* in a focused workout sense. Their minds and bodies are linked in harmony as their focus resides with play and enjoyment — all through expressed through the movement of running.

I want to capture this feeling and deliver it to every runner I've ever coached or ever will coach, and I picture myself saying, "It's easy, run like a Kang'oma girl!" It's a beautiful moment, celebrating not only women's sports in Sub-Saharan Africa, but also the simple joy of fluid, effortless running for the sake of celebration and nothing more.

Nucleus of Knowledge: Baseline for How-To

Before we dive more deeply into the harmonizing elements of the Flow State Runner model, we need to establish a common understanding of our Nucleus of Knowledge, that is, our How-To guide covering the physical techniques for efficient running.

In this chapter, I offer guidance on selecting a physical technique for further study, share what I draw from to teach form in my workshops, and then teach you how to curate your own personalized How-To Guide and integrate it into the Flow State Runner model.

Why not just run naturally?

As much as I'm in love with how easily the Kang'oma girls run, I realize that it is a fantasy to believe that a coach can say, "Run like you're celebrating the joy of sport in an impoverished land" and expect a runner to use this example to undo years of experience that leads to inefficient running and mobility constraints. While we can learn from talented, naturally efficient runners, and even attempt to mirror their styles, we're not likely to find ourselves in this extremely limited group of runners who were born with ingredients that tend to favor efficient running (walking and running required in daily life as the only means to move throughout and between villages, no shoes, movement like running and dancing as a form of social bonding, etc.). So, for most of us, studying and training technique and preparing the body to reach its optimized state is crucial to achieving our full potential from each running experience we encounter.

Nicolas Romanov, Ph.D., covers this topic extensively in his workshops, articles and books. In *Pose Method® of Triathlon Techniques* he states, "by assuming that our running style is preordained at birth, we emphatically eliminate any improvement we could make through technique, leaving only training as a means to improve performance."

On this topic Danny Abshire writes in *Natural Running*, "The problem is not that we have forgotten how to run naturally, it's more that we have fallen prey to unnatural influences in the modern world—namely running shoe designs and the hard surfaces we typically run on."

For most amateur-level runners, an unnatural style has been followed for so long that a simplistic coach's cue of "run naturally" is not going to result in much of a change. In addition, a culture of sitting too much, zero-to-hero, and high volume training approaches has led to mobility limitations and injuries from training in a damaging way. Kelly Starrett offers in *Ready to Run: Unlocking Your Potential to Run Naturally*, "Yes, you can reclaim the natural running capacities that you were born with, but you've got to do the work. Smart, patient, consistent work. If you are looking for a magic pill in a running shoe—or any other intervention for that matter—you're doomed to the treadmill of injury, with the prospect that you will one day wear something out for real."

And T.J. Murphy with Brian Mackenzie voice on technique in *Unbreakable Runner*, "More and more coaches are looking closely at the mechanics of proper running form as the body deals with gravity, balance and impact force during the running movement...it is an essential, high priority task, emphasized so that a runner both marginalizes the risk of injury and maximizes performance."

Just as swimmers, gymnasts and ski racers invest time in learning technique to reap performance gains, so should runners. The question does not concern the value of technique in developing as a Flow State Runner — that is a given. It concerns the proper subjects of focus and methods for integrating technique improvement without overwhelming the mind and rendering Flow State Running experiences all but impossible to reach.

Why I struggled to sell shoes

I once accepted a sponsorship from a shoe company, visited their annual conference and even started selling their shoes directly. While I liked their shoes at the time, I really struggled with the concept of maintaining my integrity as a coach while tightly aligning with a footwear company. The more insights I gained on the shoe business, the less attracted to it I became. My tipping point was later being invited by another shoe company to coach an event. I received an invitation for a *carte blanche* shopping spree to outfit myself in their products. They were insistent that I wear and promote a new high-tech shoe, which I tested on a treadmill and instantly knew I could never promote or recommend to anyone. That's it, I thought. No more selling shoes.

My passion resides in supporting the interests of those I coach to the best of my ability, and my duty to serve my runners' best interests must come before my own fiscal interests. If I'm committed to one footwear company and another offers something better for my athletes,

I want the freedom to recommend what's best, not an obligation to push what my sponsor is producing, which may or may not be the best for every runner I encounter. I ultimately aspire to help people learn how to make their own informed selections.

I maintain the same approach with running techniques. I want what's best for each runner, which may be a single concept, a mix, or something entirely customized or new. I thrive in the freedom and flexibility to recommend various approaches that meet the needs of a diverse set of runners, and this is exactly what drives me as an integrator versus a coach with an attitude that, "it's my way—brand X—or the highway." Understanding that as an art and science, knowledge and gear technology will always be in flux, I seek the characteristics of the sapling, whose strength comes from flexibility and energy drives growth. In other words, I advocate taking in as much information as you can to formulate what works best for you as an individual given the breadth and scope of knowledge out there and the multitude ways to convey it.

It comes down to how people learn, what resonates with an individual and what areas need the most attention. It is a coach's duty to tune in to that trio and deliver effective guidance. And part of our work here together is that we develop this coach's voice in your mind.

With that said, I share with you my guidelines for selecting a technique approach to prioritize and practice. I also offer guidance to help you build a curated How-To Guide to integrate into your development as a Flow State Runner. What I'm intentionally not providing is a detailed review or critique of specific programs from the teachers, coaches, authors and exercise scientists who offer products and services in this domain. What I will say is that there are more similarities than differences, as well as a wide range of teaching styles and available trainers and resources. I offer links in the Resources section of the Appendix and encourage you to make your own exploration.

Let's move on with my thoughts on selecting a technique to study and practice.

Guidelines on selecting a technique

Years ago I became passionate about cooking and spent time learning from a chef friend. When teaching knife skills and advising me on kitchen purchases, he once told me that the best knife to have is the one that you <u>want</u> to use. That may not be the most expensive one, the most high-tech or the classic that was forged by a blacksmith in Japan. It is simply the knife that fits your hand, that feels to you like the perfect weight and balance and that cuts like you want it to cut. It's the one you reach for without hesitation, even if there is one four times as expensive right next to it. This fits well with my dad's guidance to always choose the right tool for the job. I smile every time I'm cooking and intuitively reach for the *right* knife.

Choosing a physical running technique to rely on is the same. I encourage you to avoid dogmatism and trends and simply explore for yourself. It helps to learn and experience a variety of techniques and schools of thought. Keep these things in mind as you explore:

- **Motivation:** What's in it for the teacher/author? Is he or she selling equipment, ideas, or a combination of both? Are you able to identify the source of his or her motivation? For example, is video analysis offered as a means to sell you shoes or to help specifically with your form?
- **Experience base and fit:** What's the experience or track record both qualitatively and quantitatively? More importantly, is the track record aligned with your goals and background? Just because a running technique program has a flashy track record with a list of Olympic athletes running the 400M or with elite marathoners does not mean it fits all runners, and especially, that it will fit you. Ask yourself: does it relate to your situation and goals (as linked to the question on motivators in Chapter 1)? Is the technique tied more closely to quantitative performance than qualitative experiences, or a mix? A triathlete looking to improve her run split, an office manager using running as a form of mid-day

meditation and stress relief, and a hobby runner interested in catching up with friends with pain-free weekend conversations while running may have different results and experiences when studying the same technique. In addition, a runner's experience base and goals will evolve over time, offering the opportunity to explore different perspectives that fit his or her current needs.

- **Stickiness and sustainability:** Can you get your head around the concepts and practices enough to draw value from it in 6 months, 1 year, or 6 years without having to re-study it? Do you have "a ha!" moments when exploring it or head scratching moments where it doesn't seem to click for me? Do you need a sheet of paper with any associated drills to remember them later? Are there helpful videos and illustrations that fit with how you think and remember?

- **Fun factor:** Do you enjoy studying the concept as it is presented? Is it fun to experience and practice? Does it lead you to positive moments that you want to experience again? Are you inspired to continue down this path?

- **Resonation with my core beliefs and style:** What's your learning style and personality? Are you visual, cerebral, quantitative, sensory, auditory? As a learner, are you a scientist, musician, engineer, painter, yogi, techie, a mix or something else? Does the approach and style in which it is taught resonate with you?

- **Access to qualified teachers and resources:** Do you need a coach in-person to learn and practice this? If so, can you find one nearby in your city/country? Is it possible online, via videos or a book?

If you have ever worked with a coach or searched for a suitable coach, you will recognize that many of these guidelines apply to that process as well.

So, which technique is best? That's a fair question, but the answer is not one-size-fits-all and is ultimately your unique journey of discovery. If you have never studied a physical technique or running form model,

I recommend that you check the resources in the Appendix and begin your deeper exploration. In the next section, I offer a high level overview of how I teach physical techniques in workshops. You'll be able to glean some insights from this already and then will have ideas for where to make a deeper dive.

Teaching physical techniques

My focus is on teaching runners an <u>integrated</u> Flow State Runner model and to do so, I also bring an integrated view into teaching the How-To component. I share my approach with you here as an example of <u>my</u> integration approach. I suggest that you approach technique with an open mind and draw together what resonates with you, and if you are coaching others, what resonates with your students and their needs and learning styles.

In my workshops in Europe and the United States, I've had very good results teaching runners the Pose Method® and have used it extensively in my own running and in my coaching practice. As a part of any exploration into running technique, I recommend Dr. Romanov's books, taking a Pose Method® course and/or working with a qualified trainer. I've also found that select elements of ChiRunning® resonate with the yogi and yoga teacher in me, and aspects of it have proven effective at reaching some types of runners I work with, so I've drawn from these concepts in my approach as well. And of course, I also integrate lessons from the myriad examples I shared in Chapter 1 with concepts I've developed in-flight to help runners break through various sticking points. And when I find new concepts from fellow coaches and authors that work for a given situation, I'll integrate those as well, offering credit to the originator.

This is my humble approach to building a large toolkit that supports a wide variety of runners and learners. I aim to help unlock "aha!" moments in runners and those moments come in all shapes and sizes and sometimes when the runner doesn't expect it — sometimes even when the coach doesn't expect it! My guidance: be open to experiencing a wide range of exercises and examples and to the surprise joy of finding your "aha!" moment. And don't stress when it's not happening. It doesn't matter how many drills you try that don't resonate with you — it matters that you find key ones that <u>do</u> work for you.

In this book, I provide you with a sampler list of drills and experiences that I've found particularly effective for the 1,000+ runner's I've coached over the years. Of course, this is no way replaces a full workshop, course or book on any technique you wish to further explore. Please consider pursuing those and then incorporating your expanded How-To Guide back into the Flow State Runner model.

Key Drills

- **General:** my favorite teaching exercises do not involve equipment or a whiteboard full of checklist steps to take. They involve using the body in a manner that generates a feeling that can be transferred to straightforward, efficient running, even when the runner doesn't yet understand any details of a particular technique. I also incorporate what I call "Etch-it" moments. This is a term I derived when thinking back to the pre-digital tablet days of the drawing toy called Etch A Sketch®. If the name alone doesn't conjure up an image of shaking that iconic drawing pad and the image disappearing, then I suggest you search online for an image or video. I can only imagine today's kids asking how to install apps on it! In my teaching, Etch-it moments cover any drill that is designed to release unnecessary tension and to reset a runner's form or mind to neutral, as a reset is often needed more so than a layer of new drills or things to think about. Many of the drills below can be used as Etch-it moments, simply introduced mid-run for less than a minute to serve as a reset. I often use Etch-it moments late in a long run, to help me reorient my mind and body to efficient technique.

- **Backward Running:** Running backwards is one of the quickest ways to teach efficient running. Practice running backwards (in a safe place!) with your head neutral, eyes straight ahead (looking away from the direction you are running). Once you are comfortable with the movement, make the smoothest possible transition to standard/forward running. Run through the turn (rather, don't stop running and then change direction). Focus on smoothly rotating from backward running to forward running. Pay particular attention to the initial several steps after turning. Many runners experience a moment of perfect balance and body positioning in this drill. If that's you, then capture that feeling and repeat the exercise trying to lengthen the duration it lasts after the transition. What is happening behind the scenes is that in backward running our bodies are naturally aligned to move via an efficient fall and to land over our supporting foot with minimal impact (which is taught in the Pose Method®). It is simply harder to break backward running because of our anatomy. A runner's ability to run smoothly while alternating backward running and forward running is a foundation to virtuoso running, discussed next.

- **Virtuoso Running:** Once you've mastered backward running and seamless transitions between backwards and forwards, it is time to pursue virtuoso running. Here you will master running sideways in a variety of foot configurations (side-to-side hops, trailing foot crossing in front of leading foot, trailing foot crossing behind leading foot, alternate crosses). You may even spice it up with some playful kid-style running, agility hops and quasi-Parkour moves. The goal though isn't a chaotic free-for-all of merged running styles. Rather, the aim is a seamless flow of running that connects all directions as if it is the same movement, which it is, after all. The drills start with easy sideways hops, shuffling the feet apart and together. Now transition between these sideways motions and straight forward running, again focusing on a silky smooth transition with no discernible difference in body tension or fluidity. If the transition is awkward, slow it down and keep working through the movements until the transition moments become fluid. Build on this and work into a rotation pattern: sideways left side leads, forward, sideways right side leads, forward. Advance from there to include backward running and to vary the length of time you stay in each style.

- **Blind Running:** Find a safe area, free of vehicles, pot holes and other obstacles. Recruit a friend to guide you by the elbow or upper arm and run with your eyes closed. For many this exercise is unnerving at first. Stay with it and focus on your other senses and on staying relaxed and pulling your feet. Once you've mastered blind running with a guide, find a large open grass field or beach and try it solo. One exercise that works well is to count steps, trying for ten before opening your eyes the first time and then extending that target as far as you feel comfortable. Blind running tunes runners into valuable proprioceptive inputs that are often missed in sighted runners' overstimulation from sight inputs. I often incorporate barefoot running and color drills with blind running exercises.

- **Stairs Running:** Stairs are an excellent tool for teaching running technique. While I'm fortunate to live in a country with the world's longest staircase (11,674 steps), you don't need a set of stairs that extends all the way up an Alpine mountain to benefit from what stairs can teach us about running technique. Even a set of five steps can be of use. Pause mid-step when going downstairs and notice your balanced body position (hint: it's the naturally well-balanced pose from the Pose Method®). Now, check yourself when running. You should be close to that same position when landing. When running up stairs, pay attention to how speed is achieved by pulling the feet, quietly and quickly, rather than hammering them down like pistons. Stairs work very well when you simply mix them into a run and then try to maintain the same feeling of stairs when you return to a normal running surface. And the key to running up the world's longest staircase: you guessed it, one step at a time!

- **Zombie Run Variations:** This one is based on an excellent drill from Dr. Romanov that he refers to as framing. In basic framing, two people run in line. The person in back has their arms outstretched, like a zombie, on his or her friend's shoulders. If you learn to run smoothly in this frame, you're on a good path, as it requires both runners to organize their bodies in manner that maps very closely to efficient running form. My zombie variation builds progressively and has runners exit the frame and re-enter it, striving for smooth transitions across a range of speeds and switch durations. At a more advanced level, I have runners switch buddy pairs and alternate around the group, all the while maintaining tempo and smooth movements. And at the end of workshops, we do one long zombie run conga line, but that's more for humor at the end of a long day of learning than technique. We can all benefit from a good laugh from time to time!

- **MED and Tension Dumpers:** I covered MED in detail in Chapter 5, but I wanted to mention it here along with the concept of tension dumper exercises. Tension dumpers are quick ways to release tension from the body, tension that we don't often realize we're carrying. One of my favorite methods is simply shrugging the shoulders tight while making fists — then relaxing shoulders and shaking the hands like you're trying to shake them dry. Three of those cycles coupled with a deep inhale and exhale can quickly dump tension. Cueing a jaw and tongue relaxation is another useful tension dumper. Tension dumpers are similar to flow release triggers, as discussed in Chapter 3, so a little play and off-script movement helps here as well.

- **Skipping:** I included an example on skipping in Chapter 1. This is a very effective tool for teaching what low tension in the feet, ankles and lower legs feels like, as well as a quick foot pull. Skipping is my go-to choice of Etch-it drills. I also coach runners to practice skipping rope and alternating between rope skipping with heels lightly kissing and heels suspended, as well as tensed shoulders and relaxed shoulders. These alternation and exaggeration drills are effective at reaching delivering "aha!" moments. Skipping also serves an excellent tension dumping and flow release trigger role.

- **Soft Sand Running:** If you've got access to soft sand, you can use it as a training tool in a similar way as stairs. Your ability to float on soft sand translates directly to efficient, forefoot running techniques. In addition, high cadence soft sand running also reinforces a "relax to perform" mindset helpful in any adversity and key to reaching flow state in your running. I'll cover soft sand running, snow running, mud running, weighted running, obstacle course running and a host of other related topics in my future book on running in adverse environments. For now, when you encounter soft sand, think like you're on a mountain bike shifting gears to an easy gear and spinning. Upright torso, spin the feet (quick cadence), pull up from the sand instead of pushing forward and most importantly, stay calm and in MED. Soft sand doesn't care about your tension and anxiety or any other feelings you have about it, so keep calm and embrace the sand.

- **Cadence Overspeed and Relaxation Drills:** To teach runners to transition to higher cadence running (by that I mean pulling the feet off the ground at the Pose Method® advised tempo of 180 beats per minute or higher), I often trick them into running at a much higher cadence and then slowing down to 180. This is a technique I borrowed from my music studies, where I would practice technical sections in a range of tempos, from much slower to faster than the intended tempo. Once I landed on the written tempo, it felt easy and not as rushed as its tension-fueled first time experience. Practice running at 160, 170, 180 and in tens all the way up to 220. Then, with relaxing music in your mind (Pink Floyd, Debussy, whatever works for you), repeat the drills with the goal to keep as little tension in the body as body at each cadence. Ultimately land on 180 again and maintain that relaxed feel. Eventually I suspect that your perception of 180 will shift.

- **Hips Open:** CrossFitters know this phase well, "Open your hips." It comes into play in every movement involving the posterior chain (lower back, glutes, hamstrings) and is an area I focus on quite a bit in yoga teaching as well. Feeling and reaching an open position in the hips (hip extension) is often a challenge to achieve consistently due to a sitting-most-of-the-time lifestyle. Our psoas gets tight and hip flexors get comfortable in their shortened state. Efficient running techniques encourage opening the hips (instead of folding at the waist), so one of the simplest exaggeration drills I use is exaggerating closed and opened hip positions. This drill brings awareness to hip and torso positioning and is especially useful in illustrating the tendency of many runners on hills, which is to close the hips and send their center of gravitational mass backwards, thus making the hill harder than it needs to be.

- **Hills:** I use hills extensively in my coaching practice. That's no surprise given where I'm based and the name of my company, Hillseeker®. Aside from the given conditioning benefits, hills also offer mental strength and mindset training opportunities, as well as micro challenges for the struggle phase of flow. I use hills in workshops to highlight that form often breaks down when we're under pressure and that the natural tendency for many is to lean into a hill by bending forward at the hips, which destroys optimal form. Get it right on the hills and your likelihood of getting it right in other terrain is greatly increased. I incorporate blind running and skipping on hills, and the blind running hill experience is particularly insightful. Lastly, I featured hills in a series of 40 free hill workouts I designed and tested in 2015[9], offering a wide range of challenging and fun hill workouts incorporating sprints, stairs, skips, sleds, games and more.

Demonstration Exercises

I rely on a handful of demonstrations to make a point or illustration.

Here are my favorites:

- Impact of straight leg, heels landing: Jump up and down with both legs a few times. How does the landing feel? Repeat, but this time land with straight legs on your heels. How did that feel? Try it again, landing on one straight leg. Repeat again, with a slight bend in the knee: is it still jarring? This highly simplified demo brings awareness to the impact caused with straight leg, heel landings. In workshops I have runners do this before they watch the video I filmed of them running. They usually react the expected way when jumping with straight legs. It doesn't feel good. The profound reaction though comes when they see their videos and realize that many of them are landing firmly on their heels with nearly straight legs! It's both literally and figuratively shocking.

- **Braking Force:** Remember shuttle drills from basketball, football or simply gym class? These involve running fast a short distance and quickly turning around to run back to the start, often repeating multiple times. How do you make such a quick direction change? You throw a foot out in front to act as a brake. If you watch heel strikers on video, you'll see the same thing — one foot out in front to stop forward motion. The problem is that these runners aren't attempting to change direction — they are attempting to run forward, but applying a break with each leg movement. This one simple demonstration often explains more than a 10-minute lecture on the demerits of heel striking.

- **Falling:** Dr. Romanov, the expert on gravity-aided running teaches that running starts with falling. So, how to we learn to fall? We don't! We mastered this as a child. What we can learn though is how not to fall, that is, how to avoid getting in the way of falling. If you fall and don't react, what happens? Face on the ground! So, after falling you need to react to that fall and that reaction is pulling your foot off the ground. The simplest falling drill I use is to have a volunteer stand up and catch me as I fall forward into them. They catch me by outstretching their arms and placing their hands on my shoulders as I fall. Then I tell them to get ready for another fall, but for this fall, I lean from my head and push my chest forwards. What happens? I don't fall and they don't need to catch me. By leading with my head and chest, I send my weight back, thus preventing the fall. Again, this simple example illustrates quickly how bending at the waist breaks falling and makes it harder for runners to make forward progress.

- **MED tension:** MED is a key demo in my workshops and it is physical, but requires awareness to address. I covered MED in detail in Chapter 5.

Mobility & Yoga

As an overzealous triathlete in my mid-20s who was typically also spending 10+ hours a day at an office job sitting in a chair, I was the epitome of inflexible. I dealt with lower back pain for several years before my transformation to a triathlete and several years after it. Doctors and chiropractors addressed it as an apparent deficiency of orthotics, high-tech running shoes and spinal manipulations. One doctor, after diagnosing me with isthmic spondylolisthesis — a slip or fracture of the intervertebral joint — told me I should avoid running forever. Thankfully, I ignored that doctor. The solution that worked for me was to address my mobility. I sought out a yoga class, and a new world opened to me. I not only made a significant improvement in flexibility, notably lengthening overly-tight hamstrings, which relieved the stress on my lower back, but I also discovered an effective means to quiet a busy project manager's mind and tune in to my body at a much richer level.

Mobility and flexibility are key components to reaching flow experiences, as a supple body will support a supple mind, and vice versa. As a practitioner of yoga for 20 years and a qualified yoga teacher, I believe in the value of yoga as an integrated system to provide a solid foundation for all pursuits, athletic and otherwise. I practice yoga daily and encourage my clients to integrate yoga even at the most minor level in their lives. An entry level approach for getting started is to complete basic yoga Sun Salutations A & B three times each on a daily basis, preferably in the morning. I have included resources in the Appendix and on the *Flow State Runner* website to help anyone wishing to learn more about yoga.

For running and functional-training-specific mobility, Dr. Kelly Starrett is a leading expert in this field, so I follow his guidance personally and with my clients. Refer to Kelly Starrett's *Supple Leopard* for general mobilization and *Ready to Run* for running-specific mobilizations, notably based on the foundation of cultivating well-organized healthy-efficient positions, so that you're not constantly undoing compromises when performing athletic movements. Your vocabulary will expand to include foam roller, lacrosse ball, smashing, bashing and voodoo bands, and your body will thank you. Dr. Starrett has produced a wealth of instructional videos, available on his website.

You may also want to check out Stretch Therapy, a system developed and refined over the last 25 years by Kit Laughlin and his team. Stretch Therapy is an effective to improve flexibility using contract-relax and other PNF (proprioceptive neuromuscular facilitation) techniques combined with a range of stretching poses that allow the body and mind to safely access new range of motion, targeting one muscle group at a time. One of my coaching colleagues teaches this method and I've experienced some very good results firsthand and with our clients.

Functional Training

While conditioning and workout programming is beyond the scope of this book, I do want to include that I've found great success with the runners I've coached when we include the following in their training program:

- Strength training with barbells, kettle bells and sand bags, using multi-joint movements
- Bodyweight functional training with non-isolated core work
- Development of proper squat mechanics, focusing on posterior chain activation (glutes, hamstrings, lower back)
- High intensity interval training in running, rowing, cycling, swimming, paddling and XC skiing.
- A blend of CrossFit®, MovNat®, SEALFIT® and other themed workouts and training styles, including my own Hillseeker® challenges and hill running workouts, as well as physically demanding yoga practices, such as Budokon, Rocket, and Kokoro Yoga.
- A yin complement including yin yoga, hiking and other cross-training activities done without technology and at low intensity.

Running Classroom

Rather than save running technique work for a classroom in a seminar once every few years, in the few days after reading a book, or as a once a month practice when you happen to remember it's something worth focusing on, I encourage runners to view their entire running route, on every run, as a classroom or lab.

Technique practice can, but doesn't have to be a daily 20 dedicated minutes to a series of drills. It can be 30 seconds here, 1 minute there and 10 seconds over there, all linked into a normal run. We can work on technique all the time if we view our running environment as our lab. When taking groups on training and teaching runs at the

SEALFIT Integrated Training Center in Encinitas, California or from our Hillseeker Training Center in Zurich, Switzerland, I'm constantly pointing out elements of the environment that we can use to train and reinforce proper technique. For example, any wall offers a chance to run with backs to the wall for 30 seconds to reinforce a vertical foot pull and upright body position. Encounter a hill? Focus on an upright torso, low tension and high cadence. Stairs? Run up and down once and carry that feeling into the next 100m or more of running on the flats. Soft sand? Spin through it with a balanced forefoot landing, focusing on the pull and again, high cadence. Uneven terrain? Focus on light, agility movements, hopping from one landing point another. There are endless possibilities to map elements of the environment to positive skills to reinforce. I don't stop at structural and geographical elements either. As you'll see in Chapter 11, I also encourage runners to use colors and nature encountered in the environment to boost both physical and mental skills.

Building your How-To Guide

This chapter provides an example of a collection of knowledge that is integrated into my How-To Guide as both a coach and runner. What you need now is your own, curated How-To Guide to plug into the Flow State Runner model. My overarching guidance is: keep it simple. Pick a small list of ingredients that work for you now. Set the rest aside. You can always rework and expand your How-To guide, and you will. That's the process of learning and growth.

Placing the above or your own favorite skills into a How-To Guide can be visualized in the same manner as the Burpee example in Chapter 4. First, study a skill and search for those "aha!" moments that *click and stick* for you. Note these areas and why they resonate with you. Then, start practicing them with the Inner Coach (Chapter 9) and Dome of Awareness (Chapter 6) methods in your normal running. I advise that you not overload your How-To Guide. Start small, experiment, and grow it.

For example, let's imagine that you finished a Pose Method® seminar a week ago and you have a new How-To Guide full of knowledge, skills and drills. The top three that resonated with you include: cadence of foot pull, direction of foot pull, and no kicking the front foot forward. There's more you remember, but these are the top three you've identified. Note this in your journal. (Yes, please keep a journal, paper or electronic, to help you organize and track your Flow State Runner experiences and development.) During your run, your Dome of Awareness will scan and note which of the three is likely to have the biggest impact at the moment based on how your body is feeling. Then, your Inner Coach will keep you focused intently on only one drill or concept at a time. Eventually, you'll fire up the Dome again to run another scan and re-assess, and you'll move on, either to another How-To skill or simply to running without a specific focus.

After your run, note in your journal your progress, questions, insights and challenges with each skill you practiced today.

Take ownership of the quality and depth of YOUR How-To guide, the one you build with your studies and practice and that works for you, as it will be much more valuable to you in the long run than any specific book or resource created by someone else. Experiment, learn, integrate, record so you don't forget, and then repeat and grow.

The Glue

Lastly, and to reiterate my opening premise, the glue is often missing in what runners recall from various techniques, and this results in the underdevelopment of a runner's Inner Coach's voice. Without a strong and focused Inner Coach, the great lessons in physical techniques can easily become lost in a sea of other thoughts. To that end, we will now continue to the Net of Breath, which plays a critical supporting role in both the arousal and calm required for high quality Flow State Running experiences.

7. HOW-TO GUIDE: ORGANIZING THE BODY

8. Net of Breath: Harnessing the Breath

"All things share the same breath — the beast, the tree, the man... the air shares its spirit with all the life it supports."
— *Chief Seattle*

Learning about breath the hard way, by sucking a SCUBA tank dry

It was my 2nd dive right after receiving my Open Water SCUBA certification. My buddy and I were closely following the dive instructor in the warm waters in the Andaman Sea, off the coast of Thailand. I noticed that I was running low on air right around the time that we changed direction and began swimming against the current. I was surprised at the "sudden" resistance I felt in the current and noticed that my heart and breathing rates began to increase. I tensed up and started to breathe heavily when I noticed how quickly my air gauge was approaching the reserve level.

I notified the instructor with the pre-arranged signal, but there was a mix-up between our two different measurement systems, Bar and PSI. She misunderstood my signal and concern and opted to spend 5 minutes taking photos rather than escorting me and my buddy to the surface. I panicked at being "blocked" from ascending, began to rapidly breathe and quickly sucked my air tank dry. Once my air supply ran out, I had to breathe from the emergency regulator on her tank to make it safely to the surface.

The moment we reached surface, we argued, with me accusing her of making the mistake in reading my signals and her telling me the truth: I am responsible for my dive. She told me that the best course of action would have been for me and my dive buddy to disregard her authority role and ascend on our own. It's our dive, our breath and our life. That was a great lesson, albeit unintentional, on personal responsibility and taking ownership of solving problems in our personal sphere, regardless of cause or fault.

There was also a powerful lesson on breathing. I faced adversity, experienced a loss of control and succumbed to my body's sympathetic nervous system (fight, flight or freeze). In my case, I made the choice to fight, by arguing with underwater hand signals with an ever-increasing respiratory rate, until the Dive Instructor grabbed my gauge, understood that I was panicking and nearly out of air, and safely escorted me, breathing on her air tank, to the surface. I was lucky that my *fight* resulted in a safe ending, as this situation could have easily spiraled out of control.

The sympathetic system, part of our autonomic nervous system, controls our unconscious reactionary response, and when faced with a trigger or surprise stressful situation, the system automatically puts us into the mode of fight, flight or freeze. I did a little of all 3 actually! From a breath perspective, when the sympathetic system is engaged, the first outward sign is a rapid acceleration of the breath rate, high in the chest. Without conscious intervention, what happens next, especially if fear takes over, is often a shift to short, incomplete exhalations. This leads to hyperventilation, which leads to panic and loss of control.

I eventually earned a Dive Master qualification and used this story countless times to educate divers on their role in their own safety as well as the power of breath to either ruin or make their dive. I also integrate it into lessons on actively using breath in running and in developing awareness of the signals that breath is about to unravel you.

Breath is a double-edged sword. While it has an amazing positive power to transform the body and mind, it also has a strong negative power in unraveling both. Your ability to master both sides of the sword

147

as a runner opens a treasure chest of performance optimizers.

My journey to understand the value of breath as a tool received a huge boost when I took on SEALFIT Kokoro Camp, a 50-hour physical and mental toughness crucible inspired by the US Navy SEAL BUD/S Hell Week. A mere 15 hours into the experience, I recall a powerful lesson on the beach following a series of sprint trips back and forth from hurriedly covering ourselves in sand to racing to wash it all off in the cold December ocean, the infamous sugar cookie exercise.

The sugar cookie cycle ended in a nice long "rest" floating in the ocean, a "reward" affectionately known as surf torture. We were instructed to stand with our arms out to our sides, allowing the cool air to scream discomfort into our souls as it connected with our wet cotton t-shirts and bare skin. With blue lips and hands I couldn't feel, I was shivering and shaking and about to lose my composure. An instructor approached me, standing inches from my face, calmly looked me in the eyes and said, "Take a deep breath, exhale slowly, relax and stop shaking."

It took several attempts, but following his precise instruction, I noticed that I was no longer shivering. My body became completely still. His guidance had led me through stimulation of my parasympathetic nervous system, while also guiding me to direct my breath in a manner that created internal warmth. I was stunned that this actually worked and felt the fire of my courage stoked to a new level, because I knew that as long as I could breathe, I could overcome extreme discomfort and challenging obstacles. If I had any doubts on the power of smart, controlled breathing, those doubts vanished on that cold night.

So, using our breath in a smart way has tremendous benefits, but does that translate to running, and if so, how? We'll get there, but first, let's breathe and then examine what breathing accomplishes.

We are our breath

For a simple example of the impact of breath, complete the following exercise right now:

- Inhale and exhale short, shallow and incomplete breaths, breathing through your mouth, high into your chest only. Do this for 20 breaths.
- After the last breath, sit for one minute and notice how you feel.
- Now, inhale through your nose for 6 slow counts, drawing the air low into a relaxed belly and expanding the lungs upward to the chest. Exhale for 6+ counts, from the top of your lungs to the bottom. When all of the air is out, repeat the cycle and continue for a total of 3 rounds.
- After the last breath, sit for one minute and notice how you feel.

What's going on here? Did you notice any differences in how you feel now versus at the start of the exercise? Most do. We are our breath, and our breath allows us to accomplish the practical, the optimal and the mystical. Let's have look at each.

What breathing does: the obvious

We will examine to the obvious first: fuel. Breathing serves the primary function of fueling our muscles and organs with oxygen and transporting carbon dioxide out of the body. The magic happens in the lungs via gas exchange, whereby arriving red blood cells from the heart trade off carbon dioxide and pick up fresh oxygen. Good trade. This gas exchange occurs in the alveoli, and once the red blood cells have picked up a fresh supply of oxygen, they travel back to the heart and out to our muscles and organs.

When sufficient oxygen is available to supply the muscles' needs, we are in an aerobic state. When insufficient oxygen is available, including in the initial seconds of any high intensity movements, we are in an anaerobic state. Our bodies are designed to operate for long durations in an aerobic state, which is where we reside for endurance activities lasting over one hour. When we are in an anaerobic state, the byproduct of glycolysis is lactic acid. Its presence in our bloodstream leads to the perception of pain and of heaviness in the limbs. Most runners have experienced this feeling at one point, perhaps when doing hill sprints or a hard 5K effort with legs that just won't "go" anymore.

The nose has an important role in the obvious function of breathing, as a conduit, of course, but also as an air filter, air moisturizer and air warmer. Breathing through the nose also has an important role in the less obvious benefits discussed below.

Breathing happens automatically, driven by subconscious contraction of our intercostal muscles and diaphragm, expansion of the lungs, the resulting pressure differential and air rushing in to fill the negative pressure space. If we hold our breath and refuse to take in new air, we will eventually pass out and the body will restart respiration automatically. If our muscles are working hard and producing more carbon dioxide as waste than arriving oxygen as fuel, this imbalance is detected in the lungs and brain responds automatically by calling for an acceleration of the respiratory rate and heartbeat.

But unlike other automated processes in our bodies, breathing is also controllable. We can step in at any time and take over the controls, accelerating or decelerating our respiration, and taking it on just about any journey we choose.

As runners, we can benefit from understanding the practical aspects of breathing and oxygen consumption, as these are integrally linked to our heart rates, intensity levels, VO2 max, lactic acid production and processing, and other physiological factors that when properly considered, measured and addressed, can result in our increased fitness and performance. If you want to dive deeper, check out the references in the Appendix on breathing and exercise physiology.

Recalling the catch-phrase from old infomercials, *but wait there's more*, there are indeed other layers of performance contribution we find in breath.

What breathing does: the less obvious

Less obvious is breathing's role in our autonomic nervous system: a duality of arousal & focus on one hand and calm & restore on the other. The autonomic nervous system is our primal control mechanism that activates on automatic pilot to handle breathing, heart function, and digestion, as well as our response when we encounter a stressful stimulus and return to calm. It is an involuntary system that splits its work into the sympathetic system to control our *Fight, Flight or Freeze* response for dealing with emergencies, as well as our parasympathetic system to handle our *Rest and Digest* response for restoring balance.

For example, when an aggressive wild dog appears on the trail ahead, our autonomic system immediately responds by activating our sympathetic system. This primal function results in how we respond to the dog, with an unconscious decision to fight it, run away, or freeze. The sympathetic system releases stress hormones, the same that we see in the struggle phase of the flow cycle discussed in Chapter 3. It also rapidly responds with an increase in breath and heart rate, dilation of pupils and contraction of muscles. When the wild dog sprints away from us to chase a deer, and we recognize that the danger has passed, our complementary parasympathetic system responds by lowering blood pressure, relaxing muscles and lowering heart rate.

In Dr. Herbert Benson's 1975 classic *The Relaxation Response,* he bridges Transcendental Meditation with medical science, examines the connection between stress and disease, and advocates for a mind/body approach to conquer the harmful effects of stress. The author teaches that we have over-activated our sympathetic system with a daily self-created stress load that isn't the same as the primal survival mode stress it was designed for and that this leads to hypertension and disease. Updated to today's terms, he is saying that we've got this built-in system designed to help us deal with life-threatening emergencies, yet we overload it by reacting to an unnecessarily large array of events as an emergency, from multiple overloaded messaging inboxes to a dead smartphone battery to some opinion posted on our social media feed.

That constant overload creates a hyper-stressed state, a state of the sympathetic system operating in over-drive. Viewed holistically, this of course puts our health and longevity at risk. The counter action that Dr. Benson encourages is activation of the relaxation response, that is, the parasympathetic system, by regularly practicing a simplified deep breathing and meditation technique. As I mentioned in Chapter 3, either we lead ourselves to a balance, or nature will find it for us.

We can draw from Dr. Benson's work and guidance and consider how hyper-stressed states and the complementary relaxation response impact our running. In modern day life, it is common for runners to lace up their shoes while wearing a virtual backpack full of stress, perhaps a large collection of small daily stressors, a small collection of major stress events, or a mix of all that and more. This means that they spend a large part of each run creating a relaxation response (parasympathetic stimulation) to offset their overloaded sympathetic system, thus perhaps reaching an equilibrium only by the end of the run if they are lucky, but not often enough reaching a fully satisfying flow state experience. For this group, they are simply starting in too much of a deficit! And despite our best wishes, we often find ourselves in this group.

To counter this deficit, we need to create more time with the parasympathetic system stimulated when we are not running, and with that we will enter each run ahead of the curve and set ourselves up to sooner enter a high performance, high-fulfillment zone when we are running. This is important, so I'm going to say it again a different way: if we are entering a run hyper-stressed and spending the whole run just trying to untangle, quieten and de-stress our minds, we are missing a huge opportunity for more moments of flow, high performance training, and creative thinking during the run. If we improve our ability to more quickly activate our parasympathetic systems and come from a lower stress baseline in the first place, we are poised to get more gems out of each run instead of using all or most of the running time as a counterweight to stress.

One of the easiest ways to stimulate the parasympathetic system regularly is with a simple, deep breathing practice known as diaphragmatic or belly breathing. In this style of breathing, which I'll refer to as deep breathing for simplicity, the diaphragm contracts to expand the lungs from the bottom, which enables not only full oxygen-carbon dioxide exchange, but also an important manual stimulation of the vagus nerve, which runs from the brain stem to the abdomen and is linked to numerous parasympathetic system functions, including the heart rate.

Deep breathing is a key shortcut to activating the parasympathetic system, largely via vagus nerve stimulation. It calms the mind and body, and this calmness is an important gateway in a runner's quest for flow state experiences.

Incidentally, we can stimulate both the parasympathetic and sympathetic systems with controlled breathing, although as humans we tend to be better at creating a stress response than a relaxation response, so most of your work as a Flow State Runner will be on developing your relaxing breath techniques and baseline.

Later in this chapter in the section entitled Breath School 101, I cover techniques for deep, controlled breathing, sample exercises and daily practice recommendations.

What breathing does: the energetic and mystical

Lastly: breath has the power to transform our psychoemotional states and send us into a variety of altered states, from euphoria to serenity.

The *Yoga Sutras of Patanjali* is an ancient text that describes the science of yoga, which is an integrated system of mind-body-spirit practice with a goal that is, according to the text, "nothing less than the total transformation of a seemingly limited physical, mental and emotional person into a fully illuminated, thoroughly harmonized and perfected being—from an individual with likes and dislikes, pains and pleasures, successes and failures, to a sage of permanent peace, joy and selfless dedication to the entire creation." That's a worthy aim for most and certainly far beyond the perception of many and practice from some that yoga is simply stretching!

According to *Yoga Sutras*, in each of us is a breath-associated life force, which is called prana. This is a similar energy concept known from Chinese Medicine as qi, Korean culture as gi and Japanese culture as ki. In the system of yoga, we can stimulate and move this energy in ourselves through the use of pranayama, which is the fourth of the eight limbs of Ashtanga yoga.

Pranayama is a Sanskrit word translated to mean the extension of life force (prana = life force of breath, yama = extension). In practical terms, this means employing a variety of techniques for inhalation, breath retention, and exhalation in structured breathing sessions. The inhalation and exhalation points are typically specified (e.g., breathing through both nostrils or alternate nostril breathing, which is covering one nostril while the other is open and engaged in breathing). Timing may be specified (e.g., inhale for 3 counts, retain for 3 counts, exhale for 5 counts). Techniques may be combined or employed in a progressive manner.

Some pranayama techniques stimulate energy, such as the Kundalini Breath of Fire, which heats the body and cultivates an energetic feeling. Qigong Advanced Breath Empowerment and Ananda Mandala, similar breath practices, also stimulate energy, but in a different manner. When done correctly, these practices often result in out-of-body feelings of floating, emotional release and euphoria. I've experienced and taught both firsthand and can attest to a powerful, out-of-this-world feeling after 20-30 minutes of this intensive style of advanced breath practice.

Other pranayama techniques raise awareness or create stillness in mind and body. The techniques that target calmness are, as expected, similar to guidance we find regarding the relaxation response and activation of the parasympathetic system. Pranayama may be combined with movement, and is often linked with time spent in and transitioning to and from yoga poses, reinforcing the benefit of yoga as a moving meditation.

Pranayama may be combined with mental imagery of energy

moving up and down the spine, crossing through energy centers or chakras. This allows the breather to link and train the mind, body and spirit, connecting the rising and falling breath with stimulation of the nervous system and mental imagery of whatever the breather wishes to let go of (e.g., ego or fear), and give energy to that image (e.g., love or confidence). Pranayama works well as a gateway into concentration and meditation practices, which along with yoga poses, represent four of the Eight Limbs of Yoga.

The most important takeaway in this breath discussion of pranayama is that breath can be viewed as energy as well as a mover of energy. While it is literally fuel required to sustain our lives, when controlled and directed in a breath practice, it offers the power to move us out of stagnation, change our attitude, strengthen our minds and bodies, and much more.

Lastly, the name isn't as important as the practice. You can call it pranayama, controlled breathing, or whatever resonates with you.

If you are interested in exploring the energetic and mystical side of breathing, I suggest finding a qualified, local yoga or Qigong teacher, and jumping in with an open mind and curiosity to see what works for you.

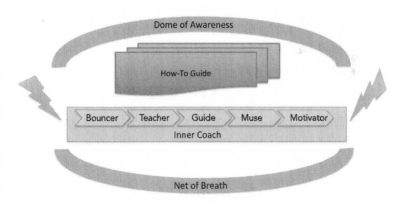

Image: Flow State Runner Model

The Net of Breath and its role in the model

I teach the image of breath as a net that supports the Flow State Runner model. It is a net to symbolize air's ability to flow through it, yet the net's strength and vitalness in supporting the entire model. It is that important. In addition, the net is pliable in that it moves with the model, with your needs as a runner before, during and after your runs.

While breathing is the most natural thing we can do, occurring automatically for us 24x7, to maximize our use of breath for gains beyond our cardiovascular needs in running, we must train breath outside of running and apply some conscious thought to it during runs.

Breath, Performance and Flow

Breath serves many roles in Flow State Running and your optimized performance. These roles include:

- Mind-Body Awareness and Dome Illuminator
- Struggle Phase Accelerator
- Release Phase Trigger
- Flow Inhibitor
- Flow Wave Generator
- Recovery Fosterer
- Stress QRF (Quick Reaction Force)

Let's look at each in more detail.

Mind-Body Awareness and Dome Illuminator

A consistent breath training practice, even just a few minutes a day, will serve an important foundation for increasing your mind-body awareness. The act of patterned breathing alone requires you to focus on one thing, your breath. The ability to focus is typically quite under-trained in our distracted, multi-tasking, high tech world. Here is your chance to change that in your life. If you want to have the ability to focus when you need it, train your focus. And breath is a great way to do that.

Consistent breath training will ultimately illuminate your Dome of Awareness, enabling you to more quickly observe what is happening in your mind and body, and more readily do something about it.

A breath practice will ingrain patterns in your brain, patterns which your brain will recall on automatic pilot when you are in flow. If you don't put those patterns there though, there is nothing to recall. My best example of this is when I found myself nearly stranded at a massively unorganized and overcrowded airport in southeast Asia in front of a ticket agent who could not locate the booking for my return flight home. I had already been in a packed bus and queuing for four hours, and was poised for 24+ hours of additional inconveniences if the ticket were indeed lost. As the agent repeatedly gave me bad news, I noticed that I had automatically shifted into a deep breathing pattern. After years of training this pattern, it was kicking in automatically during a stressful situation, and it was exactly the pattern I needed to maintain my calm and think of a solution, which is exactly what I did. So, the lesson is to put useful patterns in the bank for a time in the future when you may need them!

As runners, we also need to know where we are in terms of sympathetic and parasympathetic system stimulation, an observation that breath connection and an illuminated Dome of Awareness will strongly support. This impacts how we setup a run to stack the cards in our favor. In some runs, we may need to increase the initial stress to prompt a true struggle. On others, if we are having a particularly stressful day with our sympathetic system fully engaged in dealing with numerous real or created stressors, we're better off starting the run with stimulation of our calming parasympathetic system. Breath leads to heightened awareness, which leads to more keen observations of our emotional states, which we can address and guide, rather than react to.

Struggle Phase Accelerator

As discussed in Chapter 3, struggle is required in the flow cycle to get to release and ultimately to flow. That struggle phase will activate our sympathetic system, prompting a release of norepinephrine and cortisol and setting the stage for focus and action, as well as the follow-on stages of the flow cycle. We can use breath to accelerate or trigger the struggle phase and a sympathetic system response. This may simply happen automatically and inadvertently, as shallow breathing and an incomplete oxygen exchange accompanies the fear and anxiety sometimes experienced when training, and especially when racing.

On days when your stress level is low and fear/anxiety are not factors, you can consciously use rapid and shallow chest breathing (approaching, but not quite reaching hyperventilation), the Breath of Fire, or other energizing and stimulating breath techniques to create a stress to your system, a controlled burn of sorts, falling back to the firefighting metaphor. Breath pauses, particularly after the exhalation (thus pausing and delaying restart of respiration on empty lungs), are another method of stimulating the sympathetic system. Breath pausing in particular is an advanced technique, so if you choose to explore this path, do some under the guidance of a qualified teacher and in a safe environment.

The important takeaway is that breath is available in your toolkit as a tool for consciously stimulating your sympathetic system and the struggle phase of flow. To that end, I include breath practices early in some Flow State Runner workouts, as well as in the Flow State Runner workout template. Learn, practice and experiment with various techniques if you find yourself in need of an additional struggle to unlock flow. In addition, be aware of inadvertent patterns of breathing that may prompt a struggle and sympathetic system stimulation when you don't want it.

Release Phase Trigger

Moving from struggle to the release phase is all about triggers, and one of the most effective triggers is breath. As discussed, deep breathing stimulates the parasympathetic system, which calms and balances us, thus allowing focus to shift away from our beta-wave-centric, micro-managing brain to automatic pilot in alpha/theta states. This is where we want to be for flow.

An example of using breath as a release trigger following struggle is to take five deep breaths, each with a long and complete exhalation. You could do this while standing, walking, or running at an easy or moderate pace. I often incorporate this release trigger breath technique with mental imagery, seeing each long incoming breath as super high quality rocket fuel entering my body and each long exhale as any weakness and worry that I'm choosing to purge from my mind and body. Following the fifth breath, I feel transformed, and I am in a much stronger mentally and physically aligned position to run.

The more time you spend using breath to enter alpha/theta brain wave activity and to reach calmness in general, the more prepared you will be to call upon it quickly and effectively when needed during a run. We will revisit breath as a release trigger in Chapter 12 on Flow State Runner workout design.

Example: Breath as a Flow Release Trigger

In my research for this book, I completed a motorcycle superbike handling course in the UK. This course provided an excellent opportunity to bring me out of my comfort zone to study a sport that required flow to perform at a high level and that also required one to address fear to smoothly carve a high-powered motorcycle at high speeds through corners.

In this intensive course, we received an hour-long classroom lecture on a particular topic, and then mounted the superbikes to test the skills on the track.

The first time that we queued in the starting paddock moments before driving onto the track, I felt my heart beating out of my chest. I was sitting on a high performance Ducati racing bike, wearing a full leather racing suit, and about to start moving through corners where I imagined I would soon be dragging a knee as I laid the bike over on its side far enough, but hopefully not too far!

During that first session, I was so stressed that I was the slowest person on the track. I latched onto the handlebars like a vise and kept so much tension in my body that the bike went every direction other than where I wanted it to go. Despite my conscious efforts to provide the inputs I had just learned in the classroom, the bike would not respond.

Before the next session on the track, I spent five minutes sitting on the bike doing a patterned, deep breathing exercise. As I drove onto the track this time, I was in a different world: relaxed and focused. With my parasympathetic system stimulated, I had shifted to alpha state and ultimately on to flow. I felt connected to the motorcycle, with my mind and body moving together with the machine instead of fighting it. Everything felt so easy. My heart rate stayed low. I could see parts of the track I had been too fear-induced and tunnel-visioned to see before, and I swept through corners with a new level of skill, speed and joy.

Flow Inhibitor

If done poorly though, breath can be an inhibitor to flow and result in suboptimal running experiences. An example of poor breathing is the shallow or chest breath that takes place primarily in the upper chest and doesn't allow sufficient carbon dioxide to escape the lungs, leaving it trapped in the bottom of the lungs, which prevents an optimal delivery of oxygen from reaching and enriching blood. Its presence in the lungs sends the need for faster breathing and heart rate, which stimulates a stress response (sympathetic nervous system reaction), thus triggering additional struggle, rather than release and flow.

Imagine what happens when one blocks both the fuel line and the exhaust system in an exotic sports car. If the fuel isn't making it to the motor and the hot exhaust gases aren't making it out, it doesn't matter how expensive and powerful the motor is, how aerodynamic the shell is or how sophisticated the electronics are, the car is not going to perform. It is the same with our bodies and breathing. Breathe in a manner that allows maximum oxygen intake to fuel your muscles and maximum carbon dioxide escape. Do it for your performance. And sure, do it for the plants and trees too!

Flow Wave Generator

When you enter flow in running, you likely want to stay there. Maintaining an optimal oxygen intake with deep, belly breaths will generate a supporting undercurrent for your flow experience, like surfing an endless wave. To stay in flow, we need to maintain alpha/theta state presence, maintain focus in the moment and maintain a balance toward parasympathetic system stimulation. Deep, full breathing is an enabler and sustainer for all three.

Recovery Fosterer

Deep breathing slows the sense of time, increases awareness and focus, and via parasympathetic system stimulation, lowers heart rate and blood pressure. This facilitates our transition from training and racing into the mandatory, yet often overlooked, recovery phase of any flow experience or sustainable running program. I include a short deep breathing exercise at the end of every Flow State Run and link it frequently to an awareness and gratitude practice, to seal in the experience. I also incorporate breath-focused mini recoveries. I cover both in more detail in Section 2.

A brief deep breathing practice is also useful before bed, and highly recommended over viewing a backlit device that emits blue light. The device time has a major impact on melatonin production, thus reducing the length and/or quality of your sleep and rejuvenation time, while the breath practice will support a shift from beta to alpha and theta brain waves, which we help you drift off sooner to reach the healing delta waves of deep sleep.

Stress QRF (Quick Reaction Force)

Controlled breathing can be used as a Quick Reaction Force (QRF) to combat stress, fear and the unknown/unexpected. Runners encounter a variety of stressors while in-flight, that is, during runs and races. These span external stressors, such as terrain, weather, and aggressive dogs, and internal stressors, such as perception of pain, stomach ailments, fear, etc. If you run frequently, it is never a question of IF you'll meet a stressor during your runs, but WHEN and HOW OFTEN.

Stressors during a run are often helpful in bringing out the best in runners, while offering a sense of excitement and adventure. On the flip side, negative reactions to stress can derail you from reaching the objectives of your run, and worse, can send you into a downward spiral of negativity. Consider your breath as a Quick Reaction Force, ready to spring into service at a moment's notice should your situation and equilibrium come under attack.

Here is how: stress arrives and is immediately met with a few deep breaths. This allows you to balance your natural fight, flight, or freeze response with a calmness and control that may be a better fit for the situation. Then, assess the situation. If you train this, it will happen automatically.

My most memorable experience using breath as a Quick Reaction Force was during the final stage of the Marathon des Sables. I hadn't eaten in 24+ hours and was running on fumes with a body that was just barely hanging on to make it to the finish. Late in the stage, I tripped over a rock and crashed hard onto a hard, dirt road. It felt like I'd been tackled. My initial reaction was anger. I was angry that I had fallen, that I had run out of food early, that I was scraped up, that my knee was throbbing in pain. I shouted and slammed an empty water bottle to the ground.

My mini meltdown nearly cost me a Top 50 finish that I'd sacrificed much to earn. All it would have taken is a couple more minutes of negative self-talk, and I would have created such a snowball of negativity that it would have smothered me and led me on a slow, hobbling walk to the finish line.

Fortunately though, I chose to summon my QRF of breath. With my body covered in dirt and scraped up, I stood on the side of the road in a tiny Moroccan village and took 10 deep breaths. By breath 8, I was back in the game and more focused than ever. I didn't need to mentally will myself, to scream at myself or to throw things. I needed to breathe, and with that breath came stillness and a clean canvas, upon which I could then apply motivation and mind tricks to get the most from myself on the final run to the finish.

Breath School 101

This section includes instructions on performing several different types of breathing techniques and exercises, most relevant to Flow State Running. It also covers the basics on breathing while running and a summary of how to use breathing techniques before, during and after runs.

Deep Diaphragmatic Breathing

In deep diaphragmatic breathing, the preferred method for calming breaths, we can view our control of the breathing process as occurring in three steps.

- **Step 1:** Starting with inhalation, the diaphragm is engaged and draws down creating space in the lungs.
- **Step 2:** The lower ribs expand, drawing out as they are pulled

by the intercostal muscles, again creating more space for the lungs to expand.

- **Step 3:** The upper rib cage lifts and slightly expands.

For the active exhalation, the 3-step process reverses, with the upper chest releasing, followed by lower ribs and lastly, a drawing in of the belly, which in effect draws in the diaphragm to squeeze air from the lungs.

A helpful visualization for diaphragmatic breathing is to think of drawing air deep into the belly until it's packed full. This initial loading is why it is sometimes referred to as belly breathing. With the "belly" full, the air is drawn into the space between the lower ribs and up to the upper chest, filling up all spaces from the bottom up as high as you can go. Of course, you are not literally sending air into "space" outside of the lungs, but the visualization helps with engaging the right muscles and movement pattern to complete a full air exchange, as well as stimulate the vagus nerve and parasympathetic system, the aims of this technique of breathing.

When I was 12, I took my first lessons in playing the trombone. To play this and other wind instruments, the musician must inhale with a diaphragmatic breath and then maintain that belly pressure (contacted diaphragm) while blowing air with control into the instrument. I was struggling with the concept of maintaining diaphragmatic pressure as I moved the slide and blew into the trombone. My teacher's method for increasing my awareness was to lightly pop the back of his hand on my gut, although the surprise of it made it feel like a punch in the gut to this 12-year-old fledgling trombonist. It didn't take long for me to learn the lesson and keep my belly firm and diaphragm engaged! It is the same with deep diaphragmatic breathing. Bring your focus low in the belly for both the inhalation and exhalation and you'll be engaging the right muscles to ensure a proper diaphragmatic breath and full exchange of air. Or else, I'll give you a remote, virtual tap in the gut.

Ujjayi Breathing

An ujjayi breath is used in Ashtanga-rooted Vinyasa yoga practices. It involves breathing in and out through the nose with a very slight throat constriction. An ujjayi breath sounds to the breather like ocean waves. To learn to perform an ujjayi breath, breathe in and out with the mouth open like you are trying to fog a mirror. Then close the mouth and continue this mirror-fogging breath. The ujjayi breath technique not only draws the air in and out through the nose, thus filtering and warming the air which in turn warms the body, it also stimulates the vagus nerve, which shifts focus to the parasympathetic system and creates the associated calming effect. Ujjayi is particularly well-suited for daily diaphragmatic breathing practices as well as Vinyasa yoga, flow Release Triggering, and flow Quick Reaction Force response to deal with stress.

Other Breath Techniques and Concepts

- **Alternate nostril:** one hand is placed over the nose with the index finger and/or middle finger on the bridge of the nose, the thumb available to close one nostril and pinky finger available to close the other nostril. For the inhalation, the breather closes one nostril, leaving the other open to breathe in through. For the exhalation, the breather opens a single nostril. If a retention is used, both nostrils are lightly closed. Alternate nostril breathing stimulates different areas of the brain, thus various patterns and tempos are used to achieve different results.
- **Kapalabhati, Breath of Fire and Bhastrika:** In these techniques the aim is to build energy and heat. The techniques differ slightly in how the inhalation and exhalation are controlled, with Breath of Fire placing equal emphasize on controlling both, and the other two focusing on sharp, forceful exhalations followed by an automatic inhalation in response. Ananda Mandala and Qigong Advanced Breath Empowerment are similar to Breath of Fire, and

as mentioned earlier, lead many to feelings of euphoria, emotional release and oneness with the universe. These are all advanced breath practices that carry some risk, so I advise exploring them only with a qualified teacher.

- **Nostril vs. Mouth Breathing:** Breathing through the nostrils builds heat, as the air is warmed and moisturized. Breathing through the mouth releases heat. This is particularly useful to know when running or surviving in extreme hot or cold conditions, as the breath can be used as a temperature regulator, in addition to its role impacting the nervous system (stimulating stress or calmness).

- **Sitali Pranayama:** This is a cooling technique that releases warm air and generates a calming effect. Open the mouth forming an "O" shape. Extend the tongue past the lips and roll it into a U shape. Inhale through the mouth, taking the air in like it's coming through a large straw using a belly breath. Close the mouth, move the tip of the tongue to the roof of the mouth and savor the coolness. Then exhale through the nose.

- **Breath Pause:** Pausing after the inhalation, thus retaining the breath, or after the exhalation, delaying the re-start of respiration, is used to stimulate focus, restore a sense of calmness or even to create energy or a stress response. This technique is often referred to as performing breath holds or retentions. Pause is a soft term I teach to convey the message that it is a relaxed moment in between our normal in-and-out breathing process, rather than a tight, constricted hold or clinch. A pause may be added after an inhalation (on a full tank of air), after an exhalation (on an empty tank), or after both. Breath pauses show up in patterned breathing, as I describe next.

Patterned Breathing

Patterned breathing is controlled breathing that follows a pre-defined pattern. It is most commonly used with diaphragmatic breaths, in and out through the nose. Patterns serve different purposes, but primarily follow our common theme of instilling calm or stimulating energy.

An example pattern is 5-0–8-0, which describes a 5-count inhalation and 8-count exhalation. The zeros represent retentions, which in this example are skipped (so, it's just breathe in for 5 and out for 8).

A basic calming pattern that elicits a parasympathetic system response is 5-3-8-3. In this example, each retention is three counts, the inhalation is five and exhalation is eight. A more advanced pattern may extend the initial pause and exhalation. The aim isn't to be advanced though — it is to find and practice a pattern that works for you.

A challenging, stimulating pattern is 4-6–4-12. The extended exhalation and subsequent protracted pause on an empty set of lungs tends to create a sympathetic system response, especially in new breath exercise practitioners. This is incidentally a good exercise to train your stress response and condition yourself to react calmly to the perceived threat (a primal threat of not having air to breathe). It is also a handy tool if you're in need of creating alertness. As with all advanced breath practices I've mentioned, I recommend working with a qualified teacher to learn and practice this technique.

With any of the patterned breathing exercises, and with diaphragmatic breathing in general, make sure that on your exhalation you push all of the air out and draw your belly in (diaphragm up) to gently squeeze stale air from your lungs.

Patterned Breathing with Mental Imagery

We can build on patterned breathing exercises with the incorporation of imagery, phrases or mantras, linked to the breaths and/or pauses.

The first example is to focus your thoughts on the inhalation with positivity and the thoughts on the exhalation with negativity, thus you are breathing in and increasing your awareness of a positive thought, giving it a growing level of focus that is matched to your lungs expanding and filling with air. The exhalation is an opportunity to decrease and let go of a negative thought, with it exiting your mind just as the carbon dioxide-rich air exits your body.

Other examples are that you inhale confidence and exhale fear, or inhale light and quick legs and exhale heavy legs. Yes, you can use this patterned breathing and imagery technique <u>during</u> running as well.

It is not required that you always have a thought for both parts of the breath cycle. You can simply inhale *speed* over and over again with each inhalation! And if your Dome of Awareness identifies a worry that you know you would benefit for releasing, it's OK to simply focus on each exhale that you are letting go of this worry, bit by bit, until there is no more to let go of. It is the same with emphasizing a positive thought or mantra. You may choose to focus each inhale on the thought, "I will finish."

You can also incorporate breath pauses. I often use words like *float*, *focus* and *calm* during breath pauses, as I find them particularly useful in directing and aligning my thoughts with my nervous system and the rest of my body.

In addition, you may find it effective to incorporate mental imagery with patterned breathing, emphasizing an image on the inhalation, freezing an image on a pause and de-emphasizing an image on the exhalation. One of my favorites is to visualize that I'm being pulled forward on the inhalation and pushed from behind on the exhalation. This is particularly useful in interval training. I cover this in more detail with examples in Section 2.

How do I train breathing in general?

My recommendation is five minutes of breath practice daily, either on your own, in a yoga class or with the support of an app. Keep it simple and aim for a calming practice, using diaphragmatic breaths in and out through the nose. Sit with a straight spine either in a chair or on a cushion that elevates the hips above the knees. Closing your eyes is helpful, but not required. I often do basic breathing exercises on a train or airplane and my seat mates are none the wiser.

Basic patterns to explore and practice are as follows, with I=Inhale, E=Exhale and P=Pause.

- I-P-E-P
- 4–0–4–0
- 5–0–7–0
- 3–0–9–0
- 5-3-8-3
- 5-5-5-5

You may want to note in a journal any thoughts that arise, as this type of breath practice often prompts creativity. By the way, it is not mandatory that you are stationary — feel free to incorporate patterned breathing exercises in walking mediations or even during your runs.

How am I supposed to breathe when I run? Nostril? Mouth? Patterns? Align with foot strikes?

My overarching guidance in breathing while running is to do what feels natural and to avoid shoehorning anything that feels to you like an awkward, forced breath technique into your daily running. That said, there is benefit in employing breath as a tool while running, so your goal is to become an expert at knowing which breath tools work for you during different running scenarios and when only natural breath is needed. The challenge of course is separating experimentation with a new tool that will feel natural only after a little practice and a breath technique that simply isn't a natural fit for you. That's part of your learning and training journey of discovery, for which breath is a relatively easy tool to experiment.

The aim when running is for the breath to be natural, to integrate with an efficient physical running technique, and to foster the mindset you need for a given run's objectives. In general, allow breath to happen with as much thought and control as it does any other moment of your waking and sleeping life, UNLESS and until you choose to turn auto-pilot off and direct your breath for a specific aim. We'll come back to that in a moment.

Let's first start with the basic question of mouth vs. nose. I encourage you to avoid overthinking and attempting to over-control this. What's important to know is that nostril breathing offers a filtering and warming mechanism, as well as an additional parasympathetic system stimulation. It's there for you to tap into when needed. If you attempted to nostril breathe whenever running for the entire run, you'd likely find that it only feels feasible at very low intensity levels and quickly feels restricted as your intensity increases. This is normal, given that when intensity rises, the brain signals an *open the flood gates* need for maximum intake of oxygen, thus signaling to bring air in through both the nose and mouth. Let the body do what it naturally wants.

Your awareness of how you're taking air in and letting it out is important in moments where you want to use breath for a purpose other than fuel and for moments when you are searching for a root cause of an issue that may be linked to shallow, incomplete breath cycles. With your awareness strong, you can steer your breath as needed.

Moving on to patterns now — I'm in favor of integrating the aforementioned patterned breathing techniques into running when there's a mindset goal, thus a pattern may be plugged in to part of a run and then disconnected after the objective is achieved, allowing the breath to return to a natural state. There are other schools of thought as well.

In *Runner's World Running on Air: The Revolutionary Way to Run Better by Breathing Smarter,* author Budd Coates teaches rhythmic breathing as a method of increasing awareness, preventing side stitches and improving performance. In short, Coates' premise is that runners tend to start exhalation on the same foot and the moment of exhalation is when the core is the least stable, as the diaphragm and associated muscles are relaxed. That lack of core stability timed with a foot strike always on the same side leads to various risks and disadvantages. According to Coates, if we run with what he terms *rhythmic breathing*, that is, breathing with a pattern that alternates exhalations across foot strikes, it creates balance, improves performance, etc. He offers different rhythms that match the full range of running paces and set up an every-other-foot exhale pattern. Teaching this method is best left to the author, and in his book you'll find suggested patterns and concepts, as well as insights on pacing, side stitches and asthma.

I'm all for tools that increase awareness and have used patterned breathing in a similar manner to train the mind while running. My coaching focuses more on reducing impact and pulling the foot from the ground (per the Pose Method®), so in general, I coach runners to avoid synchronizing their breath with foot-to-ground impact. I have, however, found positive experiences adapting an alternating rhythmic breathing approach to foot pulls, initiating breaths in and out when the foot is airborne, and also as a focus tool during tempo runs.

I'm also very much in favor of the spinal bracing techniques and overall core strengthening taught by Kelly Starrett in *Ready to Run: Unlocking Your Potential to Run Naturally.* That said, the Flow State Runner model is modular, so whatever works for you, incorporate it. And if you incorporate it, experiment as well by adding imagery or mantras to the rhythms.

There are times I advise choosing to turn auto-pilot off with your in-run breathing and direct your breath for a specific aim. IF you need to draw your attention to or away from something during your run, something your Dome of Awareness has picked up in a body scan, then it is time to employ patterned breathing with thoughts or imagery link to whatever it is you wish to reinforce, redirect or otherwise impact.

Thus, in my school of thought, patterns are used by conscious choice when we need them to accomplish something. Else, allow the rhythm of your breathing to naturally occur and focus more on efficient technique that reduces your impact on the ground, and a combination of posture and strength training to support your health and performance in general.

How do I breathe deep and full when I'm running and I'm out of breath to start with?

I envision being asked this question from a gasping runner, standing at the top of a hill sprint, only able to eke out a few syllables of the question per gasp.

Yes, if you are running at high intensity, it will be challenging and sometimes impossible to feel that you are breathing deeply, especially if you compare it to sitting at home in a chair in a patterned breath training session. Again, don't overthink this. Humans have been running since the good ole primal days of chasing down dinner, and the body knows full well how to use its systems to get maximum oxygen intake and carbon dioxide expulsion during a sprint. With respect to breath, we tend to break things not at max intensity, but at lower intensity, thus attention to deep breathing serves you more during pre- and post-run rituals than during the chase. Recognize though when your higher breath rate may be caused by stimulation of your sympathetic system (stressors, including the expectation of an upcoming high intensity interval, thoughts of competition, fear of terrain, etc.). Ideally your Dome of Awareness senses these and calls for your breath and mind training to address the root cause.

This is a good opportunity to mention that I prefer to speak in this book in terms of intensity rather than speed, because speed is relative and too many runners define "their" speed against commonly accepted paces, thus see themselves as fast or slow runners, based not on their fitness and experience, but in comparison to others. "Fast" for one runner may be extremely low intensity for another, but high intensity is high intensity, regardless of the resulting pace.

In general, aim for full air exchange, regardless of your intensity and resulting respiratory and heart rate. At the highest intensity, this happens naturally. At lower intensity levels, it comes down to awareness and experience. The more you train belly breathing, the more quickly you will revert to this when needed, and it is particularly useful for recovery.

Lastly, take advantage of what I term "micro recoveries." A micro recovery is the rest window after an interval, the brief pause at a pedestrian crossing signal or even stepping off the trail to allow a group of hikers to pass. During these moments, activate diaphragmatic breathing with a focus on a full exhalation. Link it to a mantra and you've got yourself a brief moment of Inner Coach power and flow stimulation!

Summary of using breath training to support Flow State Running experiences

Pre-Post Run & Race
- Dome of Awareness Primer, part of daily mind training
- Combined with mental imagery and visualizations
- During yoga or mobilization work
- As a pre-sleep ritual
- In pre-run and pre-race rituals to build energy, alertness and focus

Workout Design
- Struggle phase stimulating struggle and beta
- Release phase triggering alpha
- Recovery (gratitude breaths)

In-flight, while running
- Before Dome Body Scans
- As a Quick Reaction Force
- Integrated with your Inner Coach's voice
- Micro recoveries

Closing thoughts on breath

In this chapter I offered three views on breath: fuel, nervous system stimulation, and energy mover. Each is important to understand and factor into your running. While I expanded this section to include a view of controlled and directed breath in the yoga domain, you will find it in many facets of daily life, from the dentist's chair to the operating room table, and even the sports locker room.

Consider a miracle drug that can bring about a heightened state of awareness and stillness, a drug that can make you feel that you are floating and that prompts a hyper focus, and a drug that can both energize and calm you. Now consider that this drug is free, requires no prescription, and has no side effects. That drug is breath and it is a very important driver in setting yourself up for successful and fulfilling running experiences.

I've included many references and referrals in this chapter and the Appendix. As always, if your interest is sparked and you want to go deeper, you have my full encouragement.

With the Net of Breath now thoroughly explored, we have gone deep with the Dome, Nucleus, and Net of the Flow State Runner model. We continue our journey with the realm of the Inner Coach.

.

9. Inner Coach:
Hiring the Best Coach in the
Business — YOU

"A coach is someone who tells you what you don't want to hear,
who has you see what you don't want to see,
so you can be who you have always known you could be."
— Tom Landry

2011, near San Diego, California: My decision is an attempt to mix spontaneity, a sense of adventure and a desperate need to shake off the lethargy of jet lag. I've just arrived in Southern California after 22 hours of travel. I'm here to teach running technique at the SEALIFT Academy. Nine time zones ahead is home in Zurich, where snow blankets the ground and winter is firmly entrenched. With SoCal's warm and sunny greeting, I quickly forget about winter and decide that what I need is a nice, long run in the sun to wake up and acclimate to a very different locale and winter lifestyle.

My general fitness is solid this winter, but I'm not in ultra marathon shape at the moment. For a variety of reasons, I've put my running on the back burner for the past six months, so my run fitness is not where I know it can be when I'm training hard for races. My latest excuse is that I don't enjoy running in the winter, that I'm up for a run anytime that the weather is nice enough for just wearing shorts, shoes and sunglasses, but not when it involves tights, Gore-Tex and a layering strategy.

I have other good excuses too: that perhaps I don't enjoy it as much now that it's my job, that it makes me less flexible for yoga, that I've done enough hidden damage through years of ultra marathon running, and on and on. Sometimes I run a lot, other times just once a week or even twice a month. And then I go through a period of running nearly every day and hopping straight back into the ultra marathon and mountain running scene.

I feel guilty at times — that it is expected of me to always love running, to always have a big race that I'm training for, and to always be a model of a passionate and obsessed runner who can't bear the thought of missing a day of running. That's not my reality, though. I have moments where I'm very much motivated to run and other moments where I have to force myself to lace up, knowing that future me (me after the run) will thank present me for getting out the door.

My longest run in the past six months was 45 minutes. And that was a few months ago. Usually I'm out for an occasional 20-minute interval sessions on my local hills or sprints during workouts. I need to up my running game again.

With this in mind, I decide to make up for lost time and lost training and do a long run—two hours should do it. Even without much training, I should be able to cruise through a couple hours of beach running.

At the 1-hour mark, I'm feeling fine and nearing my planned turn-around point. Then the following dialogue in my mind starts. Read it like dialogue in a movie script, where **V** = the Voice in my head and **J** = Jeff, me.

V: Forget about the turnaround. Run to Torrey Pines. It's just down the coast from here.

The Voice in my head has arrived.

J: Seriously? That'll add at least two hours to this run. I don't have any gels or cash to buy food. I don't have a water bottle. I don't have the base for a marathon today. Two hours is enough.

V: Come on man — you're an ultra runner. You've raced in the Sahara. This is nothing. Don't turn around. Run to Torrey Pines.

One hour later, at Torrey Pines State Natural Reserve:

V: You see, no big deal. You're here. Now go run some trails.

J: Ok, it's beautiful, but this is enough. It's gonna take another two hours to get back, more if I run the hills here.

V: Come on Mr. Hillseeker. No excuses. Set a good example by running the hills. We'll deal with the return trip later.

J: Fine.

Another hour passes.

V: What happened to your pace? You've slowed down a lot. You really should run back now.

J: No kidding. I'm tired. This run back is going to suck.

V: It sure is.

J: Thanks for the encouragement, Voice.

V: Don't mention it. But I have to say, you're the one with the ego who drove him to run this long with no base for it.

J: That was YOU.

V: And I am YOU. Let's not mince words. You're getting even slower now. Maybe running isn't your thing. You should take a taxi back.

J: No way! The last thing I'm going to do is stop a run short and take a taxi home.

V: Ego.

J: I'll power through it.

V: All the power in the world isn't going to make up for your lack of training and lack of food. And look at this, your lower back is killing you, isn't it, old man?

J: Yeah, it does hurt a little. Ok, a lot.

V: And that's why you should quit this run, which you never should have started in the first place on such little training.

45 minutes later:

V: Just walk already, although your walk is probably pathetic too. I mean, your run is — well, let's face it, it's more of a shuffle than a run, and it's embarrassing.

J: Shut up Voice.

V: Like really embarrassing. Do you actually teach people to run like this? Surely not. How did you ever manage to run ultra marathons? Just walk now. Get some ice cream and call for a taxi. Your form is terrible. You're hungry, dizzy and getting weaker and slower by the minute. At least take a nap and stretch out your back.

J: I'm ignoring you.

V: You know what? You're going to hurt yourself, and then your teaching will also be lousy. You will have flown all the way out here to teach and you won't be able to even run 400 meters, much less demonstrate efficient technique. You're falling apart right now and you'll never be able to run the whole way back. Just quit.

J: Ok, that's enough! Either change your attitude or get out of my head!

V: Change my attitude? Why didn't you say so? In the absence of you expressing your wants, I defaulted to your Inner Critic's voice. I love playing your Inner Critic. I'm pretty good at it too, don't you think? I draw my inspiration from a mix of characters, but I hear myself in the voice of Robert De Niro.

J: I don't want to hear your voice at all!

V: Do you actually want help instead? Do you want coaching?

J: Of course!

V: Ok, but I'm keeping it simple. And you get to hear me in whatever voice you want!

J: That's fine. Simple is good. And I want your help in the voice of Morgan Freeman.

V: Done. First, run a body scan.

J: Done.

V: What did you find? Prioritize and tell me your primary observation.

J: Lots going on, but my low back is the worst.

V: Run the scan again, focusing on your torso.

J: Done — I'm folding forwards at my waist.

V: Visualize yourself standing tall, with open hips and a relaxed lower back. Hold that visualization for 1 minute.

J: Ok, I see myself running tall, upright with open hips. I see myself with a low back that feels totally opposite than what my physical body feels now.

V: Stand tall, run tall. That's all. Stand tall, run tall.

15 minutes later:

J: I'm breathing so much better now. I don't feel as heavy.

V: Awesome work. You're looking stronger. You look like a runner. Standing tall helped with your breath and your ability to recapture efficient technique. Scan again.

J: Done. Cadence is slow.

V: Quick Feet. Quick Feet.

15 minutes later:

V: Excellent improvement. Your form is back and looks great. Your speed is back to what it was during the first hour.

J: This feels so much better. I can cruise this all the way back.

V: You could, but you've got more in you. You can do this last 3 miles in less than 25 minutes. Look at the ocean. Draw energy from the waves, with each arriving wave drawing your forward.

J: Ok, waves—energy.

V: Waves, waves, waves.

15 minutes later:

J: That rocked. I'm flying, but I don't think I can hold this pace any longer.

V: Yes, you can. Think of your grandfather. The last push home is for him, in his honor. Own this stretch for him.

J: I'm on it.

And with this inner dialogue playing in my mind, I finish a nearly six hour run, three times the planned duration. What an experience!

My jet lag recovery run turned into an impromptu and very slow extended marathon, minus the t-shirt. Some runs awaken us. Some runs entertain us. Some runs help us escape. This run, well, it did all three and it also taught me a valuable lesson.

Had I not tapped into the power of my Inner Coach and the ability to interdict and change the inner dialogue, I never would have learned this lesson. I would have succumbed to the negativity expressed by my Inner Critic, and it would have driven me to quit the run, thus not realizing my true potential, and likely miring me in a protracted cloud of negativity.

The Power of Coaching

Coaches are capable of offering a tremendous level of support, with their objective eyes constantly scanning your performance and psyche, looking for improvement opportunities. They have the mission to then reach you and help you extract every last bit of capability with high impact guidance given at the right time.

The chapter-opening Tom Landry quote is such a gem that I am including it here again: "A coach is someone who tells you what you don't want to hear, who has you see what you don't want to see, so you can be who you have always known you could be."

Yes, good coaches see, hear, and sense that which is overlooked, ignored, or simply not observed because of the tendency to live so caught up in busy minds, technology and a multitude of devices, and thoughts of what just happened or may happen in the future.

If you had a coach running beside you at all times, they would notice where you need corrections to your physical technique and where you need mental and emotional redirection. Good coaches are capable of getting more out of you than you believe is possible. Coaches also prioritize, so as not to overload you with so much guidance that you can't handle any of it. Then, they coach you toward the desired outcome, with compassion, ferocity or whatever combination of message and communications style that's needed to reach you.

Since it is unlikely that you're going out on every run, if any run, with a coach at your side, you need to consider some options.

Do you simply operate in *I'm Free* mode, following your whims and moods, and doing whatever you wish?

Do you hear an internal voice yelling at you to go harder?

Or, do you activate the voice of a wise Inner Coach, one that you've developed and trained specifically for this situation, for a wide range of situations you encounter as a runner?

Hopefully the answer is crystal clear. If you want to grow as a runner and want to experience more Flow State Running experiences, invest time in developing and using your Inner Coach's voice. Don't just assume that it will happen on its own. It takes work to fully cultivate, but with it in place, your running will never be the same.

Inner Critic

Before we look at building and strengthening the voice of your Inner Coach, we need to examine its opponent, your Inner Critic. Inner Critic is the powerful force that sometimes appears in your mind and works hard to undermine your progress toward your goals. Inner Critic is an expert at unraveling you. Inner Critic knows how to get under your skin, how to fan the fire of your fears and how to distract you.

Inner Critic is a control freak and wants to run the show. Inner Critic doesn't care about techniques, race medals and your fulfillment. Inner Critic loves to show up alongside adversities — fatigue, rain, hills — all are welcome opportunities for Inner Critic to "help out."

Inner Critic tries to undermine self-confidence while emphasizing worry and self-consciousness. Inner Critic loves when we worry about what others think and how we look. Inner Critic highlights our fears and mistakes and is reluctant to ever allow us to let go of them. Inner Critic has a strong dislike of flow state experiences and will go to great lengths to prevent runners from ever entering flow.

Inner Critic is in each of us, but the stronger, more versatile and more present we make our Inner Coach, Inner Critic will visit less often and with less impact. Overpowering Inner Critic begins with awareness of its existence within us and its propensity for visiting us in moments of adversity. From this awareness, we train ourselves to be strong across the five Inner Coach roles, with the energy we direct to them serving to minimize the attention we give Inner Critic.

Delegating to your Inner Coach

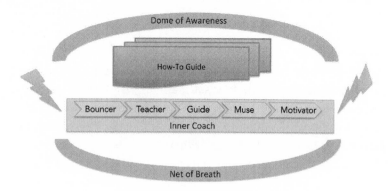

Image: Flow State Runner model

Inner Coach has five important roles and areas of responsibility. Your mission is to build a strong inner voice for each role and to integrate each voice into your running as needed.

- **Bouncer:** Deals with your Inner Critic.
- **Teacher:** Delivers coaching cues and other guidance.
- **Guide:** Guides you into moments of focus and presence and helps you deal with overload. Keeps you on task with One Cue Only.
- **Muse:** Carries you into moments of play and release, to support flow experiences.
- **Motivator:** Supercharges you with lightning strikes, positivity interdictions and spirit. Believes in you.

Invite your Inner Coach to each run and consciously activate this voice before you take your first step. Once you are running, choose the Inner Coach role you feel the most connected to at the moment, and be ready to shift to other roles as needed. Let's look at each role in more detail.

The Bouncer

Your Inner Coach works as a club bouncer, ready to deal with rowdy, out-of-control Inner Critic, either when it shows up uninvited or when it somehow sneaks in and starts to wreak havoc. The Bouncer's presence is often enough to intimidate Inner Critic into walking away. If not, visualize the Bouncer growing in size and Inner Critic shrinking and losing its voice, until it is a tiny, voiceless grain of sand that the wind blows away.

Here are some tips for allowing the Bouncer to flourish, thus minimizing Inner Critic's presence and impact:

- Float your visualized coach as the Bouncer over your shoulder, guarding the door to your mind and ready to deal with your Inner Critic should it try to get involved and force its way in.
- Whenever Inner Critic shows up and jumps deep into your thoughts, redirect your focus to Inner Coach, and send in the Bouncer. Sometimes when I notice that Inner Critic is getting too vocal, I envision that Inner Coach left me alone for just a moment to deal with something else. So, I just think, "Hey Bouncer, get in here and take care of this guy!"

It is inevitable that Inner Critic and Inner Coach will use your mind as a battlefield. It's going to happen, and often when you need it the least and when it stands to wreck your goals the most. Rather than wait for this battle and hope that Inner Coach wins, train for it by hosting mock battles. Here's an exercise to help with that:

Exercise — Host a battle between Inner Critic and Inner Coach's Bouncer Role

This is an entertaining and worthwhile exercise that is also very realistic, especially in long distance running. Your task is to host a battle between your Inner Coach and Inner Critic, allowing each to become progressively more vocal and more aggressive throughout a segment of your run. This is an exaggeration exercise, so be sure to play up each voice, focusing on the Bouncer role for Inner Coach.

During your Inner Voice Battle Run, toss the microphone to Inner Critic first and open the floor for some initial mild negativity. Pass the mic back to Inner Coach for a counter. Continue the exchange, building more energy and sharper responses. Notice how your body responds to this inner battle. Does it energize you? Does it distract you? Continue the battle to a moment of peak intensity and then shift all of your energy to Inner Coach in a triumphant finish.

Always finish with Inner Coach winning. Why? Because that's the future you want to craft for yourself if you want more flow in life. If you want flow, you want Inner Coach to be a consistent winner, and if you want Inner Coach to be a consistent winner, you have to always SEE Inner Coach as winning. Try it during different types of runs, from easy to high intensity, from short to long.

When to engage Inner Coach as the Bouncer:

- The moment you detect negative inner dialogue or fear, or that you are starting to connect and empower your observations of adversities.
- Whenever you stop believing in yourself and start doubting.
- Whenever you start revising and scaling down your goals or plan during a run, especially when Inner Critic is telling you that today just isn't your day.
- Whenever you are feeling natural aches and pains that are not a real injury and not worthy of undermining your goals.

The Teacher

The Teacher delivers coaching cues and other guidance. Based on observations of the Dome of Awareness and the Teacher's knowledge of your cultivated and customized How-To Guide, the Teacher keeps track of which perception drills and body positioning instructions have proven effective in your running. The Teacher is open-minded and creative, thus encourages you to try new things when the time is right. The Teacher is active in guiding you through Tension Dumpers to reach MED. The Teacher also steps in to remind you of flow release triggers, breathing and any other steps you've learned to help you release and stay in moments of flow. Lastly, the Teacher expects proper technical execution of movement from you, but in a constructive manner, unlike Inner Critic's unfocused attack on you. The Teacher balances out the Motivator's drive to help you ride the edge of continued development and performance without being so hard on yourself that you allow your Inner Critic to take over.

When to engage Inner Coach as the Teacher:

- Any time you need to receive How-To Guide guidance
- Tension Dumpers, returning to MED
- Recapturing flow when you had it, but lost it
- Whenever your high expectations and the Motivator Inner Coach clash in a performance that suddenly brings Inner Critic to center stage

The Guide

The Guide has a big job — keep you focused, fully in the present moment and directed with One Cue Only. A cue can be any thought or guidance, from physical technique reminders (stand tall) to mindset reminders (own this!). The Guide helps you as well in dealing with overload, and thus works alongside the Bouncer role, as overload is a quick invitation for Inner Critic to join the party, and the Teacher role, as only one of many teaching cues is to be given at a time.

In the movie *The Hunt for Red October,* Sean Connery calls for transmitting one sonar ping to the enemy sub, ordering in his unique voice: "one ping only." This single-focus concept also appears in the movie *City Slickers*, when Smiley states that the secret of life is: One Thing. You will train your Inner Coach to give you one instruction at a time, and you will train yourself to focus on just one cue at a time. Think of it in Connery's voice if that helps you remember it: *One cue only*. It may also help to visualize tuning in an old radio dial to the *One Cue* station — the aim is to avoid overlapping radio signals and static and land on one clear station. One cue.

Flow doesn't happen in the past or present. It happens *in the now* — in the moment. We are very good at living <u>outside</u> of *the now* though, with our powerful brains running scenario after scenario envisioning future events and replaying past events (often inaccurately).

We even do this with our bodies. When teaching runners about heel strike and slow foot pulls, I set them up in an inverted Y position, with both legs extended. I tell them that their front foot is landing in tomorrow and the back foot is stuck in yesterday, thus they are attempting to run in yesterday and tomorrow, but not today, in the present. Efficient running technique brings them to running in the present physically (landing under the body, pulling the foot up under the body, both per the Pose Method®), the next step is to help get their mind to the present. With mind and body *in the now*, we are best poised for fulfilling running experiences.

Have you ever been in a conversation where you struggled to listen intently and caught your mind thinking about something on your calendar for the next day or something that happened last night? Have you ever tried to meditate or simply sit quietly and noticed your mind running wild with endless thoughts, worries and ideas about both past and future events? When these scenarios happen, the Guide is there to step in and say IN THE NOW.

To stop our mind from endlessly thinking of the past or future, we need to focus our concentration on one specific thought or cue at a time. This is true presence, being focused and engaged in the current moment, and the Guide is there to remind you *One Cue Only*. If you experience too many cues at once, not a single one will reach the target. The Guide is responsible for ensuring that every cue selected indeed reaches that target.

One thing I've noticed when helping to develop new coaches is that there is a tendency for them to overload a student with cues and information. It is as if they are trying to prove their knowledge and value beyond a doubt, so rather than select one lesson or cue to teach, they offer it ALL and all at once. In doing so, they prove that they may know a lot of information, but they may not show sensitivity to what the student actually needs and how the student best learns. It is the shotgun approach of teaching, and it's not the sign of an experienced teacher successful in reaching her students.

When learning a new technique or working toward self-improvement in any area, we tend to do the same thing as self-coaches. We think about everything all at once, and then feel so overwhelmed that we hinder our ability to learn.

I notice this as well when teaching running technique in workshops and people try to focus on too many new skills at once. I'll be leading the group in an exercise on, for example, skipping, and some runners will feel completely overwhelmed in what should be a fairly playful, kid-like exercise. They ask, "How am I supposed to skip while keeping my cadence high, tension low in my body, my heel kissing the ground, thinking of the color green, breathing through my nose, tension at Level 4, etc." My answer is "you're not supposed to do all of that at once — just skip and pay attention to how it feels to pull your foot."

The Guide is there to take control and remind you to think of one cue at a time. When the Dome of Awareness detects something new to address, the Guide lets go of one cue and delivers another. When you start thinking of too many things at once, simply call on the Guide to deliver focus to you.

When to engage Inner Coach as the Guide:

- Whenever you are self-coaching and giving yourself adjustments, cues or thoughts to focus on
- Moments of overload: when too many thoughts or situations arrive at once in your mind
- When you catch yourself thinking too much about the future or past, the Guide is there to bring you to the present.

The Muse

The Muse has a simple and fun role: to remind us to play. Play is critical as a release trigger for Flow State Running experiences. The Muse reminds us not to take ourselves too seriously and to occasionally snap out of structure and rigor. The Muse helps us forget about self-consciousness. The Muse prompts us to skip, run backwards, take a quick session on playground equipment, race a kid up a hill, splash through a stream or puddle, balance on a log, roll down a grass hill, smile at someone and more. Listen to the Muse and be spontaneous — you can always blame any looney actions on the Muse as well!

The Muse is well-suited to join you on long runs and ultra marathons, moments of alone time with only your Inner Coach — moments that receive a huge boost with humorous, light reminders to smile, play and actually enjoy the experience, rather than charge through it only thinking of pacing, time and numbers.

When to engage Inner Coach as the Muse:

- In Flow State Runner workouts, after Struggle activities.
- In moments of stress and overload due to terrain, weather, fatigue and other adversities
- When seeking creativity, or a change in state or routine

The Motivator

Sometimes you need a coach to help calm your mind and focus, and other times you need a surge of adrenaline shot straight into your heart. Yes, these are the times when you need lightning to strike — the make or break moments when the right cue given in the right voice at the right time can propel you toward a high level of performance and shatter your preconceived limits. The Motivator's role is to know what works for you and to step in with motivation when you need it most.

The Motivator knows how to bottle and re-use lightning bolts of motivational energy. The Motivator pays attention to those moments when you listen to a powerful motivational speech, perhaps one of those YouTube videos that layers a speech over an inspiring video montage of championship performances and emotional examples of heart, courage and perseverance. The Motivator remembers the parts that sent chills up your spine and then replays those moments for you at exactly the right time while you are running.

The Motivator remembers that race you ran with your name printed on your race number, where people screamed your name at just the right time to motivate you to run harder up the hill or power through some low moment. The Motivator then brings that moment back to you when you are training alone and in need of the energy of a supportive crowd.

My Inner Coach as Motivator remembers the 1999 New York Marathon and has in my library the sound of New Yorkers shouting my name, in their wonderful Brooklyn accents and all. Many a run has the Motivator replayed those cheers when I'm alone on a track pushing myself to the edge on 800 meter intervals.

It takes some practice and experimentation to develop an effective voice. I'll never forget one of my early coaching experiences when I was passionately working to help an athlete, giving him a combination of technique cues and enthusiastic motivational phrases. "Chest up. Fight for this. Breathe 1,2,3 — now go! Stay with it — stay with it! Come on — beast mode!" It didn't take long before he stopped what he was doing and caught my eyes, saying, "I know you think you're helping, but everything you're saying is making this worse for me and making me want to quit." What a deflating punch to the gut! It was a powerful lesson for me — motivation is not one size fits all. I had to change my tactics and experiment to learn how best to reach this athlete.

Your task as a runner in the quest to develop a powerful Inner Coach's voice is to build a library of effective cues and motivational commands. Keep them short and simple and practice them in training runs before you need to draw on them in races. Chapter 11 offers a series of tools designed to build this library. What works for another may not work for you, so the key is to experiment and find out what works in various situations. Then just as a coach builds a mental library of what works for his or her athletes, you will build a library of what works for you. When you tap into this library, you'll draw out images and voices that will serve as your lightning bolts, prompting the release of hormones to heighten your state of awareness and presence, and increase your performance. This is your lightning in the bank, your spirit in reserve for when you need it most.

Remember the glass orb that signifies the Flow State Runner model? When you are running, see yourself in that plasma globe with the lightning bolts appearing and supercharging you as your Motivator.

When to engage Inner Coach as the Motivator:

- During key moments of competition
- During adversities (terrain, weather, speed)
- During high intensity training efforts, when training above comfortable pain thresholds
- When the Bouncer needs some extra muscle to shut down Inner Critic

Developing your Inner Coach's voice

The beautiful thing about your Inner Coach's voice is that you can make it precisely what you want it to be. The sound, accent, character — it's all up to you. Some runners like to map their Inner Coach's voice to a coach or mentor that has been or is currently in their lives. Got a favorite coach from school? Now's your chance to honor that coach by bringing their voice into your running practice. Felt motivated from a coach you've seen in film or TV? For the low cost of zero, you can now bring that coach onto your support team. How about a coach who could have gotten so much more from you if they had only done this or not done that? Now you can change that and tap back into their energy in a way that serves you today. By the way, it's OK to have more than one Inner Coach's voice, hence the reason I introduced the multiple roles that Inner Coach may play. Great potential lies in developing your ability to call upon one of many coaches on your virtual support team's bench, activating the right coach for the task at hand.

I encourage you to make the effort to visualize the sound of this voice and the appearance of your Inner Coach, floating over your shoulder, running beside you, in a vehicle following you shouting through a megaphone — whatever works for you!

There is value in seeing this voice as a 3rd person and not yourself. There is also power in visualizing your Inner Coach as being totally dedicated to helping you get the most out of yourself, even when you don't feel like it. You want to make your coach proud, and feel comfort in knowing that your coach is there to support you, to push you and to get the most out of you. Ultimately, you trust your coach.

For some, perhaps it is easy to instantly see and hear your Inner Coach in your mind. For others, this may prove extremely challenging. For most, it requires some conscious effort to specifically define a voice (or voices) to represent your Inner Coach and to hear this voice as different from your own. This is mind training, and it is what makes the difference between status quo running and Flow State Running experiences. It is worth the investment.

Here are four exercises designed to help you cultivate your Inner Coach. I highly recommend that you take time to try them and to journal about your experiences with each.

Exercise 1 - Sample voices from prior coaches

Think of some coaches or mentors you've had in your life — ones that really reached you in a way that made a difference in your performance, or even in your life. Remember their voice and perhaps things they used to say to coach you. Assign a single cue to each, one that is a fit for their style of coaching or teaching. A cue could be an instruction on your body position or simply a motivational word or phrase.

Hear each coach repeat their cue, over and over in your mind, for at least 10 repetitions. Now go out for a run and invite each coach, one at a time, to coach you. *Hear* them, in their voice, give you the pre-selected coaching cue. Notice how you respond. Perhaps you need to hear them repeat the cue or change the intensity of their guidance. Experiment and have fun with this exercise. Try swapping the cues around your coaching "team" and notice how your mind and body responds to different coaching personalities and voices.

This exercise works well when combined with a meditation or visualization practice. For example, visualize a successful run with a specific coach's voice and guidance, and then later complete that run following the same script you created for the visualization.

Exercise 2 - Experiment with new voices

For both a technique and mindset skill, pick an area you want to practice. Preselect a single coaching cue for each skill.

Here's an example:

- Mindset: perseverance during last 200m of 800m intervals

- Technique: quick foot pull

Map each cue to a new voice. Imagine this voice, female or male, age range, accent, language, and any detail you wish to add. Pick at least two voices to test. Give them names if you wish.

Two of my favorite voices mapped to the above needs include:

- Mindset: the wise coach in his 60s or 70s with a gray beard and weathered face; old school approach; blend of my thick-necked, gregarious WWII US Navy veteran grandfather and Rocky's coach, Mickey Goldmill. He tells me "Fight Jeff, Fight. This is your life. Fight for it. Make me proud."
- Technique: feminine voice; patient, but firm and extremely clear and precise in cues given; high expectations of my technical execution of her instructions. She tells me "pinpoint your focus, like a laser that starts in the ball of your foot and shoots straight to your hip. Fire that laser on each pull." Later she offers a simple, "laser pull" and I understand exactly what's needed.

Feel free to use voices similar to my favorites or go with your own. Try at least two distinct personalities and visualize each coach running with you, watching you and then giving you their guidance. Then go out and run, repeating the same exercise on the move. Lastly, experiment with switching their roles, with the mindset coach guiding you in a technique cue and vice versa.

Exercise 3 - Be a coach for someone else

One of the most effective methods of developing your Inner Coach's voice is to practice your Outer Coach's Voice on others. If you've got a background as a coach or teacher, you are ahead of the game, as you likely have experience that you can readily transfer into your Inner

Coach's voice. This doesn't mean that it comes naturally though. While it is said that we are our own worst critiques, we can also be our worst self-coaches! It takes continual practice and awareness to cultivate and direct this inner voice to best support us and to avoid turning into our Inner Critic.

When cultivating our Inner Coach's voice, don't worry if you feel that you may not have the expertise to coach running or sport in general. The best way to fully learn a skill is to practice teaching it to others, so select a skill you've learned from this book and teach it to a friend or family member. Go on a run with them and offer your voice as their Coach's voice. Observe them running, the way their body moves, the tension levels you notice and anything you can glean from their mindset. Pick out one observation to offer and follow it up with a coaching cue. Then shift back into observation mode to see if and how the cue works. After a while, either reinforce the cue or offer a different one. Don't be afraid to experiment. Try a mix of cue types and tones to your voice to see what works best for the person you're coaching. Try it first under simple running conditions, and then put them under pressure. I routinely use this technique in my Flow State Runner workshops, teaching and practicing a skill first under simple conditions (easy-to-moderate pace, level terrain) and then adding complexity and intensity (speed, steep hills, tricky terrain, unknown route). The added complexity provides an opportunity to practice skills under conditions, likely to be encountered in "real life." Notice what happens when you overload them with too many cues and too much guidance.

After practicing your outer coach's voice on another runner, try those same cues on yourself, in your own internal voice or any coach's voice you prefer. Notice if you respond in the same manner or differently.

By the way, I mention internal and inner voice, as we are training and developing inner dialogue and a mindset to help direct you toward desired outcomes. While it is generally more socially acceptable not to talk to one's self out loud, if it helps you with the coach's voice concept or an any running situation, do it! I'm just as comfortable shouting an encouraging word to myself in the throes of a challenging interval than I am to the runners I coach. I couldn't care less what others at the track or on the trail think about the crazy runner yelling at himself to *give more* or to *fight for it*. If it works for you and helps you get more out of yourself, use it.

Exercise 4: practice voices across all five roles

Assign a voice or personality to each of the five Inner Coach roles: Bouncer, Teacher, Guide, Muse and Motivator. Perhaps you have a couple examples from your past experience with coaches or mentors that perfectly match one of the roles. Plug those in, and then invent a coaching personality for the others. Run a separate run to practice each voice. Observe the impact, and then practice combining voices, working yourself from two Inner Coach voices up to all five during a single run. Observe and note what was helpful or unhelpful and continue to craft a model that works for you. Notice in what roles your Inner Coach's voice feels natural and what roles require more focus and development to make your Inner Coach's voice as well-rounded as possible.

Closing Thoughts - Hire Yourself

One of the most powerful aspects of working with a real coach, not a visualized or Inner Coach's voice, is trust and confidence — your trust of each other and your confidence and belief in each other. I will always remember how Coach Lisa Smith-Batchen enabled me to profoundly exceed my expectations by simply believing in me and persuading me to believe that my abilities were higher than I thought. In the 2008 Marathon des Sables, she told me in the final few days before the race that she expected me to place in the top 100. At the time, my goal was simply to finish this epic weeklong race, not to have some specific standing, certainly not in the top 100. Her stretch goal and belief in me created a powerful energy, an energy that took on a life of its own and drove me to a level of intense focus, pain tolerance, and relentless drive that resulted in a top 50 finish and the best athletic performance of my life. What's important is that the right coach was on hand with the right guidance for me, and I surrendered to that guidance, placing my faith and energy in it.

For those moments when a coach isn't present, you can achieve something similar by having faith in yourself, by believing in your power, and by using your Inner Coach's voice to keep you focused, faithful and motivated. Changing the paradigm to envision your coach's voice as a 3rd party is a tool to separate your physical body and (over)thinking mind from your mind's true potential to serve you and elevate your performance to unimagined levels. This is your game-changer — a very important method for getting more from yourself and being the best version of yourself possible.

Believe in yourself and hire <u>yourself</u> as coach — you are the one who will always be there when you need YOU.

10. What do I do when ... ?

"I like nonsense, it wakes up the brain cells. Fantasy is a necessary ingredient in living, it's a way of looking at life through the wrong end of a telescope. Which is what I do, and that enables you to laugh at life's realities."
— Dr. Seuss

The power of the mind: hitting rock bottom and digging out at the Ultra Trail du Mont Blanc

2009, Swiss-Italian border: More than 24 hours have passed since we set off in Chamonix on a 166KM (105 mile) run that will take us up and down the mountains of the Mont Blanc massif. Climbing a total of 9,400 meters and covering ground in three countries in the Alps (Switzerland, France and Italy), the Ultra Trail du Mont Blanc is in a class of ultra marathons at a high level of difficulty and with borderline lunacy.

The race started in the early evening with much fanfare as nearly 2,000 runners full of nervous energy embarked from idyllic Chamonix like Spartans marching into war. The send-off music was heroic, the setting festive, and the feeling in each runner's gut a mix of nervous energy, lingering doubt, and tenuous hope. The first big climb broke up the field, as the course took its first of many swipes at our collective egos. French villages came and went through the first night, and with sunrise came the Italian border and a run through Italy's side of Mont Blanc that will take most of the next day.

In Switzerland, following a descent of Col Grand Ferret, where I give in to adrenaline and ran much faster than I should have so "early" in an ultra marathon, I now find myself alone on a 20KM (12 mile) section of mostly flat running through a valley, with the proverbial wheels coming off. The blistering pace I'd enjoyed on both the climb and descent of the last pass is replaced by a physical and mental meltdown. Now on some of the easiest terrain in the race, I can barely hold any sense of a running pace. This confuses me. Hours earlier I felt superhuman. I'd passed a hundred runners on that pass and had even found the energy to shout out loud my joy while passing through one incredibly scenic area.

Now I am crashing, and crashing hard. Physically I feel spent, with cramping quads, an aching lower back, and feet so sore that I'm wincing with each step.

My breathing is labored. I feel lethargic and unmotivated. I start on the endurance sport math game — calculating my current pace and dwelling on every worst-case scenario of continuing with that pace. Hello Inner Critic. I'll barely make the next time-cut off. This is easy terrain that's killing me. I've got three more mountain passes to climb. There's no way I'll make all the checkpoint time limits to finish this race. Each calculation brings new worries and doubts.

Every few minutes, I try to run again, with the shuffle lasting 30 seconds before being replaced by walking. My body language is dismal: eyes down, sunken shoulders, frown. I look beaten. I am in a dark place that is normal for ultra endurance events, but never an easy dragon to slay in the moment.

With self-pity consuming my mind like a dark cloud stretching its menacing tentacles to claim the sky, I pass by a local farmer — he glances up and offers a simple, yet perfectly timed and profoundly helpful, "Bon courage." While French for good luck, the word *Courage* spoken with a strong French accent brings about an intense emotional response in me, as I choose to hear it in English and think of courage. I smile and offer a breathless "Merci monsieur. Merci beaucoup."

As tears form in my eyes, I repeat the word: Courage. Courage. Courage.

With each repetition, I feel more deeply connected to ancient warriors. Courage. Spartan. Courage. Samurai. Courage. Fight for this, Jeff. Courage.

I look up at the immense mountains surrounding me and tap into their power. Courage. Mountains.

I look at my legs. Courage, legs.

I breathe in deep, fresh, crisp Alpine air. Courage, air.

I feel my heart. Courage. Heart.

I experience a massive transformation, as if I've stepped out of a dark, damp, and cold cave into bright and warm sunshine. I find myself once again running, once again smiling and once again laughing (laughing alone is a key skill for ultra marathoners). My running form returns and my legs lighten. My attitude improves and I hold my head high. As my mind gets back on track, everything else responds positively. I've dug myself out of this dark pit, a pit that nearly took this racing dream away from me. Will I return there again? It doesn't matter, because in this moment, I'm running. I'm happy. I'm doing what I love. The next moment doesn't matter until it's upon me. I'm a runner. I'm in the mountains and I'm alive, so very alive.

Putting it all together

The Flow State Runner model is here for you as a skills development and orientation tool. It works as a foundation to support you in developing and calling upon the unique blend of elements that results in the highest performing version of yourself possible. It Is also intended to support you in those moments in running, learning and life when you feel disoriented and overwhelmed.

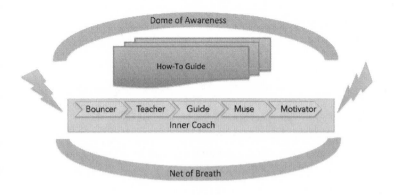

Image: Flow State Runner Model

You now have a much deeper understanding of the Dome of Awareness, the Support Net of Breath, Inner Coach and the integration of a skills How-To Guide. Your investment in practicing the offline, baseline skills in each of these areas (the work you do when not running) will lead to their reliable and effective presence when you are running, and especially in moments of fatigue, stress, and other adversities. It is not enough to simply read once about it, so I encourage you to practice the suggested exercises, journal your experiences, and to continue to grow. Then, put it all to use in your running and incorporate your own ideas as you go.

In practice, once you've made progress developing yourself in all aspects of the model, the aim is that you check your orientation occasionally and perform the tasks of the model primarily on autopilot.

It's like you are a sophisticated satellite in a geosynchronous orbit of the earth (at the appropriate altitude to stay in the same space above a point on the surface). The satellite has sensors and thrusters that automatically correct position when it is interrupted by solar wind and gravitational effects. It has been programmed with various triggers that pull it back to into the correct orbit if it veers too far off, but those triggers aren't used during the times when the flight path is safe and all systems are nominal. For most of us, it takes focus and dedicated practice to develop our inner flight control systems, and that is the work I encourage you to keep doing until it is well-honed and embedded in your daily life.

In the story above, I was lucky. I was lucky to receive a trigger from someone else. Had I run under the Flow State Runner model, I would have inner-coached myself away from the issue in the first place. The Dome would have recognized long before the issues started that I was on a path toward unraveling myself and my Inner Coach would have started redirecting my focus to a positive aim, which would have avoided a very long and nearly race-ending meltdown. This lesson learned has been used as a catalyst for much of my motivation to help others avoid similar mistakes. I remain grateful for the Swiss farmer who wished me luck and nudged me back on track to reach the finish line in Chamonix that day. Merci beaucoup, Monsieur.

Bridging Section 1 and Section 2

We're nearing the end of Section 1 of this book. In Section 2, I share my collection of Flow State Runner mind tools, training insights and racing tips. I also share my thoughts on technology and personal growth. These are all practical topics that I layer on top of the philosophy and structure of the Flow State Runner model. Before we go there, I have devoted the rest of this final chapter of Section 1 to covering frequently asked questions that have surfaced in my running workshops and coaching interactions over the years. The answers and insights round out my Flow State Runner philosophical basis and segue us into the hands-on guidance in Section 2.

FAQ

What do I do when I hate running in general or occasionally just don't feel like running at all?

At the start of all of my running workshops, I ask some simple intro questions to learn why people decided to spend their valuable time with me for one or more days on the topic of running. The most common response isn't to help them get a new marathon Personal Best, run their first ultra marathon or avoid injury. The most common response is that they HATE running. Sometimes they say simply that they hate it, but have to run to pass an assessment or to perform in CrossFit workouts. Other times they say they hate it, but <u>want</u> to love it because it is portable and they usually feel better after doing it. They express dislike for a variety of reasons, perhaps because it hurts, is boring, or isn't comfortable in whatever the weather is. The funny thing is that very often these runners love their running experience after it's over, yet forget that post-run feeling right before the next opportunity to run is there.

If you are in this group, hopefully by using the concepts from *Flow State Runner,* you will find yourself moving out of the "I hate running" camp in general and find yourself, at worst, only in the "I sometimes don't want to run" camp.

I've observed that people who don't enjoy running, but still do it begrudgingly, are typically running with poor physical technique. Solve that and you're well on your way to positive running experiences. Next, it's a question of mindset, and that's something you are tackling by spending time with this book and its associated concepts.

Sometimes even runners who LOVE running and are incredibly fit for running aren't motivated to go out and run on a given day. This is normal, but frustrating for these runners.

You can improve your technique and fitness to make progress toward enjoying to run, but attitude remains the most important, so let's tackle it. Here are my top three tactics for dealing with times you just don't feel like running:

1. Fill out the Flow State Runner LUNP Evaluator described below (LUNP = **L**ikely-**U**nlikely (probability of occurrence) and **N**egative-**P**ositive (potential impact)
2. Gamify your run (explained below)
3. Use your lack of motivation as fuel by completing the *I don't want to run* session in Chapter 12

Let's look at each in more detail.

<u>LUNP Evaluator</u>

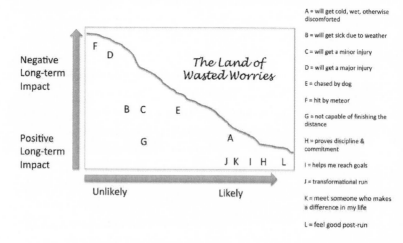

A = will get cold, wet, otherwise discomforted

B = will get sick due to weather

C = will get a minor injury

D = will get a major injury

E = chased by dog

F = hit by meteor

G = not capable of finishing the distance

H = proves discipline & commitment

I = helps me reach goals

J = transformational run

K = meet someone who makes a difference in my life

L = feel good post-run

Here's how this handy tool works. Simply write down a list of things that could happen during the run or that you somehow have associated with this run. Give each a letter. Start with any excuses in your mind. Then, add any other events that based on your prior experience running or your wildest thoughts could happen from the moment you lace up until you are safely back in the door. Now, plot them to the chart, over the continuums of likelihood (from unlikely to likely) and long-term impact (from positive to negative). Next, step back and review the chart. Notice what shows up in the positive and negative long-term impact zones, as well as the area of vast uninhabited real estate, which I call the *Land of Wasted Worries*. The LUNP Evaluator helps remind you that there's nothing to see in the *Land of Wasted Worries*. I've included a blank copy in the Appendix for you.

Whenever you are wavering on whether or not to get out for a planned run, imagine your coach asking you to fill out this evaluator and to review it together. You are often, if not always, your own coach, so print out a couple empty copies and have them on hand. Then, when you're feeling unmotivated to run, but motivated to think of numerous excuses, grab the sheet and fill it out. Often just the thought of writing down excuses and the host of likely benefits is enough to urge us out the door!

Gamification

Gamification is another useful tool. Make your run a game of numbers, a mission or some other type of adventure. I used this technique in many of the workouts I designed in 2015 as a part of my *40 Hill Workouts Project*. A simple example is 5-4-3-2-1. It works like this: Run 5 minutes. Walk as much as you wish. Run 4 minutes. Walk. Continue this ladder until you finish the final 1-minute run. The running parts can be a hard run or sprint, and the walking parts an easy run, based on your needs. What is important is that the game serves as a gateway to get you running. I've used decks of cards, dice, and a variety of the mind hacks from Chapter 11 to gamify workouts.

The "I don't want to run" Training Session

This motivational technique is inspired by my friend Guy Spier, author of *Education of a Value Investor*, who mentored me on the writing process by encouraging me to deal with writer's block days by forcing myself to just write something, even if it's page after page of the words, "I hate writing." Most of the time I'd laugh and snap out of my block just thinking about this, but occasionally I did what he suggested, either writing those precise words over and over, or writing about how I had no ideas and didn't feel like writing. Every single time I broke out of the mind block, and many of those sessions turned into my most productive and fulfilling moments of writing. In Chapter 12, I offer you a workout designed to help you go deeper in your lack of motivation to run and to hopefully use that to turn it around for you.

How do I deal with my weight and body composition?

Over the years I've experienced many runners opening up to me about their challenges with weight and body composition. Running attracts people as a weight-loss tool, so this is not surprising. In addition, with many high performance, competitive runners, it is not uncommon to find those who obsess about weight, even when, to most, these runners would appear under-weight with an extremely low body fat percentage.

I've struggled with body composition and image as well since my teen years, when I started running to lose weight while on my school's wresting team. I've performed well in ultra distance races when my stored fat was far more than I prefer for vanity reasons, but optimal for my performance. And conversely, I've leaned out for photo shoots and felt physically wrecked in the process.

From my earliest days as an overweight teen runner, I was exposed to key lessons, such as how it is not possible to out-train a bad diet, numbers on a scale do not equal happiness, and our performance is tied to what we eat. That exposure didn't equate to an instant solution though — rather, it taught me the valuable lesson that for many, nutrition and body composition are a constant struggle and work-in-progress. Later, after thinking I "solved" nutrition for myself, I learned that not only do our metabolism and nutritional needs change as we age, so do the requirements for our mindset to evolve.

Our approach to the intersection of nutrition, body composition, performance is out of the scope for this book, but it is an important one for any runner to explore and test on themselves.

My general guidance on the aforementioned is as follows:

- Eat real food as much as possible. Skip all fast food, avoid processed foods and soft drinks, and go easy on bread, pasta, sugar and alcohol, especially if you are interested in reducing body fat.
- Catalysts are OK (shakes, cleanses, diets) for creating initial momentum, but avoid quick fixes and rapid solutions, as they are not sustainable.
- Consider the three perspectives that author Robb Wolf describes as how you "look, feel, and perform." Avoid over-focusing on one perspective at the expense of the others.
- Experiment on yourself like a scientist: change a variable, stick with it for 2-4 weeks and observe your mind and body's response.
- Recognize the impact of stress and sleep deprivation, and make changes in your life to impact each.

What do I do when I'm in a funk and my running feels heavy & slow as a result?

This "in a funk" feeling most often hits runners on a rainy, cold day when they are considering bailing on a run, because of a number of invented excuses. It also appears during the first of several intervals, late in a long run and any time Inner Critic wishes to throw it at us. We've all been there in some form or fashion, but this doesn't mean it is not challenging. The more prepared you are to deal with it, the less time and energy you'll waste if and when this feeling arrives.

Here are four steps I advise immediately taking when this feeling hits you:

1. Redirect your energy to someone else. Race them, cheer them or honor them. See the *Other People* section in Chapter 11 for ideas.
2. Send in the Bouncer to deal with Inner Critic.
3. Replace the words "Heavy and Slow" with "Strong and Steady," "Alive and Kicking," or whatever serves you. Replace the words

and repeat that as a mantra until your mood shifts.

4.   Take a physical action, any action, just move. Get outside, run for a few minutes, run a hill or stairs, run a different route. Take action.

Remember, your mind will adapt to the patterns you expose it to. If you repeatedly teach it a pattern of experiencing an emotional low point, followed by inaction and wallowing in self-pity, this will become a habit, thus a comfortable pattern for the mind to recall again and again. And that's precisely what the mind will do. If you instead teach the mind a pattern of immediately responding to an emotional low point by taking ownership of the reversal and taking action to make that happen, the mind will adapt to that pattern, making it a habit — a very powerful habit.

What if I'm bored and stagnating in my running?

For runners who are always stimulated and excited about running, this section isn't for you. Keep doing what you're doing! For the rest, maybe you're running for fitness and getting tired of the same 5KM loop in your neighborhood, or you're training for your 20th marathon and just not finding your daily runs as exciting. Boredom and stagnation happen in hobbies, routines and life. The key to breaking out of this and keeping yourself stimulated is to change some variables. Here's my top 10 list for introducing new things and changing variables in your running:

1. Sign up for a different race distance or type if you are an experienced racer, or your first race if you are just getting started. Get out of your comfort zone with this.

2. Make up a challenge and invite others to complete the challenge with you. Be creative — challenges can include obstacles or features in your area (like running long sets of stairs), distance goals, connecting various points, etc. My *40 Hill Workouts Project*

includes lots of ideas for challenges, and most can be adapted for non-hilly areas.

3. Experience new terrain and/or running surfaces. Run trails if you normally are just on the road or the track if you're a trail runner. Reverse your normal routes.

4. Get a ride somewhere and run home, or run your commute in part or full.

5. Introduce elements of play into your runs. Be spontaneous at times, and also plan for it, with specific activities and locations. This can include adventure and mission-themed runs. I include some examples in Chapter 12.

6. Coach or mentor a new runner.

7. Change a variable on your body: leave your watch at home or use a new one. Add a new fitness gadget, wear different clothes, wear a new hat or sunglasses, run a race in a costume or carrying a Swiss Alphorn or some other musical instrument.

8. Run with a different running partner or group.

9. Mix in some mid-run functional training, such as squats at the top of a hill and push-ups after sprints.

10. Do the workouts in Chapter 12 and experiment with the mind tools in Chapter 11.

What do I do when I feel overloaded and stressed?

I trust that running is already a default tool you use in response to stress and overload, as it is a powerful one. Thus, my answer is intended to address when running isn't enough, or when the overload and stress happens during your running or racing. Here are five key suggestions.

- **Eliminate self-created stress:** Make a conscious effort to identify and eliminate stress that you are creating, based on external expectations that you've accepted or internal expectations that simply don't serve you. Read up on the abundance and scarcity mentalities, starting with Stephen Covey's The 7 Habits of Highly Effective People, which brilliantly covers this and other key life topics.

- **Start your day NOW:** Your day doesn't start with the morning alarm clock, at a certain time, with the first cup of coffee, first run, or first meeting. Your day starts when <u>you decide</u> it starts. If your day or your run isn't going in a direction you want, hit the reset button and mentally start fresh. Let go of the past and focus solely on the present.

- **Let go of stuff:** Clean your slate, starting with letting go of something that's annoying or troubling you. Just pick one thing to toss, and worry about the rest later. It helps as well to do some decluttering, both mentally and physically. Clean out and donate unused and unneeded sports equipment and clothes. Clear your desk off. Don't worry about making "Operation Declutter" perfect. Just take actions and get rid of what you can in a time-boxed flurry of decluttering. Get out of your comfort zone with respect to caring about what others think. Write and share something creative, play music, sing, speak a few phrases of a foreign language with a native speaker — all without caring about what the listener thinks. Lastly, identify something to quit caring about right NOW, today in this moment, and let it go!

- **Change some social variables:** interact with more, less, or different people. Spend more time with people who help you cultivate growth and positivity, not take you away from each.

- **Cultivate more yin in your daily life:** As I discussed in detail in Chapter 3, evaluate your Yin-Yang balance, and if there is not balance, make some changes to highlight the lacking area, which is usually yin.

What if I can't do meditation and visualization, or find it incredibly challenging?

Many, many people find concentration, meditation, and visualization practices challenging, so you're not alone. Our minds are incredibly powerful machines and they love to show off by constantly running what-if scenarios and running off to chase ideas, just like a dog runs to fetch a ball and never wants to stop playing fetch. Our minds excel at playing fetch with 1,000 balls at once — usually without caring if any of the balls are actually retrieved. So, the mind can be a challenge to quieten at times.

The most important guidance I offer on this topic is to start simple with smart expectations. Notice I didn't say low expectations. I said smart expectations. For a very busy mind, a smart expectation is to sit with your eyes closed for three minutes a day, first thing in the morning. Just sit, with no other exercise or expectation. Think about whatever you want while sitting. Do this for three days in a row. Then, for the next three days, continue the 3-minute exercise and pay attention to what you are thinking about. Just notice it — don't attempt to control it. Journal about it afterward. The journal entry can be a simple bullet point list of what you recall that popped into your mind. Whenever I do this exercise, I think briefly in the moment, "interesting, that's a funny thing to show up and earn a spot on the list." Then, on to the next thought. After those three days, continue for another three days where you pick one thought you want more of in life. For example, confidence. Think of just the word, or a moving or still image it conjures in your mind. Now, sit for three minutes and redirect all arriving thoughts to your focus thought. When you think of that team meeting coming up in a few hours, redirect your thought to confidence. When you think of a relationship worry or frustration, redirect your thought to confidence. Don't get caught up in worrying about the fact that thoughts are arriving, just keep redirecting, like you are a tennis player hitting balls served from a machine. Just keep hitting balls back, regardless of their speed or angle, or if you miss any.

See how you do with this exercise before worrying about more advanced practices.

Experiment as well with nature, with something as simple as a walking meditation, where you walk surrounded by nature and just observe.

You could also experiment with technology. While I believe we have a tendency to over-indulge in technology, often to the detriment of our ability to reach flow states and connect authentically with one another, I have found technology useful in supporting breath training and meditation. I cover this in more detail in Chapter 14.

What if I find this whole Flow State Runner model too much to remember?

Keep it simple! Always go back to the plasma globe image. It's got a top, bottom and magic inside. That's pretty much what I've taught here, slightly changing the terms into Dome, Net, Inner Coach and How-To Guide.

Another way to remember: Look up, look down, look inside of yourself, look in a book. That's the model. Up is your awareness, down is your supporting breath, inside is your Inner Coach, and lastly, a book—that's your knowledge and skill.

Aside from that, it's all about doing your work in each of these areas. Do the mind primer exercises and the breath exercises. Practice the fundamentals of an efficient physical running technique. Work on developing your Inner Coach. The more experience you build with each, the more the model will become ingrained in your mind as a successful performance pattern rather than something you need to memorize.

What if my emotions keep getting in the way during races? What if I struggle to let go of things?

Let's face it — it's likely that you're going to feel (insert a list of emotions) during races. Emotions that surface in races map closely to daily life, including anger, joy, frustration, jealousy, fear, happiness, doubt, euphoria, admiration, apathy, surprise, hope, shame and pride. One or more of these will visit you during races and perhaps will visit frequently, with an interest in staying for a while, and when negative, in wreaking whatever havoc possible during the visit.

The danger isn't in experiencing the emotion, as this is a normal part of living life, especially when you are putting yourself out there "in the arena," as Theodore Roosevelt described in *The Strenuous Life: Essays and Addresses*. No, the danger is in your mid-race reaction to emotions and unwillingness to let go of or redirect those that aren't serving you and your race goals. In the absence of focused concentration, the mind will often default to negativity when placed under stress, so when you notice this happen, give it a positivity bone to chew on. That said, there is some risk of getting overly attached to positive emotions, and crashing when those are not present. Rather than attempt to micromanage the arrival of positive and negative emotions, focus more on recognizing their presence and your typical reactions to each type of emotion.

In addition to keeping your Dome of Awareness scanning capabilities sharp and able to detect your emotional state as it evolves during an event, it is also worth TRAINING those emotions, even the ones that seem negative. Train them and observe the response on your mind and body. In Chapters 11 and 12, I include mind tools and a workout designed specifically for this purpose. You will learn how to recognize and harness these emotions to improve your running experiences. Then, it is up to you to detect, leverage, redirect or release the cascade of emotions that are certain to arrive in your racing experiences.

Lastly, refer to my advice in the aforementioned question on stress and overload on letting go of things and decluttering, as it is applicable here as well.

I try so hard to be in the zone and have flow experiences, but it just doesn't happen. Why is that?

My first reaction when hearing this question is to tell you to stop trying so hard. Rather than try to be in the zone, or to desperately seek it, commit to the fundamentals I've taught on setting the conditions for flow. Do your homework with the Dome of Awareness and Net of Breath exercises. If you skip this basic daily work, which is essentially breathing exercises and basic mind calming or meditation, don't expect flow to happen when you are running just because you try for it or want it.

If you are consistent with the baseline practices, then analyze where you are with distractions. Are you using a lot of technology? Are you checking email and social media right before or even during runs? Tracking your performance with various devices, uploading your stats to sites to compare with others, wondering how best to "market" your run or workout on social media? Are you multi-tasking during the day like popcorn kernels popping, moving from one action or thought to the other instantly, like pop-pop-pop? With today's tech-fueled lifestyles, none of us is immune to the above; however, these are not effective behavior patterns for cultivating flow. If you want more flow and are struggling to find it, start with getting yourself off the grid more often with tech, even if that grid escape only happens in short yin runs, as I described in Chapter 3.

Are you setting up the conditions for struggle and release? In your running, are you putting yourself under a brief period of pressure early in the run, pressure that draws you out of your comfort zone and requires a focused, intense response? Following that, are you taking a brief moment to snap yourself out of that focused mode, with an element of play or unusual pattern variation?

With extra attention to these areas, my expectation is that you will open the door to experiencing flow in your running. Remember, cultivate the soil, plant the seeds, wait patiently for them to grow, and then do all the things you do normally with garden metaphors. Lastly, when flow happens, regardless of the duration or magnitude, notice it, and be grateful.

What do I do when I'm injured or sick and can't run?

When it comes to sickness and injury, the tendency is to allow the mind to create a bigger story than the physical reality. This isn't to say that you are inventing the excruciating pain of torn ligaments from a rolled ankle. Some injuries and illnesses indeed sideline us completely. Other times, we give the situation more power than it deserves and allow a sniffle to grow into a major cold and an aching knee to grow into a gait-compensating, show-stopping snowball of an injury.

The number of injuries or mystery colds that I've observed arriving the night before big events is significant. Yet, I can't recall a single example of a failure to start or finish because of it. In most cases, it was a non-factor during the race, some of which were Personal Best experiences. Even in the Marathon des Sables, when I limped to the starting line with knee pain daily, after toughing it out through the first hour each day, the knee pain went away and I was able to perform.

So, recognize that the perceived illness or injury may be caused by stress, and deal with that stress with deep breathing and whatever meditation, stillness, visualization or PLAY practice works for you. That's right, play … do something that has nothing to do with running and get out of your head for a while.

For those situations when it is a real injury or illness, and running is definitely not possible, the thoughts usually turn to 1) losing fitness, 2) gaining weight, and 3) derailing race preparation plans.

If there is a way to maintain cardiovascular fitness (rowing, Ski-erg, cycling, swimming), then do that. But don't neglect your mind, especially if you are so injured that no physical training is possible. Rather than feel sorry for yourself, channel the time spent healing the injury into growing your knowledge and expanding your mindset. Use the time to make some headway in mind training. Do more breathing exercises. Dive deeper into meditation and visualization practices. Read up on areas in this book that sparked an interest. Use this mandatory rest period for the benefit of training other areas in sport and life that you may tend to neglect.

Also, embrace the opportunity for the deep rejuvenation that forced recovery brings. The year I won a lottery slot for Ironman Hawaii was the same year I had a serious snowboarding crash six months before the race, broke three ribs and partially collapsed a lung. I wasn't cleared to run for several months. Even worse, I couldn't laugh for months. Terrible! I recall what a great victory it was to go on my first "long" walk of 45 minutes during my recovery. That forced winter rest did wonders for my training and health though. Had I not been injured, I would have leapt immediately into an over-eager training mode, as I was hyper-motivated to prepare for my dream race.

Lastly, give yourself credit for what you pursue and accomplish during this forced period away from running, rather than mope about not being able to run or missing a planned race. Some of my best knowledge building experiences occurred during forced recovery, and those experiences made a huge difference in training and racing efforts once I was able to run again. I'm grateful for every injury I've had, because I learned something important from each one, either from the injury itself or from what I chose to do with the forced rest and time away from running.

Is it ok to walk the hills? What about any walk breaks in general?

First, the only one whose judgement matters on the topic of how you approach a hill or walking during a run or race is YOU. It frustrates me as a coach to hear new runners describe how they "failed" in their first 5K race because they had to walk at some point. They covered the distance on their own, so that's not a failure in my book. Running is human-powered locomotion, moving from one place to another. So is walking. Elite race-walkers finish 20KM races (1.1 KM short of a half marathon) between 1.25 and 1.5 hours.[10] Average half marathon times for <u>runners</u> are roughly between 2 and 2.5 hours.[11] So, elite walkers are covering a half marathon by <u>walking</u> significantly faster than average runners run that distance. Does that mean that average runners or any level of racewalkers are "failing" in their race efforts? No!

The concept of "not walking" in a run can be a useful motivator, so if it helps you push harder and get more performance out of yourself, then use it. I've seen the dark side of this concept though, and it is largely about losing control of one's ego. I recall a mountain bike race I was in where I spent half an hour on a climb fighting like mad to pedal up a steep incline, refusing to get off my bike and walk. Ego on, impact neutral. The whole time there was a guy in front of me pushing his bike up the hill, at the exact same speed, but much lower intensity and frustration level than me. He was showing me that there was a smarter wave to move on this part of the course, but I was a slow learner. I thought to myself, "There's no way I'm going to give in and succumb to the walk of shame." I wobbled and growled my way a bit further up the hill, veins on my forehead nearly bursting and a grumble of cursing in my head. Ego on, impact negative. I eventually let go of my ego and walked — smart choice. I caught and passed the "walker" and a few more wobbling, riding holdouts, recovered along the way, and rode the descent full of energy. I later scolded myself for not wising up and dropping my ego sooner. Lesson learned.

The same applies in running. Be smart — if walking and running are the same speed on a given terrain for you, walk. This is especially useful in trail races and ultra marathons. During that walk though, shift your intensity to your mental effort. Tap in to one of the mind tools from Chapter 11 and build your mental fuel reserve for what is to come.

In addition, use the time to tend to your fueling and hydration needs, check your map if you're in that kind of race, and sort out any gear or clothing adjustments. I used walk breaks extensively in the Marathon des Sables, always tending to my hydration, nutrition or equipment during these very short recovery breaks. It was a challenge to let go of my ego to do each planned break in full, but it enabled me to pass dozens of runners late in each stage, faster runners who didn't give enough attention to maintaining their bodies early in the run.

While on the topic of hills, I highly recommend that you establish a habit of always running beyond the crest of a hill before stopping to rest or slowing your pace. This tactic accomplishes important mind shifts. It builds your resiliency towards false summits that the trails and life often put in the path. It also minimizes the hill's power while maximizing yours, reinforcing the concept that your strength is limitless, rather than bound to the arrival at a summit.

And by all means, when you need to run a hill to reach your race goals, run it. And if you've got hills near home, train on them. They are good for the mind, body and soul! Remember to use an efficient technique when you're running up hill, upright posture (don't hunch your torso over at the waist) and quick feet.

I find it difficult to go fast, to really push myself hard in interval training. What can I do?

My favorite coach's answer is "Suck it up, Buttercup." That said, there are mind tricks that will help. For novice runners, especially those who have never done high intensity interval training, the feelings of rapid heart and breath rates coupled with lactic acid buildup are foreign and frightening.

The first step in addressing this is to build an experience base of high intensity sensations and map moments of high intensity training to a positive feeling. For example, I coached a group of college-age runners once, and I focused on adding elements of play and humor to their high intensity intervals. They all performed very well. One of them approached me after the workout and said that this was the first time in his life that he ran intervals that weren't for punishment. He said that his football coach always used sprints to punish the team for mistakes, so over the years, he had developed an instant negative reaction to running intervals as a punitive experience. When he experienced play, humor, and a positive release in the interval session I led, it completely changed his paradigm.

It is therefore important that you consider how you frame interval sessions and how you build the associated expectations in your mind. Hint: don't frame these sessions as punishment. If you always dread interval sessions, guess what? The dread will become a self-fulfilling prophecy. Find a way to make this type of training adventurous, humorous, team-oriented, and even fun.

The second part is how you react to feeling the physiological effects of high intensity efforts, because yes indeed, it hurts, sometimes a lot. Train yourself to embrace the discomfort with the knowledge that it is precisely the discomfort that will make you stronger. Sure, that cough medicine tastes nasty, but it is worth it for how it will make your throat feel.

You are investing in yourself with high intensity training, and that investment requires patience and tolerance of risk, uncertainty and discomfort. Endure the pain with the knowledge that you are making a wise investment. I share techniques in Chapter 11 to help you push yourself while in the pain dojo, that is, the zone of discomfort brought on by high heart and respiratory rate and lactic acid that makes it feel like you're dragging tires behind you when you're not!

Doing long runs all alone is driving me crazy — what do I do?

The term long run is relative. My first long run lasted 20 minutes — about 15 minutes longer than I thought I could make it. Later I'd do 6-hour or even 12+ hour solo long runs. But if I take a year off from ultra running, then 90 minutes starts to feel long again. Regardless of what "long" is for you, I know it can be a challenge at times to run solo for an extended period of time.

Here is a collection of approaches to help:

- **Entertainment and/or education:** audio books, podcasts, language studies
- **Mind Training:** Plan segments as mind training, using tools

from Chapters 11 and 12.

- **Go deep:** ponder and analyze your life, family, relationships, aspirations, fears and other juicy stuff we often only go deep in thought about when issues arise.
- **Stay shallow:** replay favorite movie scenes, think about your first crush or first anything, try to recall song lyrics, practice language accents and jokes.
- **Be creative:** write a haiku, compose a song, ponder a new idea for business or your other interests.
- **Make it a mission or adventure:** refer to my guidance on the boredom and stagnation question and the ideas in Chapters 11 and 12.
- **Work:** dictation, running meetings and calls. I often only meet with people if it's during a run or hike. I've done conference calls mostly on mute during long runs and dictated articles and book sections while running. It is not my favorite long-run activity, but it's proven an effective use of times during periods of high work and training pressure.
- **Involve others:** Get other people to join you for part of the run, hopping in and out wherever they like.

My partner doesn't like that I'm always off running. We don't run the same pace, so can't run together, and we're not into the same distances and training goals. What do I do?

As someone in a happy three-decade long relationship, my overarching advice is to get comfortable doing different activities and don't expect your interests and hobbies to always perfectly align. Actually, embrace that they don't. That variety and independence does wonders for the longevity and health of long-term relationships. That said, whenever you'd like to run together at times, but have a mismatch on speed and distance aims, try the following:

- One bikes, the other runs. Switching off from time to time makes for an interesting game, but one person on an easy spin while the other runs is a nice way to be together in fitness without forcing one runner or both to run at paces they are not comfortable with or are not suitable for their training needs.
- One partner wears a weight vest or a weighted rucksack, drags a tire, pulls a sled, or pushes a baby jogging stroller.
- One joins later in the run, like the partner joining the last 30-60 minutes of a long run, or joins after interval training.
- One incorporates intervals and sprints away from and back to the other. This works particularly well on hills. Just see the fast one as a hyper, playful dog sprinting to chase a toy and bring it back. Who wouldn't want to sprint for a tennis ball, right!

When I try to focus, I think of 100 things at once. What can I do to better focus?

You have to cultivate an environment of focus, like soil prepared in a garden, else the seeds will never grow.

- Declutter - physical and mental. Refer to my guidance on the above question on overload and stress.
- Practice concentration via very short meditation exercises.
- Practice One Cue Only, thus simplifying your self-coaching.
- Change your expectations and patterns around mindless multitasking during all waking hours, with non-stop social media checks and always-on responsiveness to instant messages. Be the change in focus you wish to see.
- Breathe deeply for a few minutes before you need to focus, or whenever you've lost it and need to return to focus.
- Play what I call the Czar's Court game. Take a simple task and perform it with the precision, smoothness and perfection required

as if you were performing in front of the Czar in some ancient time and the slightest flaw would result in you no longer living in said ancient time. A lighter version of this, but still inspiring the same level of concentration and mindfulness, is to complete any task with the awareness, grace and precision of the Japanese Tea Ceremony I described in Chapter 1.

I get depressed after big events. How do I come out of it and prevent it for the next time?

I featured this topic on Episode 11 of the coaching podcast I host, the Hillseeker Podcast, so please listen if you'd like to hear my discussion on the topic. My overarching guidance is to know that it is a normal part of the process, part of the lifecycle of living life in the arena, of training and racing and being an athlete. Plan for it, expect it and be kind to yourself when it arrives.

If you are going through post-race or post-event blues or are interested in preventing it or lessening the impact, I advise you approach it in three stages: preventative care, triage and after-care. Here's a deeper look:

Preventative Care: your most important investment

Ask yourself some questions about your "story" in the months before an event:

- What does the event I'm training for symbolize for me? Or does it? What have I mapped it to? E.g. Does it symbolize that I have control over my life? That I'm young and vibrant? That I'm faster than last year? That I'm faster than other people my age? That I'm fulfilled and happy? Or more fulfilled and happy? That I'll keep the weight off and stay healthy?
- Is the event, or my desired performance at it, the only way for me to experience what I've mapped it to? In other words, in the absence of the event, are there still ways for me to experience the

desired feeling or end-state?
- If the race or event isn't the only way to experience what I've mapped the event to, what story or outcome would also serve me? What other ways could I experience feeling the desired way (young, healthy, vibrant, fast, smart, fulfilled, happy, whatever)? What can I put in place now (well before the race) to ensure that I continue to experience that which I'm seeking, even after the event?

Often our races are about showing us that we have what is already inside us (courage, confidence, energy) and perhaps proving to ourselves again and again that we have this. Sometimes it helps to just remember that it's all inside already and that the race doesn't define who we are. This helps especially if you have to quit a race. Just do this as a thought exercise, and check-in on it throughout your training.

Less on the philosophical level, it really helps to preselect your next event and sign-up for it early. It can even be an adventure, instead of a race (like a bike or ski tour).

Triage (in the moment of feeling down and not wanting to leave the sofa)

- Direct your energy to other people. Volunteer for something, coach someone or teach a skill.
- Learn something new! This can be physical, like rocking climbing or Lindy Hop dancing, or music/language.
- Do yoga. The days and weeks post-race is a great time for exploring Yin Yoga.
- Play with a child or spend time with an elderly person.

After-care

- Review your preventative care questions on your "story."
- Get coaching, or make sure you reach out to your coach. If you are a coach, then be there for your athlete at this time. Some of the most important moments of the coach-athlete relationship occur in the hours, days and weeks after a major event is completed. Good coaches will help guide you through a period of gratitude, reflection and ultimately refocusing.
- Ask yourself, what would the 80-year old me advise? Or be the proudest of?
- **Debrief:** Document your lessons learned. Think about how could these help others who are pursuing the same event in the future. Engage in online or in-person communities to share your experience.

Closing thoughts and segue

This concludes Section 1, so grab your Flow State Runner plasma globe and join me in Section 2, which kicks off with a super hero utility belt of mind tools.

10. WHAT DO I DO WHEN ... ?

Section 2

11. *Mind Tools*

"Though we travel the world over to find the beautiful,
we must carry it with us or we find it not."
— Ralph Waldo Emerson

Super Hero Utility Belt

In this chapter I share with you ten highly effective mind tools. You may think of these as Flow State Runner (FSR) mind tricks, techniques or hacks. They are all tools designed to help you get more out of yourself, from quantitative performance to qualitative experience.

These tools when practiced, customized to you, and aggregated represent a well-developed, expansive toolkit of skills, insights, experience, and practiced behaviors — a super-hero's utility belt, so to speak.

This utility belt is a source that can ultimately be called upon when the going gets tough during a training session, race or emergency in life. It includes tools that fit a wide range of situations and circumstances, and if you invest the time to customize it to your personality and needs, you will have everything you need when you need it. You'll also know how to find the right tool instantly and have ingrained the pattern of using it so that it happens on automatic pilot.

Even if you have the most modern super hero tools and gadgets, they will not be effective if you don't recall how to use them when you need them most (when you are under pressure). To repeat one of my common coaching themes, practice with your tools when you don't need them, so you'll be ready to use them when they are needed. This will also put you in a constantly-learning mindset, so you can continue to experiment and grow your toolkit.

Self-experimentation: the right tool for the job

Your aim is to experiment with these tools, to learn how you respond to each, and to understand how you respond under a variety of situations. Then, keep what works and hold on to the lessons learned for any tools that do not resonate with you.

Remember, an important overarching goal is to become familiar with how your mind, body and spirit responds to a wide range of tools and situations in the safe space of training, *before* you experience them in races, adventures and other times when a lot is on the line. You want to return to a place you know, know what to leverage when you get there, what to allow or drive yourself deeper into, what to use as a catalyst to create a specific state or response, and what signs to recognize in your early warning system so that you may redirect.

When to use

All of these tools are well-suited for times of adversity, from weather to terrain to intensity. Interval training and hill running are excellent training situations for practicing these tools because they put you in a place of discomfort and usually in need of a mindset tool to get more from yourself. In addition, use these tools in different sections or stages of a run, whenever you encounter a specific adversity you want help overcoming, or over the course of an entire run. Once you know what works for you in training, use them in races, events and your other adventures in life.

Bonding

Creating a positive bonding experience with each tool is a strong method of amplifying its power and your ability to draw it into action when needed.

Just as people typically forge a strong bond by enduring a hardship together, we may also bond with mind tools via an intensely felt experience with them. The greater the adversity, intensity or adventure in the bonded tool experience, the more secure the bond will be.

For example, I've had intense experiences running in mountains and deserts and it's the intensity of those experiences that locked in specific mind tools and lessons learned in the journey. When I need to feel I'm capable of a stretch goal or operating on a level higher, I tap into images of running in the Sahara, as it's the scene of a strong bonding experience for me. Once you've created that bond, you will always have these tools at-the-ready to help you perform at your very best.

Sealing in or capping experiences is another powerful bonding approach. When you accomplish something special to you, such as a personal best on your local running loop or running up a hill nonstop for the first time, take a moment to seal in that experience, to lock it firmly into your memory. Before continuing your run or trying immediately to overcome another challenge, take some deep breaths and look around. Notice what you see, hear, smell, and feel, and file those away, as they can be used as triggers to help you tap into this positive feeling in the future.

What follows is ten FSR Mind Tools, each with an Intention, Instructions, and helpful Insights for employing the tool.

FSR Mind Tool #1 - Emotions

Intention: Train emotional management

Instructions:

- Assign an emotion, such as anger or joy, that you will self-induce or act as if you are feeling.
- Work hard to get "in character" — into the targeted emotion, and stay there for the duration of the exercise.
- This mind tool works well when trained in pairs of contradictory emotions, experiencing a self-induced state on both ends of an emotional spectrum.
- Practice awareness and note your observations:
- What fuels you?
- What hinders you?
- What surfaces that you may want to let go of?
- Train emotions you will likely encounter training and racing. Also, occasionally train emotions with a low likelihood of occurrence in a given event, but if they did occur, would have a significant negative impact.

Emotional pairs to train

- Anger-Joy
- Jealousy-Admiration
- Fear-Courage
- Doubt-Confidence
- Apathetic-Passionate
- Hate-Love
- Entitlement-Gratitude
- Shame-Pride

Notes & Additional Insights:

I've discussed emotions on several occasions in prior chapters, with an important inclusion in the FAQ in Chapter 10. Here's an overview of key points on emotions:

- Experiencing emotions is a normal part of running and racing and absolutely impacts performance.
- Experiencing emotions is often different for everyone, and perhaps even different for you from one moment to another.
- Rather than attempt to micromanage the arrival of positive and negative emotions, focus more on recognizing their presence and your typical reactions to each type of emotion.
- Awareness is key. Learn to detect and then decide if you want to emphasize or redirect an emotion. Also, learn to "create" emotional moments by tapping into memories of people and/or situations you associate with certain emotions.
- Training emotions offers you the opportunity to develop yourself in areas of prior emotional challenge or volatility, while also offering a chance to increase your performance by self-inducing emotional states.

Inspired by reading about sentic cycles, a touch art form technique developed by Manfred Clynes that uses self-induced emotional states, I developed and tested this FSR mind tool for the first time at a weekly track workout I coached in Zurich for several years. After warming the group up, I set them off with the goal of running eight 400 meter intervals. I assigned an emotion to each interval and only informed them of one emotion at a time.

It was an eye-opening evening on the track, with a mix of personal bests, breakthroughs, tears, and even one injury that offered a valuable lesson.

The first emotion I assigned was anger. I asked the runners to close their eyes and identify something that made them feel angry, at a situation or a person. I gave them a 30-second countdown to dwell on that anger and then launched them with the mission of running the entire 400 meters with that anger as their sole focus. While this proved effective for several runners, one of them tapped into so much anger-fuel that he pulled his hamstring 200 meters in! So, anger was rocket fuel for this runner, a volatile rocket fuel!

As the session continued, I observed a fascinating mix of responses from the runners, some I predicted, others a complete surprise. I had hoped that each runner would have at least one self-induced emotional experience that would offer them insights or help them in the future when the emotion arrived uninvited. As I prepared the group for the final interval, I was worried about one runner in particular, as she had run each interval at exactly the same speed and in the same emotional state, telling me that she simply couldn't "act" an emotion and "feel" anything she didn't intrinsically feel. Through seven intervals she said it wasn't working for her. That all changed with the last interval, which I briefed as being Love. She finished that interval several seconds faster, with tears in her eyes. The thought of Love connected her to a memory of a family member and that emotion allowed her to soar through the interval, releasing a higher level of performance than she ever imagined possible. She found her fuel.

FSR Mind Tool #2 - Other People

Intention: Race, cheer, and honor other people.

Instructions:

- Use this tool on three levels
    - » **Level 1:** Race Someone — Identify a runner to catch, pass and/ or stay in front of
    - » **Level 2:** Cheer Someone — redirect your energy to the support of another runner
    - » **Level 3:** Honor Someone — tap into emotional power by dedicated your running to someone special
- Each level can be activated with other runners present or as an in-flight visualization
- In my experience, Honor is the most powerful and works well in clutch moments, such as major adversities and late in a race.

Notes & Additional Insights:

On a warm spring evening at the base of Zurich's scenic Uetliberg mountain, I assembled a group of runners. After warming up and working on some technique drills I led the group up a steep hill, pointing out the starting and ending points for a series of upcoming intervals. We ran back down the hill to the start and I counted them down for their first hill interval.

3, 2, 1 Go! And off they went. They returned, and I sent them off again for their 2nd hill interval. For both of these intervals, I had given them little guidance other than a coach's direct and simple, "run fast up that hill." There was a mix of enthusiasm, groaning and pain faces during the interval. Their running was decent, but far from their best.

When I had them all back together again at the start line, I introduced them to the Other People tool.

Other People operates on 3 levels. I introduced the first level by challenging them to pick someone in the group to race up the hill. Their mission was to race this person, and if they passed them, to chase down the next person. The lead runner's mission was to stay in the lead. The results showed a marked improvement for the whole group over their first two attempts. Heads were held higher, and the paces quicker. I could instantly feel the group's spirits lift and intimidation of the hill fade. In the quick post-interval debrief, they mentioned feeling a spark of energy from the sudden competitive focus, especially for those not often competitively driven.

Now, on to Level 2. I tasked them with focusing entirely on cheering any runner around them, in front, behind, beside — it didn't matter. My instructions: just pick someone and cheer them. I launched them into the interval and watched with a smile as they not only stormed the hill, but did so with great energy being poured into each other, especially in the later stages where the incline increased along with their fatigue. We debriefed back at the start line, and the runners shared how they momentarily forgot about their pain when they were encouraging someone else. This was precisely the intention, and I was happy to see them experience it firsthand.

To prepare for Level 3, I handed them each a paper and pen and asked them to close their eyes and take three deep breaths. Then, I asked that they focus their mind and soul on someone who holds an extremely high value in their lives, perhaps a parent, child, partner or friend. Following some quiet reflection time, I asked that they write down the name of this person on their paper, and then asked them to fold the paper and place it in their palm. Their mission was to run up the hill with every movement and breath serving as a passionate reflection of the honor they feel for the person whose name was being held in their palm. Everything they would do from the moment I said *GO!* until the moment they topped the hill was to be in this person's honor.

There was an immediate change in the atmosphere at this moment. No one said a word. Their eyes said it all. We had just created a sacred space, a small group all focusing on someone special to them and about to offer a physical performance in their honor. Years later, I still get goose bumps when I recall this moment — actually, I get them every time I coach this exercise to this day.

When they received the call to start, they soared away from the start line. I saw a level of performance from each and every runner that I had never seen before. That peak performance state, which is inside of each one of us, surfaced in a profound way in this group. It was such a heightened and emotional state that there was very little conversation on the way back down the hill. The group was numb from the experience. A few had selected such a dear person to them that they cried during the interval. Others were emotional afterward. We went on an easy cool down run to allow everyone to reach a calm state and to process what they had just experienced. It was an inspiring night of training.

I once taught this tool to a group of several hundred teenage cross country runners before the European International School Championships. The next day during the race, a parent commented that she overheard an exchange between two runners on a hill where one runner was cheering the other one to go faster. The runner being cheered, who was in front, replied "you're only cheering me so you can get stronger and beat me!" Music to a coach's ears!

Level 1, racing someone, is effective at tapping into one's competitive spirit and is an effective tool at just about any stage of a run. Level 2, cheering someone, is useful especially when you are suffering in a run and want to get your mind off of your suffering (because you know now that continuing to dwell on it will not make the suffering or adversity vanish).

The final level, honoring someone, is the most special — it is rocket fuel. Rocket fuel is extremely powerful, but it is also volatile, expensive and in limited supply. So, use this level wisely and conservatively for those key moments. Level 3 works well in visualizations, like the visualization I shared from the Marathon des Sables when I "saw" my closest friends and family members running with me in the desert. It also works well when writing names on slips of paper and looking at the names at different pre-planned stages of a race. I can't tell you how many marathons I've run, where I focused the last few kilometers on honoring my mom or dad!

FSR Mind Tool #3 - Focal Points

Intention: Control your vision and points of focus

Instructions:
Select one of the three vision techniques below:

- **Single Point Focus:** Pick any object in your sight and focus as intently as possible on that object. Focus so hard that everything else fades away, out of focus. This tool is especially useful in hill running, where you can select as your target a tree or plant at the top of the hill, or simply on the path in front of you. This tool combines well with the BLUE Colors tool, coming up later in this section.
- **Wide Scan:** Expand your vision as wide as possible. Think in terms of using the maximum power of your peripheral vision, while keeping your gaze soft. This combines well with the GREEN Colors tool, coming up later in this section.
- **High Speed Tunnel:** Create tunnel vision, but with a soft focus toward the end of the tunnel instead of a strong, narrow focus. Allow the sides to rush by quickly in a blur, just like you're in a train speeding through a tunnel.

Notes & Additional Insights:

A single point of focus works well when you need to focus your concentration or redirect your Inner Critic. As an energizing focus, it is very effective in short intervals and when you need to redirect your brain from overload mode into a problem-solving mode. It's also a useful tool in reinforcing micro goals, such as running hard just to the next tree, the next rock or the next switchback on the trail.

A wide scanning focus is effective for pulling in new energy and inputs from your environment. It is a calming focus and one that reminds you that you are part of the world around you. It is effective in tempo runs, which are longer and at a lower intensity level than interval runs, thus requiring a sustained level of intensity, which the wide scan fosters.

The high speed tunnel technique supports detaching mind and body to endure a higher pain threshold. Keeping the gaze soft at the end of the tunnel serves as a calmness reminder, allowing the tunnel itself to support your concentration, without a specific end point to focus on. It is also a good tool to use when you need to let go of something that isn't serving you in a run or when you need to quickly shut down your Inner Critic.

For example, we have a very long tunnel in Switzerland that goes under the Alps — the Gotthard Tunnel. It is known as the magic weather tunnel, because it often seems that separate seasons are occurring on both sides of the tunnel. Winter rages and lingers on the North side, while spring arrives early and often on the South side.

When using the high speed tunnel technique, I often think of the magic weather tunnel. When you are in it, that snow storm which was just hammering you suddenly vanishes. In the tunnel, there is no weather, and for fifteen minutes, no sign of the other end. You simply drive straight ahead with faith that you'll eventually exit the mountain. In running, this equates to going to a safe mind space when you escape into the tunnel, thus removing weather from the equation. While in the tunnel, you are free to simply run, with no expectations. Once on the other side, you will enter a different season, sometimes even with sunshine and warm temperatures.

This tool is helpful when running in a lane on the track during intervals and during races.

FSR Mind Tool #4 - Drone Cam

Intention: See yourself viewed from an imagined drone

Instructions:

- Envision a camera drone flying above you and sending a live video stream directly into your brain. The video feed shows you running, including your facial expressions and overall body language.
- Vary the position of the drone: just above, high above, from a runner directly in front of you, from a runner behind you, from the finish line, and from the side.
- Change camera angles as you run and discover which angles elicit different reactions.
- Experiment with the integration of different focus types as described in FSR Mind Tool #3.
- This tool well on a track or in any speed work session, where you need to endure the pain of high intensity effort and direct your mind away from Inner Critic's desire to convince you the intensity is too much to bear.

Notes & Additional Insights:

I used to teach this tool as *Blimp Cam*, instructing runners to imagine a blimp with a camera flying above them. But several years ago, I modernized it to drone cam. It likely won't be too long before we'll be able to simply "see" this view, as our personal drone will hover above us, sending video back to our smart contact lenses! Until then, and even when that happens, I suggest you train your mind to do this for you.

Separating your focus from your body allows you to reach a reserve of energy and to avoid obsessing about your discomfort, particularly in high intensity efforts. Use this opportunity to "see" yourself in the most positive light possible, as strong, confident and fast. Remember, you own your mind, so put whatever images in it you want, and live that image.

FSR Mind Tool #5 - Color

Intention: Associate colors with energy and concepts

Instructions:

- With the colors associated with energy and concepts, assign a color or colors to moments of your run where you need additional support.
- Use the color mappings below, or create your own. Included in the Appendix is a handy table version as well.
- You can integrate colors with patterned breathing, emphasizing one color and its association with the inhalation and another with the exhalation.
- You can also integrate colors with visual focus techniques.
- Use this tool to train your powers of observation and awareness.

Green

- Energy that pulls you forward and supercharges your system
- Plants / trees giving off oxygen, visualize breathing 100% pure O2
- Wide scan focus
- With each inhalation, allow your eyes to relax and see WIDE angle
- Allow the green to enter and charge the body.

Red / Orange

- Energy that PUSHES you forward like solar waves arriving on your back
- Warm energy
- With each exhalation, allow eyes to focus on a single point and feel the red energy push you forward

Blue

- Energy like a blue laser or refreshingly cool blue lake
- Cooling energy with wide scan focus
- Warming energy with narrow, laser beam focus
- With each inhale, the blue intensifies, along with its associated concepts

White

- Energy that envelopes and calms you
- Peace, stillness, cerebral
- Inhalation: white energy descends from clouds and wraps you up in peace and calm

Brown

- Energy that pulls you forward and faster
- Earth – gravity
- Falling toward the earth, as it spins
- Exhalation: surrender, and gravity does the work for you

Mixed Colors

- Energy pulsations, waves or sparks
- Like wildflowers or twinkling stars
- Runs up and down the spine, as a quick charge or boost, tapping into each color briefly and making you instantly more alert

Notes & Additional Insights

I have a love-hate relationship with a 1600-meter trail run hill next to my home. It is one of my least favorite and most favorite benchmark runs. Here is how I experience on it using this tool:

Two minutes in, and my heart rate is elevated such that I'm dancing the edge of my lactate threshold. The Dome of Awareness scans and determines that I'm not at MED and calls my Inner Coach into action to get me to drop tension and calm my mind and body. Inner Coach selects the color tool and draws my attention to the green undergrowth in the forest. With each inhalation I feel the extra oxygen and an associated boost in power. I look up and see the white of a cloud, so on the exhalations I feel the peace of the color white float down and envelope me. Inhale energy-green — exhale peace-white. Four minutes in, and I pass a red park bench. Like waves of solar energy, I feel red pushing at my back, pushing me up the hill. Now at the 6-minute mark, I need a new fuel and notice a descending runner wearing a blue shirt. I focus on blue, which I associate with laser focus. I narrow my focus to a small field of view just ahead and up, and I keep charging for that circle. At the crux of the climb, I notice some spring wild flowers popping up. I link these with little sparks of energy running up and down my spine. I feel this energy, straighten my posture and ride this last energy wave to the finish.

I love using this tool on a track as well. In Switzerland, our running tracks are always red with grass in the infield. During intervals, I open my eyes wide to draw in the green energy of the grass as I inhale, narrow my gaze to the next corner and feel the red surface under my feet rise to push my back as I exhale. I see the white lines dividing the lanes and feel an inner calmness. I draw from the blue sky to feel cooling energy that refreshes my overheating legs. These visualizations happen in a matter of seconds, but the impact is profound. It is a simple, yet powerful technique.

Increasing your awareness of your environment will build a stronger general awareness foundation, thus a stronger foundation for entering heightened performance states, such as flow. On your next run, simply notice how many colors you see, in what amounts and frequency. Really tune in your awareness. Even in winter, when brown may seem predominant, there are typically a wide range of colors available when you really open your eyes and enter a hyper-aware state. Some of my most powerful color experiences have occurred in the desert or snowy mountains, because the colors that do appear really pop.

These color inputs are freely available to you. You can assign any significance you want. Colors offer a target rich environment. The *Colors* tool doesn't have to be just for intervals. It is also available as a calming technique before, during or after running, or simply anytime in your life. While there are always colors available for use in the environment, you may also choose to wear specific colors with helpful meaning attached, or associate a meaning to colors you are already drawn to, or to your favorite gear.

Lastly, for yogis and anyone interested in chakra meditation and visualization, you can link the chakra colors and associated concepts to the *Colors* tool and tap in to your energy centers while running in a chakra language you speak. I like to include color in pre-race running visualizations, linking a specific color to a performance concept, and then using that color in my race gear.

FSR Mind Tool #6 - Humor

Intention: Laugh and tap into humor

Instructions:

- Consciously use humor. Make it happen, especially when under adversity and stress.
- Smile, joke, laugh, act, set the stage by bringing or wearing something funny, train with funny people
- Run like a kid. Lose self-consciousness and lighten up by briefly running with the fluidity and borderline loss of control like a young child

Notes & Additional Insights:

As a runner, you are putting yourself into challenging situations often and as a matter of choice. Many people would only run if chased, so if you can't laugh at the fact that you've <u>chosen</u> to introduce a voluntary strain on your body and mind without being chased by a lion, then what can you laugh at!?

So, we've got humor already present in the often-ludicrous nature of the challenges that endurance runners seek and sign up for. That's worth a laugh now and especially at the moment when we are a few hours into a marathon and a thunderstorm arrives or you encounter the big hill at the end of a 10K and see lots of grim faces around you!

During training and events, visit with humor as often as you can. It will lighten up your mind and help you avoid the self-pity and self-dwelling that so often unravels endurance athletes when adversity shows up to play.

Graveness feeds negativity and negativity feeds fear and weakness. Humor feeds positivity, and positivity feeds courage and strength. Smile and laugh — be courageous and strong!

Here's a quick How-To Guide for applying Humor as a mental toughness tool:

Smile

Want to raise your pain threshold? Do it with a smile. The next time you are doing a high intensity interval, try smiling a big toothy SMILE — even if you have to fake it. During events, smile as often as you can, especially at the times you are feeling the least happy. Feeling sorry for yourself because your legs have seized or your stomach hurts? Sort out your hydration and while doing so, smile at a child or the beauty of your scenic surroundings. Don't undervalue this — it is simple, effective and free!

Joke

Joke with a volunteer worker at an aid station, joke with your fellow athletes, joke with yourself! Do something funny just for a brief moment, and it will lighten your mood and those around you.

Set the stage

Pick at least one race a year to dress up in costume or carry a prop. I once ran a marathon carrying a 10-foot / 3.3-meter-long Swiss Alphorn, playing it along the way. I had the time of my life and especially enjoyed distracting other runners from their suffering late in the race. You could also incorporate a funny shirt or sign. This works particularly well on a day when you know the weather is far from suitable for training or racing. If you're going to run in bad weather, it's worth a little preparation time to make it a humorous outing.

Make fun of the challenge and laugh

Look the obstacle in the face, and laugh at it, seeing it as anything from goofy to outrageously hysterical. An enthusiastic, positively framed reaction — even when faked — will set a tone for the mind that will enable the body to perform above expectations — and that's exactly what we want to tap into! And when that reaction is ironic, it will bring you a smile or a laugh — which delivers enough of a boost to extract just a little more performance potential.

When I coach running at the SEALFIT Academy, I introduce one important rule. When you see a hill, the immediate reaction is to shout "Hooyah Hill!" which translated means, "I'm happy to see this obstacle — bring it on!" The counter-reaction (and the one most common for people) is to see a steep hill in the path and react with "Arghh … hill." With this reaction, they've lost already and their bodies will absolutely under-perform. When runners express enthusiasm in the face of an obstacle, even if that enthusiasm is less than authentic at first, they've diminished the obstacle to its true lesser stature and will outperform their expectations when taking on the obstacle.

One of the best ways to "Embrace the Suck" as Commander Mark Divine at SEALFIT terms it, is to introduce an activity so bizarrely funny to a stressful situation that you can't help but break into laughter and break out of a pity party tendency.

In my experience, on a cold night in the Pacific Ocean lying on my back in the surf while waves crashed overhead, this meant singing the Canadian National Anthem. You see, we had two Canadians on our team at SEALFIT Kokoro Class 13 (the 50-hour mental toughness crucible referenced in earlier chapters) and they remarked in calm voices (while most of the team chattered teeth and shivered uncontrollably) that what we considered freezing winter water temps felt like Canadian lakes in the summer. The instructors overheard this, thus we honored Canada and her "warm" lakes each time we entered the ocean for surf torture.

One instance, as we focused our efforts on singing the opening "O Canada," a massive wave rolled over the team. We surfaced, coughed and cleared the salt water, and then pushed onward with the singing … "Our home and native land! True patriot in …" Crash, another wave hits. Soon we were laughing so hard we could barely sing in between the waves. And herein lies the beauty — we had forgotten about our "suffering" and had embraced the moment. With our minds distracted with humor, our bodies endured the "suck" — the adversity of cold-water immersion, darkness, waves, etc., without us thinking about it. We stopped shivering and whining. We were stronger as individuals and as a team because we sought humor and then embraced it! This will work for you as well, so find something to laugh at the next time adversity visits you.

FSR Mind Tool #7 - Music

Intention: Listen to or imagine music to support different energies and stages in a run or race.

Instructions:

- If you run with music, setup and run with a variety of playlists from a range of music genres. If you respond to music, but do not wish to run while listening to music, then try to imagine or visualize it. Experiment by stepping outside of your comfort zone and using both logical and inverted mappings, as described next.
- Logical mapping: map the tempo and style of the music to the intensity and speed of your running. Map loud, intense, fast music to sprints and intervals. Map relaxing string, piano or trance music to easy pace, long runs.
- Inverted mapping: map the tempo and style of the music to what seems its opposite in running. Map relaxing music to intervals and intense music to a chill-out, slow run. The inverted mapping surprises many runners, as its effects are often counter-intuitive, especially the use of relaxing music with high intensity efforts. In my experience, I've attributed this to the relaxing music helping runners drop unnecessary tension to reach MED and transition from sympathetic nervous system stimulation to parasympathetic system stimulation, from beta brain waves to alpha, and ultimately into flow.
- Experiment using the collection of Flow State Runner playlists I've created on the major music streaming services.

<u>Notes & Additional Insights:</u>

As a musician and music lover, I often utilize music as a source of additional energy and power, as well as a tool to support reaching MED during high intensity efforts and for recovery. For short and yin runs, I'll go without audible music, but still find myself "hearing" music in my head. For long runs, intervals and ultra marathons, I run with music whenever possible. My playlists cross a wide expanse of genres, from acoustic blues to symphonic Mahler to trance, bluegrass, heavy metal, dubstep, epic soundtracks, classic rock and more. Each serves a different purpose and elicits a different response for me, even during the same run.

FSR Mind Tool #8 - Mantras

Intention: Use powerful words or phrases to generate self-encouragement. Repeat them, and use them to redirect your thoughts if your Inner Critic becomes too vocal.

Instructions:

- Make a list of words that represent a feeling, trait or state you wish to highlight. For example: strength, speed, confidence, power, fast, go, honor.
- Make a list of short motivational phrases to accomplish the same aim. For example:
  » My race, my day
  » For Mom — for Dad
  » I am a runner
  » Carpe diem
  » I will finish!
- Use these words or phrases as mantras to redirect or maintain state. Practice them during training, and learn how your body responds to each.
- Integrate with breath work, as described in Chapter 8, emphasizing the mantra on the inhalation.

Notes & Additional Insights:

I've had some powerful experiences with mantras, most often in extreme weather conditions. I have experimented with mantras that range from single words to memorized quotes and poems. My personal favorites are simple and short, such as "keep going" — a good one when being blasted in the face during a sudden blizzard, "easy spin" when on a long running climb up a mountain, and credit to SEALFIT, during any long, challenging training session, "Easy Day."

FSR Mind Tool #9 - Nature

Intention: Use nature and terrain

Instructions:

- Assign meaning to features of the nature in your running environment.
- When you observe a given element of nature, bring your awareness to its associated meaning or the symbolism you've assigned to it. Or, when you need to emphasize a feeling, seek out its associated feature in nature.
- Here are some of my favorites:
  » Trees = strength
  » Streams and rivers = flow
  » Ponds, lakes, mountains = calm, stillness
  » Birds singing = people cheering
  » Birds flying = lightness, effortlessness
  » Rocks = inner strength, resiliency
  » Flowers = sparks of energy
  » Insects = our challenges are small compared to grandeur of universe
  » Moss = calm and cool, flow
  » Movement (ocean, rivers, wind, tree branches, leaves) = surging energy pushing or pulling you forward
  » Wild animals = inner primal energy
  » Dogs = play, curiosity
  » Forest = restoration
  » Terrain:
    › Hills = thrive and spin
    › Flats = fly
    › Sand = float and spin
    › Snow = calm and float
- You can incorporate color, vision, awareness and listening tools

into this approach as well.

- There are endless features in nature available to which you can map motivational thoughts and other helpful cues, including: pine needles, grass, fallen leaves, mushrooms, fog, rain, smells, fire, and much more.

Notes & Additional Insights:

"Believe one who knows: you will find something greater in woods than in books. Trees and stones will teach you that which you can never learn from masters."
— *Saint Bernard de Clairvaux*

The above quote is so beautiful and relevant to this discussion that I wish to share it with you in the text of a chapter. Yes, time spent is nature is an opportunity to learn, grow, and remember that we are all part of something greater. It offers an environment full of reminders and ideas for your Inner Coach to help you enrich your life experience and optimize your training and performance. Remember the concept of a yin run from Chapter 3? Yin runs are well suited to experience in nature, as you will be able to better tune in to the fascinating natural world around you once you have removed the headphones, smartphone, camera, and other attention-requiring devices.

Start with going on a trail run or run through a local forest or park. Open your eyes to a deeper level and see what you can observe that you haven't paid much attention to in this location in the past. Take your top three observations and assign a motivational thought or cue to them. Repeat the run, and when you make the same observation, receive the associated thought. This tool can become as intense or as light as you wish, based on how you wish to connect with nature.

FSR Mind Tool #10 - Smell

Intention: Create a positive association between certain smells and your performance and re-use them when needed

Instructions:

- Brainstorm for memorable smells in your life, especially smells that you associate with strength, positivity and any other traits or feelings you wish to tap into in your running.
- Bring the smell with you when you run, either physically (captured on a small piece of cloth or perfume sample strip) or virtually (from memory and via visualization).
- Smell sources: essential oils, perfumes, nature, food, tea, spices, etc.

Notes & Additional Insights:

Freshly cut grass. For me, there is no stronger link between wringing myself out for a maximum effort sprint than with freshly cut grass. It stems from a memory of football practice when I was twelve years old. I remember doing sprints at the end of practice, feeling exhausted but powering through what felt like two hours, but was probably less than a few minutes of sprinting. The memory is strong enough though that whenever I smell freshly cut grass, I want to sprint.

From the perfume of a girlfriend or boyfriend from your teen years to the scent of a leather baseball glove or a freshly opened can of tennis balls, smell is an incredibly powerful link to memories and emotions.

Spend some time brainstorming memorable smells in your life, especially smells that you associate with strength, positivity and any other traits or feelings you wish to tap into in your running. Then find a way to bring that smell with you as a supporting performance tool. I've observed positive experiences from runners who put a tiny scented piece of cloth in a plastic bag in their rucksack or a pocket and opened the bag for a smell when they needed an extra kick toward the end of a race. This tool works well with *FSR Mind Tool #2 Other People*, as you could bring with you on a small piece of paper the perfume or cologne of a person you wish to honor, thus integrating the powerful sense of smell with your emotional connection to the honoree.

You and your new super hero utility belt

You now have 10 FSR Mind Tools at the ready for your selection, experimentation, refinement, and integration into your personal super hero utility belt. You can use these tools in any run, on the go, as directed by your Dome of Awareness and Inner Coach. The more depth and breadth you build into your personal toolkit, the better prepared you'll be to thrive in a wide variety of situations. You can also use these tools as an integral component of workouts by design, which is the focus of Chapter 12.

Remember as well that it is critical to your ability to call upon these tools that you BOND them into an experience that is personal and unique to you, so put that virtual lab coat on, latch on your super hero utility belt, head out for a run and start experimenting!

12. Training

"Information's pretty thin stuff unless mixed with experience."
— *Clarence Day*

Why plan, design or structure a run?

If you are seeking quantitative performance gains, preparing for a race, or looking to unlock more flow state experiences in your running practice, then a must-have tool in your toolkit is the incorporation of an appropriate level of structure and planning. This is important at both a high level and for each run.

The primary benefits of a structured training approach include:

- **Training Adaptation:** varies the stimuli to which you expose your body, which is required for a change in performance across elements such as speed, endurance and durability.
- **Flow enablement:** sets the conditions for flow in a consistent manner, not haphazardly. Ingrains high performance, success-oriented patterns.
- **Injury and Burnout Prevention:** helps prevent overuse injuries, while consistently introducing elements of fun, adventure and gamification.
- **Flow State Runner knowledge reminder:** primes the mind, body and spirit to recall key elements of the Flow State Runner model consistently, thus ingraining patterns.

What is structured training?

We can view structured training at macro and micro levels.

At a macro level, it means having a high level training plan that leads to an event or accomplishment of a goal. This plan includes benchmarks, milestones and progressions, such as an increasing distance of long runs over a multi-month period or decreasing time for a set distance. High level plans may be simple, including only a series of training races that lead up to a big event, or complex, including periodization, built-in recovery windows and a host of data-driven elements based on heart rate, VO2Max, anaerobic and lactate thresholds, volume and even power output.

Incorporated into the high level plans that I design for runners are a mix of run types:

- **Interval:** high intensity effort, from very short sprints up to about 10 minutes. Favorites include Tabata (8x20sec sprint, 10sec rest), Fartlek (spontaneously selected targets) and 800 meter repeats.
- **Tempo:** lactate and anaerobic threshold training, at an intensity level lower than intervals and near that of a hard 5KM or 10KM run pace level, depending on the runner's background, fitness and objectives. Duration can be from 10 minutes to over an hour.
- **Adventure:** mission, game or play-focused, at a variety of intensity levels and often incorporating functional training, novelty and adventure.
- **Hills:** up hill or down hill, incorporating other run types, as well as skipping. See the Hillseeker® 40 Hill Workouts projects for lots of free ideas.
- **Yin:** zero active technology utilization, zero time goals, focuses on awareness and experience
- **Easy / Long:** low to moderate intensity, steady effort. Includes active recovery runs as well as long runs.

Each run type is important in creating a physiological and/or mindset adaptation in the runner, as well as a spark for their continued motivation and enthusiasm. When incorporated into a high level plan, some of these run types are planned in progressions (such as long runs and 800 meter intervals). Others are incorporated with variation and spontaneity (such as Fartlek intervals and Adventure runs).

There are myriad philosophies and training program design approaches out there. High level training plan design for specific event types is outside the scope of this book, but I suggest incorporating the above run type "ingredients" into whatever plan you develop. High level plan design is certainly an area worth exploring with the help of a personal coach, as they can target your specific background, goals and personality.

Moving on to the micro level: the micro level of structured training is on a per-run basis. It's a run plan that you write before lacing up your shoes, one that you follow during the run, and then review afterward. This plan may or may not be tied to an overall training program, yet it remains an important tool even for runners who are not training for an event or following a high level plan.

The run plan is where we can be smart and incorporate what we know about the Flow State Runner model to organize a run in order to experience that which we wish to experience, from a mind-quietening meditative escape to a challenging set of intervals.

The run plan I teach, termed the Flow State Runner (FSR) Run Plan, gives you a place to think through flow elements you want to consistently incorporate and elements you want to vary, such as intensity, duration, terrain, etc. The FSR Run Plan offers a simple tool for preparing yourself in a consistent way to actively practice setting yourself up for flow state experiences. The plan takes into consideration key aspects of the FSR model as well as important flow enablers, such as clearly defined goals, Struggle micro challenges, and Release Triggers. It also reminds you of yin-yang balance as well as Dome of Awareness primer activities.

You may have noticed in the opening section of this chapter I stated that a must-have inclusion in your toolkit is incorporation of an appropriate level of structure and planning. I chose the word "appropriate" with intention, as I'm encouraging you to find an MED (Minimum Effective Dose) balance between structure and lack of structure in your running. For those times when you are training for an event or to reach a performance goal, the structure level will be higher than times when you are running simply for the joy, peace, and escape of it. In either scenario and all along the continuum of our individuality, finding an effective dose of structure will help you ingrain flow patterns and success habits. Let's now look at how the FSR Run Plan template helps with this structure.

FSR Run Template

The FSR Run template is a tool that helps you plan your runs in a consistent, FSR-friendly manner. It highlights key areas to consider in the planning stage, whether that planning takes place via detailed preparation for each run or a quick checklist to scan before heading out the door.

It is not required to use the template, especially if the thought of planning and journaling isn't your style, but understanding the template will help you understand questions to ask yourself when you are designing or considering the structure of your runs.

The FSR Run template is shown below with helper text included, as well as later in the chapter with eight official FSR Runs. There is also a blank version in the Appendix. In addition to providing you with a strong initial sets of FSR runs to experience, my aim is to arm you with the tools and motivation to build your own ever-expanding library. With this in mind, let's look now at the template and a review of its components.

Theme	*Yin, Adventure, Interval, Tempo, Long, Adversity Training*
Objective	*Specific objective for this run or a reminder of your overall motivator*
Stats	*Planned duration, distance, route or any other relevant data points*
Setting	*Track, road, trails, park, beach, mountain, snow, sand, etc.*
Yin - yang	*Approximate split of yin and yang intended*
Guide focus	*Any technique areas you want your Inner Coach "Guide" voice to focus on*

Pre-run ritual	*Select one:* • *Breathing exercise* • *Meditation* • *Visualization* • *Music* • *Journal or drawing* • *Brief yoga flow*
Warm-up focus	*Awareness exercise: activate Dome and observe any active or predominant emotions, activate Inner Coach*
Micro Challenge	*Select one:* • *Time Pressure* • *Terrain* • *Out of Comfort Zone* • *Movement Patterns* • *Equipment* • *Obstacles*
Release trigger	*Select one:* *Breathing* • *Imagery* • *Movement patterns* • *Play / Game* • *Humor* • *Other*
Workout Plan	*Description of your training session, for example: Run ten 100M hill repeats, skipping the last 20 meters of each*
Post-run ritual	• *Gratitude Breaths* • *Sealing in positive experiences* • *Lessons Learned* • *Journaling*

Image: FSR Run Template

FSR Run Template Components

While all of the FSR Run Template components are covered in prior chapters, a review in the context of structuring runs is useful, and therefore is included below.

FSR Run: Objective

Clearly defined goals and concentrated focus are key elements of flow, so we define an objective for each run, including yin runs. This is also a good opportunity to check in with your motivator — your overarching goal, as discussed in Chapter 1. During some FSR runs we also bring intense focus 100% to various targets, including *One Cue Only*, physical and visualized objects or concepts.

FSR Run: Themes

Each run has a theme, type or intention. This serves a practical purpose of organizing and distributing training types (e.g., intervals, recovery, tempo), but perhaps more importantly, it offers a chance to make each run special and a session worthy of anticipation. Even a treadmill session, which some runners find boring, can be spiced up with the addition of a mission or warrior theme, or game. Some runs will have play themes, others mindset themes, such as gratitude. You also have the opportunity to incorporate mind training into themes, such as training emotions.

FSR Run: Yin and Yang Balance

In Chapter 3, I discussed the topic of yin and yang balance and how we tend toward too much yang in our daily lives. Here we have a reminder to consider the yin and yang split for a given run. Remember, it's not about intensity or speed. Yin doesn't mean slow and yang doesn't mean fast. It's about the total impact of mindset, expectations, active technology usage, social media engagement and the other activities of your day. Just by considering this concept, you will increase your awareness of how you live this duality and will hopefully cue yourself to shift the balance as needed.

I did this regularly for the year I lived in Amsterdam. During my nightly post-work runs, I would turn off my music and experience 30 minutes of peaceful yin running along the tranquil canals and Amstel River, simply bringing my awareness to the lights, charming old houses and reflections on the water. Then, I would put my headphones in, crank the music and experience ten minutes of yang chaos as I dodged tourists while running straight through the middle of the Red Light District. I'd close that run with ten additional yin minutes of canal running, giving myself a nice 80/20 yin and yang split. This did wonders for offsetting a 100% yang job and the highly yang (stressful) nature of a first year living abroad.

FSR Run: Pre-Run Ritual

Completing a brief ritual before running offers the opportunity to prime your Dome of Awareness and specifically link this pattern to positive running experiences. All of the Dome mind and body primers discussed in Chapter 5 may be used here, as well as your own techniques. Pre-run ritual activities include: breathing exercises, meditation, visualization, music (playing or listening), journaling or drawing, and yoga.

These activities don't need to take much time, and can be done at home or work, or on the trail or track in the moments before you start the physical part of your run. Quality and focus are more important than quantity and the ticking of boxes, so select an activity that resonates with you and give it a focused effort of 3-5 minutes.

An effective visualization exercise to use for the Pre-Run Ritual is to close your eyes and see yourself running in what you recall as one of the best runs of your life. Maybe it's a race or a simple, meaningful run with a loved one. Just spend a few minutes watching this "film" of the memorable run and tapping into the positive feeling associated with it. If you can't think of an experience, then visualize seeing yourself running in the most positive scene you can think of (happy, confident, fast, strong, finishing a race, in the mountains, etc.).

FSR Run: Warm-up

The warm-up serves the normal purpose of priming the body for movement. Some runners warm up only with the steps it takes to reach their "start line." Others experience a gradual increase of intensity, starting with walking, followed by progressively faster running. Warm-ups become very important with high intensity sessions, where the risk for injury is significant if a runner goes from a work desk to a track sprint without a suitable transition and warm-up period.

Regardless of the duration, we can make the experience a <u>smart</u> warm-up by incorporating a mental focus area to accompany the activity. Activities include visualizing activation of the Dome of Awareness, observing any active or predominant emotions, heightening awareness of the environment (nature, colors), activating and hearing your Inner Coach's voice and an initial cue on technique, and using one of the breathing techniques suitable for running.

FSR Run: Micro Challenge

In Chapter 3, I covered the importance of Struggle in the flow cycle and introduced the concept of including micro challenges early in a run. A micro challenge occurs toward the end of your warm-up, spans a 3-7-minute block of time, and can draw from a variety of activities, including:

- Time pressure and intervals
- Terrain: hills, technical, grass, mud, sand, snow, streams
- Movement patterns: jumps, precision landings in technical terrain, downhill trail running, skipping, body weight exercises

- Getting out of your comfort zone: terrain, weather exposure, uncertainty and exploration
- Equipment: tire drag, sleds, weight vest, resistance bands
- Problem solving tasks and obstacles

In my own training, my micro challenge toolkit includes push-ups and flutter kicks in cold streams, jumping in a lake or ocean, sled and tire drags, and sprinting up a new trail. Even a few hill sprints or fartlek intervals can make a big impact in progressing through the Struggle phase of the flow cycle.

FSR Run: Release Trigger
Again, looking back to Chapter 3, recall that the Release phase follows Struggle, and an effective release is aided by going off-script, that is, doing things that you normally do not do in a run. Release activities include experiencing different movement patterns (skipping, backward running), a brief moment of play and loss of self-consciousness and humor.

Another very effective technique for Release uses breathing exercises and mental imagery. Here's an example: following your micro challenge, take five deep breaths, each with a long and complete exhalation. Do this while standing, walking or running at an easy or moderate pace. With each inhalation, visualize super high quality rocket fuel entering your body and with each long exhalation, visualize as any weakness and worry released from your mind and body.

Post-Run Ritual
The Post-Run Ritual offers a moment to seal in a positive experience or capture observations from a negative experience. The ritual occurs on two levels: experiential and journaling.

Experiential

The Post-Run Ritual starts with Gratitude Breaths. These are 3-5 deep breaths where your entire focus is on gratitude for a body that allows you to run, for the time you made available to run, for having a place to run, and anything else for which you feel grateful. You may wish to use the Sitali Pranayama breath technique in your Post-Run Ritual, especially on hot days. This technique is described in Chapter 8.

Following Gratitude Breaths, focus fully on the experience, replaying it in your mind like a film. Mentally note any moments of flow, your overall feeling and satisfaction with the run, observations and lessons learned. Lock in the image of yourself in positive moments, as you can use this for future visualizations.

Lastly, remember to treat recovery with the same focus and respect as training.

Journaling

I encourage you to journal your runs, especially insightful ones, in a holistic sense — that is, more than simply tracking distance and time. This is an important step in recognizing and accelerating your growth and development.

Sample journal questions to address include:

- Overall quality of the running experience, as it relates to your underlying motivator for running.
- Yes/No: did you have any moments of flow?
- If yes, describe how it felt, how long it lasted, what you recall right before it happened, how you transitioned out of it (gradually, abruptly, never ... the run simply ended).
- If no, describe any observations. How's your day going? Any specific thoughts or patterns?
- A feeling of flow that you transferred into this run or transferred out of it (including experiencing it later in the day).
- Experiences that you had with tapping into Inner Coach and any

experiences with Inner Critic.
- New ideas that arose

Official FSR Runs

With an understanding of the template and underlying components in place, we move on to the final section of this chapter, which includes eight official FSR Runs. I encourage you to try all of these, keep what works for YOU, and then create more for yourself. When you develop a new one that you are really excited about, please share it on the Flow State Runner community Facebook page, or send it to me and I'll share with the group. In addition, more FSR Runs are included in the *Flow State Runner* Online Companion Course.

FSR Run #1 - Emotions

Theme	Emotions
Objective	Learn how your mind and body respond to training different emotions
Stats	8x 200M or 400M intervals
Setting	Track, treadmill or any route where you can mark off 200M or 400M start/end lines.
Yin-yang	10/90 split: almost entirely yang, with a few minutes of yin in the post-run ritual and during rest breaks
Guide focus	Quick foot pull

Pre-run ritual	5min patterned breathing: 5-3-8-3
Warm-up focus	Awareness exercise: activate Dome and observe any active or predominant emotions while warming up for at least 5 minutes.
Micro Challenge	2x200m 70% effort sprint. 1min rest in between each.
Release Trigger	3 rounds skipping 20M, backward running 20M, bear crawl 10M
Workout Plan	Choose an interval distance of 200M or 400M. Map a single emotion to each interval. Feel or act as if you are feeling the emotion intensely during the entire interval. Complete the intervals sequentially in pairs. Rest 2min in between intervals. Anger-Joy Fear-Courage Doubt-Confidence Hate-Love During rest breaks or immediately after the session, make a quick journal entry or audio recording of your reactions to each emotion.
Post-run ritual	Gratitude breaths, eyes closed

FSR Run #2 - Other People

Theme	Other People
Objective	Get more from yourself by redirecting your thoughts to others
Stats	8x45sec hill sprints
Setting	Hill or treadmill on incline
Yin-yang	10/90 split: almost entirely yang, with a few minutes of yin in the post-run ritual and during rest breaks.
Guide focus	Upright torso, no folding

Pre-run ritual	Write down the names of four people who are important to you on small slips of paper, one piece per name, and bring these on your run. Set a 5min countdown timer. Close your eyes and visualize winning a race, cheering a friend in reaching their goal, and being with someone important to you.
Warm-up focus	Warm up running for at least five minutes. Activate Inner Coach and map its voice to two people from your past. Imagine hearing each voice offering you words of encouragement.
Micro Challenge	Run up hill at an uncomfortably quick pace for as long as you can hold that pace without slowing down. Hold it for at least 2 minutes, but no more than 5 minutes.
Release Trigger	Smile non-stop for 2 minutes while running downhill
Workout Plan	Complete 8 x 45sec hill sprints with 1-2 min rest breaks in between each. Referring to the slips of paper with names, run two intervals per person, whereby you focus on "honoring" this person with your best effort during each of "their" intervals. See yourself in the role of running hard to protect them (e.g., blocking the wind / storm / heat), to support them (help them get through a challenge) or to perform in their honor.
Post-run ritual	Gratitude breaths, eyes closed. Journal.

FSR Run #3 - I don't want to run

Theme	Motivation & overcoming Inner Critic
Objective	Get out the door to run when you don't feel like it
Stats	8x1min intervals, plus choice duration post-interval run
Setting	Any, including treadmill
Yin-yang	50/50 split
Guide focus	Quick cadence

Pre-run ritual	Draw an image of yourself running — the funnier, the better — the lower your drawing skills, the better — the less time spent on it, the better. Take it with you.
Warm-up focus	Skip 24 times
Micro Challenge	Run for 3 minutes non-stop. For this session, just starting is a sufficient micro challenge.
Release Trigger	Look at your drawing and act it out. Set a countdown timer and make yourself laugh out loud for 60 seconds. Don't be shy — train your confidence and lack of self-consciousness with this exercise.
Workout Plan	8x1min intervals, plus choice duration post-interval run.
	This is an alternating focus interval run, where one interval is totally focused on the run being terrible and the other interval a mock celebration of the perfect run. Really exaggerate both emotional states, including body language, facial expressions and any sounds or comments that seem fitting. Four of the intervals should leave no doubt to any observer that you are unmotivated and not enjoying running today. The other four intervals should send the opposite message.
	The best thing to do when you need a run, but aren't in the mood, is to just make it happen. This run accomplishes that, and also gives you a chance to make fun of yourself and use humor and distraction to get yourself engaged.
Post-run ritual	Gratitude breaths, eyes closed. Journal.

FSR Run #4 - Yin Run

Theme	Yin
Objective	Introduce more yin in your running to offset stress and imbalance
Stats	Intentionally undefined: runner's choice, decided spontaneously without judgement
Setting	Anything goes
Yin-yang	Almost entirely yin
Guide focus	Quiet, calm mind

Pre-run ritual	Complete a 3-5min meditation, eyes closed, with your focus on the sound and feel of each breath.
Warm-up focus	Warm up at least 5 minutes. Let go of something right away: a worry, concern, thought, frustration, etc. Just identify something, and let it go.
Micro Challenge	20-30 burpees, focused on maintaining lightness and calm (a challenge worth pursuing with this oft-challenging bodyweight exercise)
Release Trigger	While running, take 5-10 deep breath cycles. With each inhalation, visualize rocket fuel entering your body and super-charging your muscles. With each long exhalation, visualize any weakness and worry released from your mind and body.
Workout Plan	Run any duration or speed you wish. Decide spontaneously. Follow these rules: • Leave all non-passive tech at home • Go dark, off-the-grid: no social media related to this run. No photos, no tweets — just presence and memories. • Get as many people to smile at you on this run as possible • Alternate heightened awareness across your senses, tuning in to each sense, one at a time and drawing out more information from your environment.
Post-run ritual	Gratitude breaths, eyes closed. Journal.

FSR Run #5 - Czar's Court Run

Theme	Focus - Tea Ceremony Inspiration
Objective	Develop a heightened sense of awareness and deep, focused concentration
Stats	5 kilometers
Setting	Trail, road or beach
Yin-yang	40/60 yin-yang split
Guide focus	Smooth, no bounce

Pre-run ritual	Set a 3-5-minute countdown timer and use that entire time to take two steps. Focus intently on every micro-action required to take a step, as if you are a robot and require a command for even the slightest shift in weight and muscular contraction. Move as slowly as possible.
Warm-up focus	Alternating high foot pulls: stationary and while running, pull left foot high 3 times, then alternate and pull right foot high 3 times. Complete 6-9 rounds of 3 pulls per side.
Micro Challenge	While running, nostril-breathe only for 3 minutes, then complete 20 high skips.
Release Trigger	Play: take 1-2 minutes to do something out of the ordinary for a run. Hop on some playground equipment, toss a kid in the air (with permission and care, of course!), skip, hop over some natural obstacles, etc.
Workout Plan	Run 5KM with intense focus on 2 or 3 actions, movement patterns or tasks, which you must perform to absolute perfection, as if your imagined medieval life depends upon it. Examples: • Tension in your hands — each hand must have the exact same shape and tension level. • Contact of your foot on the ground. It doesn't have to be every single time the foot contacts the ground, but commit yourself to some very specific landing spots throughout the run. "I'm going to land just to the left of that root." • Focused gaze — looking at a specific spot with tunnel vision. Alternate the focus on and off, just like with intervals. When on, bring your entire focus to the flawless execution of the task. If you make a mistake, repeat the action until you do it to perfection.
Post-run ritual	Gratitude breaths, eyes closed. Journal.

FSR Run #6 - The River

Pre-run ritual	Option 1: Play a musical instrument for 5 minutes or more.
	Option 2: listen to Debussy's La Mer, Smetana's Vltava, Philip Glass or any of the tunes in the *Flow State Runner*: Water Themes playlist on the major music streaming services.
Warm-up focus	Complete 3 rounds of a Body Scan, followed by any needed adjustments toward MED while warming up for at least 5 minutes.
Micro Challenge	Complete six 10 second sprints up-hill / up-stream.
Release Trigger	For 60 seconds, bounce up and down quickly while shaking your hands like you're trying to flick water off of your fingertips.
Workout Plan	Complete 10 downhill Fartlek intervals next to a river or stream (or listening to water sounds). Spontaneously select the interval duration — identify an object and sprint to it. Notice the high yin intention coupled with high intensity.
	Bring your awareness to the flow of the water. Listen intently and tap into the energy of the water, visualizing that it is the same energy driving you.
	When your mind starts to wander, pull it back to the water sounds and let it power your interval.
	Use a water-themed mantra, such as "I am flow" or "through the rapids."
Post-run ritual	Gratitude breaths, eyes closed. Journal.

Theme	Water
Objective	Connect the element of water with your Flow State Running pursuit
Stats	10x Fartlek intervals, 30-45min run
Setting	Trail, park, near moving water if possible
Yin-yang	80/20 yin-yang split
Guide focus	MED of tension throughout the body

FSR Run #7 - Auditory Environment Run

Theme	Nature
Objective	Tap in to the sounds in your environment as a live source of motivation and energy, particularly using auditory inputs.
Stats	30 minutes or longer
Setting	Forest, mountains, trails, park
Yin-yang	80/20 yin-yang split
Guide focus	Ninja-quiet ground contact and foot pulls

Pre-run ritual	Complete 3-5 rounds of yoga Sun Salutation A, wearing ear plugs if possible (to increase your awareness of the sound and quality of your breathing).
Warm-up focus	Run several minutes easy, and then for 2 minutes, alternate every 10 seconds between loud foot strikes and soft foot strikes. Exaggerate each.
Micro Challenge	Get out of your comfort zone. Options include: Run through a stream and stop to do push-ups in the water. Do some burpees in the mud. Run with a layer less or more than you normally would for the climate. Wear a weight vest. Run off-trail or in challenging terrain (soft sand, snow, rooted trail, etc.). A very useful micro challenge for this session, if you have a suitable trail, beach or grass field, is to run some with your eyes closed. This is an excellent tool for increasing your awareness leading in to any sensory focus drill.
Release Trigger	Take 6 deep breaths with long inhalations and exhalations. Pause in between each for as long as you wish, practicing a heightened sense of awareness during each pause. During the odd breaths (1, 3, 5), bring your awareness fully to the sound and/or feel of your heart beat. During the even breaths (2, 4, 6), bring your awareness fully to the sounds of your environment.
Workout Plan	Your aim is to accumulate as many focused-listening minutes as possible during a 30-minute run. Identify as many different sounds as possible and listen to each with deep focus as if you must memorize and describe the exact sound. These sounds may include anything, from nature to an urban environment.
Post-run ritual	Gratitude breaths, eyes closed. Journal.

FSR Run #8 - Color Run

Theme	Colors
Objective	Tap into colors in your running environment as a source of motivation and energy
Stats	Track: 8x400M or 4x800M
Setting	Urban, track or trails
Yin-yang	Almost entirely yang, with a few minutes of yin in the post-run ritual
Guide focus	Mental Toughness, breakthrough speed

Pre-run ritual	3 minutes of patterned breathing using 4-6-4-12 (I-P-E-P), followed by 100 Kapalabhati breaths
Warm-up focus	Practice deep breathing while running. On each inhalation, notice a color and imagine that this color intensifies with the depth and strength of your breath. Sample as many colors as possible.
Micro Challenge	Run two 400M intervals, with 1 min rest in between each. The speed should be a progression per 100 meters, from moderate to fast.
Release Trigger	Run 400 meters alternating between backward, sideways and forward running. Practice your running virtuosity, smoothly and seamlessly cycling through the different running orientations.
Workout Plan	Complete eight 400 meter intervals or four 800 meter intervals. Rest 90 seconds in between each.
	Every time you inhale, focus on green. Connect the color with incoming oxygen, super-charging you with each breath.
	Every time you exhale, focus on orange, as solar waves pushing your forward.
	Alternate this visualized imagery by seeing yourself from an imagined drone, flying high above, just in front, and just behind you.
Post-run ritual	Gratitude breaths, eyes closed. Journal.

13. Racing

"You've got to learn your instrument. Then, you practice, practice, practice. And then, when you finally get up there on the bandstand, forget all that and just wail."
— Charlie Parker

Like a hungry lioness surveying the Serengeti as she prepares to launch into an intense chase to claim her next meal, the runner stares ahead in deep focus, as her brain processes potential outcomes in numerous scenarios. Both the lioness and runner hold their breath momentarily, with twitching muscles and dry mouths. Their pupils dilate, hearts beat faster. The lioness moves her giant paws slightly forward and hunkers down, on the razor sharp edge between tense stillness and an explosive sprint. She is ready to burst into motion in milliseconds once the moment is right.

The runner's nostrils flare as she takes a deep breath, nods her head, and moves her hands forward. The air is thin and charged. The moment is here. The lioness twitches and growls. The runner — she taps on her keyboard, scrolls down, agrees to the waiver, and enters her credit card details.

The lioness leaps, and the runner clicks the enroll button. Both experience a moment of courage and surge of adrenaline — the chase is on. It is a flurry of activity, and there is no turning back for either. As the lioness races across the plain on the heels of her prey, the runner marks her calendar and laces up her shoes, ready for her first official training run in the race journey for which she just enlisted.

Whether you are a racing veteran or a newbie eyeing your first 5K, there is great energy and power to harness from the act of signing up for a race. It is a formal commitment that you are willing to put yourself into a public challenge, that you are driven and not satisfied remaining, as Theodore Roosevelt described in the *Strenuous Life*, "with those poor spirits who neither enjoy much nor suffer much, because they live in the gray twilight that knows not victory nor defeat."

Racing offers a wide array of benefits, including:

- Motivation to train, especially during times of competing priorities or less than desirable weather conditions
- A catalyst for lifestyle change
- A test or benchmark against yourself and others
- An opportunity to learn, grow, and expand perceived limits
- A journey and adventure, with an exciting dose of uncertainty
- A feeling of being vibrantly alive and inspired
- New friendships, shared struggle, and shared success
- A chance to get out of our comfort zone and take risks
- A lifestyle of travel and exploration
- Creation of work-life balance
- An opportunity for heightened states of awareness, struggle, and flow

These benefits await the runner who clicks the enroll button and adds their name to any start list. It is a nerve-racking moment for many people, especially for a first race or first time at a longer distance. It is not uncommon for runners to experience doubt when pondering a race. What if I fail? What if I don't make my time goal? What if I am the last person to finish? What if I don't make the race time limit? These are all common Inner Critic questions, thus an excellent target for your Inner Coach to address. When they arise, send in the Bouncer to toss them out the door.

Keep in mind though, that the existence of these doubts illustrates the powerful growth opportunity in committing yourself to a challenge. The more nervous it makes you, the more growth awaits.

The more emotional attachment you assign to it, the more extreme the emotional peaks and valleys you will likely encounter. The parallels between taking on running challenges and living a fulfilling life could fill this chapter, so keep in mind that the seemingly innocuous act of committing to a race offers far more potential impact on your life than covering a set distance while wearing a number and surrounded by like-minded runners.

My aim is for you to experience high quality running for as long in life as you wish and at your maximum potential toward the performance you seek. To make running viable and fulfilling over many years, it is important that you plan for sustainability and avoid overtraining and burnout. In addition to its multitudinous benefits, racing is often the cause of runners burning out and hanging up their shoes.

When this occurs, it is not <u>racing</u> that's the problem though — it is the approach to setting goals and expectations, selecting events, preparing, and approaching the race experience itself. There are numerous potential pitfalls in each, and these stand to derail the efforts of even the most dedicated and focused runners. We are going to explore these pitfalls and consider an expanded, smart approach to avoiding them, and thus prepare for thriving in race experiences.

This chapter teaches the Flow State Runner lifecycle of racing, starting with setting goals and concluding with recovery. Along the way, you will find insights on goal-setting, race selection and preparation. This chapter offers a powerful pre-race ritual, guidance for thriving during races, and instruction on maximizing your recovery experience. All of these topics are covered with a level of depth and breadth that extends beyond typical numbers-only training plans. This is an exciting topic with vast potential when considered holistically, so let's jump in.

A moment of reflection and self-assessment

Before selecting a race, and especially before planning a whole season or year of races, take a moment to reflect on your driver and ask some key introspective questions.

Is your driver behind a desire to race an external force, such as pressure from a friend or family member? Is it internal, such as a desire for a transformation or to serve as an opposing force for a hectic work schedule? Is it self-imposed pressure to equal or beat someone? Is it about the outcome or the journey? Is it simple or complex?

This self-assessment exercise isn't about you judging your reflections. It is about asking the questions and observing your thoughts. While doing so, keep in mind that it is less important that you have a quick and concise answer to these questions than it is that you ponder them briefly before committing to a race.

Also check in with yourself on your capacity to achieve readiness for the race in the timeline you are considering. I am very much in favor of setting audacious stretch goals. I love the energy and excitement that comes from runners pursuing big challenges, and I thrive on seeing people accomplish seemingly impossible goals. I believe that audacious goal-setting is a key ingredient to fulfillment in life.

That said, I've seen some runners load their plates so full with audacious goals, responsibilities and high stress activities in sport, work, and life, that their house of cards comes tumbling down in the first gust of wind. The same is true within a set of sports goals. I've coached runners who wished to continue setting marathon personal bests in their 40s, but also wished to travel the world racing hard every couple of weeks. I passionately support the performance goal, but not the conflicting expectations of achieving the goal while pushing the body beyond its ability to recover.

On the flip side, I've seen runners who juggle the seemingly impossible and pull off a phenomenal race experience while working as a corporate executive, managing a household with three children, and volunteering for a charity. It is certainly possible to "do it all, and all at a high level," but it fits some years and times in life better than others.

Ask yourself the following questions. What is happening in my life during this period of time? What is fixed, and what am I able and interested in changing? Is there self-created pressure and stress in other areas of life that I can remove or lessen to make room for this race experience? Am I setting myself up with conflicting goals and priorities?

Consider the total package, including the mix of events within and external to running. Investing a little time up front to explore these questions is a valuable thought exercise and helps you prevent stress that some runners create for themselves downstream, that is, months into training for a big challenge, when their lack of effort spent preparing the soil in the metaphoric garden results in wilting sprouts. And preparing the soil doesn't mean avoiding races — it means taking time at the river's headwaters to reflect on the big picture and organize how you view your expectations, priorities, and activities to best align with the race decision.

Once you have completed these reflections, it is time to make a selection.

The Menu: types of races, events and adventures

Obstacle course races, cross-country, track & field, 5K and 10K road races, marathons, trail races, ultra marathons, adventure races, duathlons, triathlons, and more — there is no shortage of options for running-related events to consider. Aside from the normal pallet of distance, terrain and format, consider grouping the races you are evaluating into the following categories:

- **Moonshot:** epic, audacious and extreme challenge, likely once in a lifetime. Worth taking major risks and significantly disrupting other areas of your life, including social and family time, job, hobbies, etc.
- **Everest:** major challenge, stretch goal, considerable test of mind and body, well out of your comfort zone. Worth sacrificing time from other activities and priorities, and requires significant training and preparation effort

- **Apprentice:** experience building and training races, progressive distance build-up races (e.g., 10K to Half Marathon, then Marathon), races to test equipment, nutrition and hydration
- **Walk in the Park:** All about fun and adventure, yin events (like a yin run), running to support someone, guerrilla "invented" races with friends

I encourage you to include **Walk in the Park** and **Apprentice** events in your program of races in any given year. These are very important in keeping it fun, while fostering your growth and enjoyment of running. They also serve as opportunities for exploration, experimentation and risk-taking in an environment where less emotional connection is at stake.

For example, you may wish to use an **Apprentice** 5KM race in the off-season to experiment with fast running — knowing that if you fall apart at Kilometer 4 because the pace was too high, you will use the experience to build your knowledge rather than feel gutted at walking the last kilometer. Another example: as an experienced, quick marathoner, you may wish to run alongside a friend in a **Walk in the Park** run to support them in their first Half Marathon, thus experiencing the fulfillment of friendship and serving others.

Moving up the ladder of a runner's emotional connection to events, **Everest** races are excellent drivers for transformation, breaking through to new levels of fitness, and spicing up life. In these races, the stakes are high from both physical and emotional perspectives, as it is normal with an **Everest** event to tie yourself strongly to achieving your goal. A race may earn your **Everest** label in distance (such as your first ultra marathon), in a time goal (such as a sub 3-hour marathon) or some other measure (such as your first race after giving birth or turning 80). Remember, one runner's **Everest** may be another's **Walk in the Park**. What is important isn't how an event is externally viewed, but rather how you see it in the total picture of your life, at this moment in time.

At the top of the ladder is the **Moonshot**. This is saved for extremely special events, perhaps considered only once in your lifetime. Committing to a **Moonshot** event means you are willing to make major, potentially life-changing decisions and sacrifices to achieve your goal. To *reach the moon*, you may need to use all of your vacation time to attend training camps and participate in **Apprentice** races. You may consider moving temporarily to another city or country to train in a more suitable environment. You may find yourself putting relationships and friendships on hold, risking their loss. You may be tempted to dial down your career aspirations, miss out on a promotion, or even quit your job. You may make a significant investment in coaching and equipment. The costs, risks and stakes in **Moonshot** events can be extremely high, yet so is the passion, excitement and fulfillment. **Moonshots** aren't for everyone, but if now is a time it suits you to go big, just be open and clear with yourself and those close to you about the path on which you are embarking and bring your full passion into the journey.

The following factors are also useful when considering races in a given year.

- **Variation:** there is beauty in tradition, but if you are looking to grow and stay engaged over the long haul, don't keep doing only the same races year after year. Change the variables occasionally and get out of comfort zone with speed, type, terrain, setting, distance, etc.
- **Yin and yang:** consider at least one yin race per year, where you run to support a slower-paced friend, run with no time pressure or goal, or simply volunteer to support the race.
- **Next race:** plan an event after Everest or Moonshot races. This helps with Post-event Blues, as well as serve the role of a Plan B, should your summit bid or rocket launch need to be delayed or scratched due to a life circumstance.

I've signed up! Now what?

Once you've completed the evaluation process and taken action to get your name on the start list, it is time to frame the race, set any performance goals and take a few other important steps to set the conditions for success.

- **Frame:** consider quantitative goals, qualitative goals, or a mix. Set any performance goals.
- **Apprentice:** decide if you need any apprentice events along your path
- **Dedicate:** consider dedicating your race to someone or using it as a fundraiser or awareness event for a charitable cause.
- **Set Milestones:** set milestones or toll gates to check your progress and stoke your motivational fire along the preparation journey, especially with Everest and Moonshot events. Milestones serve as micro goals, which add energy and provide feedback on the effectiveness of your preparation approach. They also allow you to course-correct along the way should you begin to deviate from your committed path.
- **Synergize:** consider spanning goals across life categories. For example, connect an Apprentice race with learning a new art, instrument, or life skill, and an Everest race with breaking through to a new career level or attaining a bonus at work. This allows you to bridge flow between multiple areas of life and transfer your focus and drive across your various pursuits. Just be cognizant of your situation and the need for balance when riding the razor's edge between thriving in flow across multiple areas and burning yourself out.
- **Embrace the Journey:** Remember to embrace the journey of preparation, as this is often the experience that will have a more profound long-term effect on you than the event itself.
- **Go public:** Share your commitment with friends and family. This creates an automatic sense of accountability and offers an opportunity for both an in-person and virtual network of

supporters at your side.

Now that you have committed, it is time to start preparations.

Ingredients of a successful training program

In general, runners tend to spend significant focus on the quantitative aspects of race preparation. Off-the-shelf and data-driven automated training plans are full of guidance on distance, duration, intensity, and pace. While the quantitative training aspect is of course critical, it is only the tip of the iceberg for what goes into a successful race experience and a sustainable endurance sport lifestyle.

In addition to physical training, effective and sustainable training programs deliver on the following requirements. Ask yourself, "does my program …?"

- deliver on my full mix of goals, both quantitative and qualitative?
- keep me engaged and enthusiastic?
- prevent overuse injuries and mental burnout?
- consider my big picture, current personal/home/work activities, desires, stress, responsibilities, and cycles?
- consider how I frame the event (Moonshot, Everest, Apprentice, etc.), not just a template of the event distance?
- address my total fitness, mobility, imbalances, core, and any other athletic interests?
- integrate mind training and address my weaknesses and development areas in a style that resonates with me?
- foster knowledge development, including how I will grow my physical and mental skills, choose and use gear, and design a race strategy?
- integrate recovery and nutrition, in a macro sense, as well as during and immediately following the event? This includes after-care in the weeks and months after an event.

Master coaches, a team of coaches, or self-coaching

If you are missing any of these aspects either in training programs you are evaluating or in a program you are designing for yourself, I highly recommend that you invest time in ensuring their inclusion. It is not required that you go to one source or person for the above. It is more important that you find a way to include all aspects and plan for at least a modest level of integration.

You may find a master coach who will fill all of these needs. If so, you are fortunate, so hang on to that coach. You may find a combination of coaches that meet your requirements — perhaps you assemble a team of three: a running coach, nutrition specialist, and yoga teacher. You may also choose to use a coach for one area, an automated program for another, and self-coach for the rest. Lastly, you may decide to be your own coach for the entire set of requirements.

Regardless of your choice, keep in mind that there is great benefit from learning from those with more experience, as well as having someone to challenge you and with whom to bounce ideas, vent, and be accountable.

If you do decide to hire a coach or team of coaches, please refer to my advice in Chapter 7 on selecting a running technique, as those same questions apply when evaluating coaches. Also, I encourage you to select a coach with passion and experience helping people like you, that is, with your style and goals. This isn't necessarily the coach with the flashiest set of certifications, academic titles, or list of famous or fast runners on their team. More important is their experience getting results with runners like you, and your belief that there is a fit in terms of energy, communications style and personality.

Once you have hired a coach, a team of coaches, or yourself as a coach, the next step is to organize and document your plan. The technology or approach you select for this is less important than the ease of use in reviewing and adhering to your plan once your training program is in-flight and you are metaphorically *over the ocean*, managing your training on top of all of your other life activities. I suggest keeping it simple and as integrated into your life as possible.

Race preparation tools to include in your training program

On top of workouts, nutrition, mental training, and all of the other aforementioned training program elements, there are five Flow State Runner race preparation tools worthy of integration:

- Visualization
- Adversity Checklist
- Emotional Elevation Profile
- Race Day Plan
- Mental Taper

Visualization

As discussed in Chapter 5, visualization offers a powerful opportunity to consciously see yourself performing in a state you aspire to, which helps you chart that destiny and make it happen in reality. Applied to race preparation, visualization takes place in mental training sessions, such as imagining in full detail the moment you cross the finish line and seeing envisioned moments where you face and thrive in adversity while en route. The lifecycle is: want it, believe it, visualize it, and then live it. You'll use visualization as well with the tools below.

Adversity Checklists

I introduced the concept of Adversity Checklists in Chapter 2. This tool is extremely useful when preparing for events. Used in many professions, sports, and hobbies, checklists are the basis for establishing patterns we want to repeat in given scenarios, actions to avoid, and response patterns to ingrain via practice, so that the desired actions occur automatically in stressful and even chaotic situations.

Guided by optimism for a great race experience and in the heat of the moment, runners sometimes forget that things may not always go smoothly. They forget that they will be tested in complex ways, sometimes off-script. They forget, and then they react to the situation in a manner contrary to how they would like to see themselves reacting as they sit in the comforts of their homes months before or months after the race.

Here we can learn from airplane pilots. First and foremost, pilots rely on preparation, through education and significant practice. Next, they make extensive use of well thought-out and well-tested checklists, ultimately practicing them in a flight simulator and being ready to use the checklists to guide their actions whenever needed in flight.

Transferred to running, this means thinking through potential adversities and addressing them in advance via preparation and mental rehearsal. Adversity comes with the territory when racing. Things will go wrong. Equipment will break. The weather will be unpredictable and maybe even lousy. Clothes will never be cool enough or warm enough. Skin will rub, blisters will appear, and the body will go through highs and lows. There will be discomfort. That's what you signed up for, right? Well, it was somewhere in the fine print, at least! And when any or all of these occur, there will be some type of reaction, and that reaction can define the difference between a DNF (Did Not Finish) and the most incredible race experience of your life. Your use of Adversity Checklists allows you to greatly influence your reaction in-flight.

Here is how to build your Adversity Checklist:

1. Think about all scenarios that could threaten your desired race success. Get into brainstorming mode, but don't allow the exercise to create anxiety. Just note potential situations with gear, your body, the weather, terrain, attitude, food, drink, etc.

2. Apply the *LUNP Evaluator* from Chapter 10 here, in terms of evaluating likelihood and impact for each listed adversity. There is a blank copy in the Appendix. Leave all the potential scenarios on your list, but note the likelihood of each and note any that fall in the *Land of Wasted Worries*.

3. Think about and document the best way you can imagine ad-

dressing or responding to each situation to achieve the most positive outcome.

4. As you expand your racing and life experiences, update your checklists and mentally rehearse the new scenarios. Read race reports and other adventure stories. Talk to other athletes and take away positive lessons to strengthen your knowledge base.

The act of simply creating an Adversity Checklist is a valuable training experience. When possible, train the identified adversities. For example, run at night in heavy fog, run in the rain or snow, or run on an empty or full stomach.

To take it to another level, incorporate visualization. Play a film of the scenario in your mind and then read the checklist that you have prepared. See yourself encountering the challenge and then working through it step-by-step, toward a positive outcome each time. Incorporate small blocks of visualization time in your training plan well in advance of the race. If you invest time in this area, then you will have significantly reduced the odds of being surprised during the race!

Some uncomfortable events will likely occur regardless of how well you've prepared physically and mentally, but with the calm and professionalism of an experienced pilot, you will recall the checklist response, apply it to the situation, and thrive as you work through it.

Emotional Elevation Profile

For some types of races, it is common for race organizers to provide an elevation profile map. The elevation profile plots the course into a graph showing the distance on the X axis (horizontal) and elevation on the Y axis (vertical). In some races, this map looks like a smooth sign wave of rolling hills. In others, it is a jagged saw, with steep climbs and descents and very short distances on the peaks and valleys. Studying the elevation profile gives runners a sense of the type of terrain to expect and a method of estimating the resulting pace. It also offers insights into the relative challenge of various sections of the course, and for competitive runners, opportunities for tactical moves.

Elevation profiles make it clear to all racers what to expect in terms of when the terrain goes up and down during a race course. If the profile shows a steep climb for the first 5KM, no runner should be surprised when they spend the first 5KM going uphill.

Here's an example of an elevation profile, noting some steep terrain over a 100KM course, spanning an elevation gap of 200 meters up to 1700 meters above sea level.

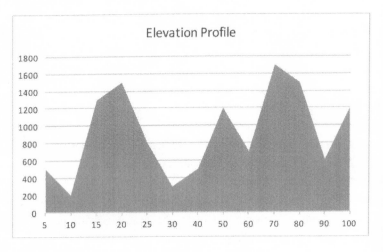

Image: Elevation Profile Example

We can borrow from this concept and apply it to <u>emotional</u> peaks and valleys. It is rare for a runner to complete a race, especially a long one, without expressing some level of emotions. It is human nature. As discussed in Chapter 11, the impact of emotions has enormous make-or-break potential on your running experiences. You have an opportunity to get in front of that impact by utilizing an Emotional Elevation Profile.

To make an Emotional Elevation Profile for a race, replace the concept of elevation points with potential emotions you may experience along the way. High, positive emotional states are mapped as peaks, while low, negative emotional states are mapped as valleys. These emotional waypoints may be linked to logical moments, such as terrain features (during a steep climb), distance (late in the race), aid stations (after receiving support), and other predictable moments along the course. They may also be plotted as random surprises, moments of sudden euphoria or doubt, and reactions to weather changes and other unexpected events.

This is only a simulation game, as emotional states may be driven by many factors, often unpredictable, but it serves its training purpose even when you are making educated guesses based on your prior experiences and self-knowledge.

Make at least three versions of your simulated emotional elevation profile per race, one that reflects an extremely positive emotional experience, another that represents a very challenging negative emotional experience, and a third that includes a mix of ups and downs. Build in logical waypoints (when there is high likelihood of feeling a certain emotion) and surprise emotional states.

Visualize going through the race according to each profile. See your reaction, facial expressions and body language under each emotion as you run through the course.

Next, study all the moments of negative emotional states and mark an X on the profile noting an opportunity for an early interdiction. That is, note a moment when your active Dome of Awareness observes the emotion's presence and calls on your Inner Coach to redirect it.

Here's an example:

Emotional Elevation Profile

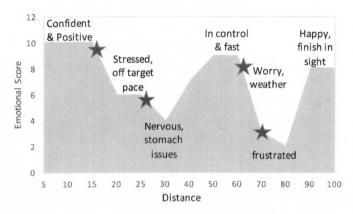

Re-run your visualization and focus on the performance of the Dome, your Inner Coach's voice, and the resulting shift in your emotional states. Visualizing this process is a powerful tool in training you to steer your performance through emotional adversities that happen to all runners. The more time you spend visualizing and training this, the better prepared you will be to react the way the best serves you when you encounter this in a race.

You can use this process on shorter runs, as well as life. For example, envision looking at an upcoming work project and seeing the expected peak moments of high volume, high focus work — perhaps in the days before a deadline or presentation, or when client demand is known to spike — and the moments lower intensity education and planning work. That maps to the elevation profile, showing the steep climbs and descents.

Next, imagine where emotions and stress may be high or low based on workload. These are the logical waypoints. Throw in some unexpected peaks and valleys as well, as emotions often arrive unexpectedly and off-script.

A valuable exercise is to map a prior race or life experience into an

Emotional Elevation Profile, and to review where it fit logical waypoints, other variables you encountered along the way, and where surprise emotional states arrived.

Race Day Plan

Prepare a Race Day Plan well in advance of the race. It is a critical tool for setting a foundation for minimal distraction, maximal focus and optimal performance on race day. Review and fine tune your Race Day Plan with the help of experienced friends or coaches, and then mentally rehearse it. An effective Race Day Plan covers the following:

- Strategy and pacing
- Nutrition, hydration, and self-care
- Logistics, Clothing & Gear
- Pre-Race Ritual
- Post-Race Ritual
- Recovery approach

Let's look at each component in more detail.

Strategy

The strategy component addresses your planned pace, including times when pace may vary, such as on major climbs and descents and across technical terrain. Included in pacing are breaks (aid stations, check points, micro recovery), as well as any key milestones. If you are running a race with pacers (volunteer runners who hold a specific pace and carry balloons or signs so that runners may follow them to hold that pace), include this in your plan.

For competitive runners, the race strategy section includes identified opportunities to take risks, attack, and any other tactics you wish to employ. For example, in a trail marathon, a runner may know of a particularly technical descent, which is his specialty, so he notes this as an opportunity to gain time, while also impacting his competitors' psyche with an assertive surge forward in this section.

Lastly, a key strategy element is to consider that races can be divided into strategic sections that you may wish to approach differently. An *Apprentice Race* may have an *Everest* section where you wish to test yourself with a maximum effort performance, such as a timed hilly section or climb of a mountain pass.

At the more extreme end of the spectrum, a race may be an *Everest* race for you, but include a *Moonshot* moment. For example, I approached the weeklong Marathon des Sables as an *Everest* race and selected the long stage (80 kilometers) as a *Moonshot*. I put in a massive physical and mental training effort to perform during that challenging stage, and I was willing to risk a DNF and potential injury for a big performance that day. The strategy worked, yet I ran out of food for the last two days of racing, as I had chosen to carry the minimum amount of food required in the race rules. My *Moonshot's* physical impact resulted in me consuming on the rest day the limited number of calories I was carrying for the remaining two stages of racing. Those two days of desert racing on an empty tank were not comfortable, but it was worth it to me, and an acceptable price for my strategy.

Nutrition

For races long enough that you will need to refuel during the race, this is where you record what to eat and drink, when, how, how to carry or transport, etc. Failure to pay attention to this important topic carries a high price tag, including performance far below your potential or even being forced to abandon the race.

Simply having food and drink with you isn't enough to ensure you consume it when needed. Too many endurance athletes have stories about feeling so good in a race that they forget to eat or drink. Almost all of these stories end with a description of a particularly awful bonk, a term that describes a sudden loss of energy, and for some, the loss of the will to even continue in the race. Remember, race day is not the day to try something new or change any of your nutrition variables!

Logistics, Clothing & Gear

The less you have to worry about in the hours before a race starts, the better. This is a prime opportunity for checklists. There should be nothing left to memory, not even your socks. I've encountered more than a few runners on race day with forgotten socks, shoes, and other items that are the first to be forgotten because they are so ubiquitous in daily running!

Pay extra attention to travel logistics as well. I once found myself on the morning of a marathon caught up in a traffic and parking snafu. I finally secured a parking spot. When I heard the start gun fire, I was a mile from the start line. I sprinted that bonus mile and arrived at the start line as the volunteers had begun to disassemble it. Lesson learned — arrive <u>very</u> early on race day!

Include the following in your checklist:

- Logistics: public transportation schedules or route options. If driving, where you'll put your wallet and keys
- Clothing: all clothing items, including gear for inclement weather and pre- and post-race clothes, hair ties (for long-hair runners)
- Gear: race number belt or pins, watch and other tech gadgets & based on the race type: water bottle, backpack, survival gear
- Mind tools: notes, photos and any other helpful reminders and tools

Be hyper-disciplined in your planning. Walk through these checklists in your mind multiple times, and for more gear-intensive races, with a hands-on rehearsal.

Pre-Race and Post-Race Rituals and Recovery

All three will be included in your final Race Plan. They are explained in the rest of this chapter.

Mental Tapering

For major events requiring a demanding physical training program, the final week or couple of weeks before the race will include a taper phase. This physical taper allows the body to heal and realize the full effects of training. When following a taper plan, the goal is to arrive on race day at your peak fitness.

I encourage you to also incorporate a mental taper period in the final days before a race. During this time, give your mind a chance to rest and rebuild its energy reserves for the day you'll be asking for its highest level of performance. To accomplish this mental taper, start with removing or at least reducing as many of the stressful parts of your life as possible. This could mean taking some time off from your job or just changing your expectations around your work briefly.

When possible, outsource some of the tasks on your plate, or ask for help from friends and family members, including help with childcare, cooking, cleaning, home projects, etc. This is a good time as well to put some life worries on hold, such as thoughts about career, finances, and relationships, as well as general expectations. Just hit the pause button on things until after the race, as now is the time to focus on YOU, and that starts with create a period of calm. Try as well to be at peace with as much as possible, with relationships, how well you did or did not adhere to your training program, your weight and fitness level, your race times or places in the past, etc. Let go of judgement of yourself and others, and just be. The time for analysis, evaluation, and consider lessons learned consideration.

Your time investment in each of the above areas will pay dividends on race day and on your general emotional health along the way.

Pre-Race Ritual

Race day has arrived, and now is the time to put all of your hard work
in mind and body training to the test. By following a set ritual for every
race you start, you will train your mind to quickly orient itself toward
optimal racing experiences that draw from the Flow State Runner
patterns you've established and ingrained. The FSR Pre-Race Ritual
serves to activate your flow patterns, calm your pre-race jitters, focus
your attention, and charge your energy system.

Here's how it looks in a simple checklist format:

Pre-Race Ritual

1. Review logistics checklist and care for yourself
2. Create solitude
3. Breathe deeply
4. Visualize flow
5. Move and connect to the race
6. Activate FSR systems

Next, we explore each step in greater detail.

1. Review logistics checklists and care for yourself
Execute the checklists you created and rehearsed well in advance of
race day. Shoes? Check. Water bottle? Check. Race number? Check.
   Review your pacing and race strategy plan.
   Follow your pre-race hydration and nutrition plan. Avoid changes
or experiments today. Put on sunscreen, anti-chafe cream, and anything
else your body needs.

2. Create solitude
When feasible, physically separate yourself from the *herd* of other often-
anxious runners. Walk away and find the quietest, most serene space

available within practical reach of the start line. If you are stuck in a corral by race numbers or pace groups, find a safe place to close your eyes and activate your inner quietness. Stay in this space of solitude for as long as possible. Avoid pre-race chats with other runners and listening in on other conversations.

3. Breathe deeply

Breathe for several minutes in the following pattern or any other pattern that you've found calming: 5-3-8-3. (Inhale-Pause-Exhale-Pause)

4. Visualize flow

See yourself running in flow state and performing at your best in several sections of the race. You may wish to see this in a series of still images or like a film. Visualize the faces of your supporters and anyone you've dedicated your performance to.

5. Move and connect to the race

When feasible, go for a short warm-up run or run in place. End this warm-up with a few yoga Sun Salutations and the Warrior 2 pose with your leading arm's fingertips pointing in the direction of the start line or any visible major challenge of the race, such as a mountain.

Draw your gaze from your fingertips to that challenge and mentally connect with the race course. Like a martial artist bowing to an opponent, this is your moment of humble and respectful warrior connection with the race course. This is the moment you formally embrace the challenge and link your warrior spirit to all obstacles that lie in your path. Repeat this exercise on both sides, and seal the experiences in a brief moment of reverence.

6. Activate FSR Systems

Imagine what it would feel like on spacecraft preparing for launch. You are wearing your flight suit, strapped tightly into your seat, on top of a giant rocket. One by one, you are activating all of the systems that will deliver you into space. You are focused, but also very much excited. Transfer that perception to an image of yourself standing at the start line of a race, and go through the following actions:

- Activate your Dome of Awareness and envision an illuminated dome appearing above your head, with an initial body scan taking place. Imagine the sounds and images. Dome is active and ready.
- Invite your Inner Coach to appear, in whatever voice or character you wish. See and hear your coach offer an initial encouraging word. Inner Coach is engaged and ready.
- Take a deep breath and feel your Net of Breath engage, ready to support you in moments of stress and low emotional points. Net of Breath in place and ready.
- Fire up your energy systems, tapping into mental stimulants such as music, your race mantras, photos of loved ones, captured scents, and written notes of support. Energy Systems are on and at maximum charge.

In-flight Tools

Once the race is in-flight, you will largely rely on the patterns you have trained and the core of the Flow State Runner model. In short, keep your Dome of Awareness and Inner Coach active, and employ FSR Mind Tools as needed.

Here are some other useful tools and thoughts to leverage during a race:

- Look at photos or notes from loved ones. In very long races, use technology to receive real-time messages of support.
- Visualize your virtual support team running beside you and pulling/pushing you through challenging parts of the course.
- Visualize your Inner Coach on your shoulder or running in front of you, especially in the role of Bouncer, Motivator, and Muse.
- Return to the fundamentals: breathe and remember your goal

and why it is important to you.
- Smile and thank the volunteers.
- Believe in yourself.

Post-Race Ritual

Just as with training runs, the Post-Race Ritual includes a very important moment of reflection and knowledge development at the end of a race. By all means, embrace all the moments of euphoria, celebration and social interaction. Do the normal things immediately after the race (get the t-shirt and medal, drink, eat, put on comfortable post-race clothes). You have earned all of it. But also, take a few minutes to yourself to complete the following ritual at the end of each race. Doing so is a wise investment in your future race experiences and a valuable preventative measure to counter post-event blues.

Post-Race Ritual

1. Create solitude
2. Seal the positive
3. Capture the negative
4. Express gratitude
5. Journal or record

1. Create Solitude

Find a quiet place to sit, away from the finish line energy. If no quiet places are available, close your eyes and create your own quiet space. Visualize powering down your Dome of Awareness and releasing your Inner Coach. Lower your focus level and release your energy.

2. Seal the positive

Seal the positive moments in your memory. Replay the highlight reel of your race experience, zooming in and pausing the moments you consider the most profound and fulfilling. Memorize the details of what was happening before and after these key racing moments. Memorize the sights (colors, people, buildings, nature), the sounds (cheers, music, exchanges with other runners), your predominant thoughts and emotions, smells, and any other noticeable sensations.

3. Capture the negative
Capture your observations from any negative experiences, moments with unhelpful emotions, or low performance points. This isn't a time for judgement or self-pity. Simply think through what happened and note any initial root cause assessments. Then, let it go.

4. Express gratitude
Close your eyes and breathe several gratitude breaths. Regardless of your performance, express gratitude, especially for the big picture realities, such as your life, health, relationships and ability to even pursue running and racing. Express gratitude for your supporters, including any virtual supporters or other supportive memories you tapped into in the journey.

5. Journal or record
Make a quick audio recording or selfie video, just to record as many thoughts as possible about your experience. Journal in writing if you wish, but don't put this off if it is logistically not feasible until well after the race. The sooner you capture your thoughts, even in rough, unprepared format, the more likely it is that you won't miss anything. Later, you may wish to use these captured initial impressions to create a race report or more detailed journal entry.

Post-Race Recovery
Post-Race Recovery is one of the most important aspects of a sustainable training program, yet it is the area most often overlooked from a plan-

ning and execution perspective. This suboptimal approach to recovery tends to happen on the edges. On one edge, runners either skip or rush their recovery, jumping immediately back into physically and mentally demanding training programs, until one day they finally succumb to an overuse injury, frustrating performance plateau, or full burnout. On the other edge, runners tend to just check out for a while, eating and drinking whatever they want, and losing fitness by not moving at all. Even if you find yourself in the middle, there is much to be gained by wisely considering your recovery as a critical component of your lifestyle as a runner.

Your recovery needs will vary depending on the duration and intensity of your race, as well as its relative meaning in your life. These needs will also vary across the domains of physical, mental, and spiritual. *Everest* and *Moonshot* races may require a significant mental recovery. Expect this — it is normal. That said, *Apprentice* and *In the Park* races may also require a mental recovery, based on the experience.

Let's start with the most common recovery area to consider: physical. Your top consideration is fuel. Make sure that you consume nourishing, real food. Sure, enjoy that post-race drink and treat, but also include sufficient healthy food to nourish your body.

On top of high quality fuel, add sufficient sleep, especially when you are crossing time zones and traveling long distances to and from races. It is not just the sleep the night after the race that's important. It is the sleep in the days and weeks after the race that will have a major impact on the response of your immune system, physical recovery, emotions, and mindset.

Lastly, utilize an active recovery approach that is inclusive of cross-training, yin activities, adventure and social fitness activities. The latter is especially important if you took a break from social time with friends and family to focus on your training efforts in the weeks and months leading up to the race.

When runners skip recovery, it is often due to fear of losing their hard-earned fitness. Keep in mind though that deconditioning after major events is part of a healthy lifecycle. When a recovery is structured and managed holistically, your starting point toward the next event will be at a higher plateau, thus ever working your way to your max potential, rather than starting over from scratch every time. The easiest way to find yourself starting from scratch is to skip recovery or approach it with zero structure or forethought!

Mental and spiritual recovery are also invaluable focus areas, especially after peak experiences. After a period of holding yourself to high expectations in training and racing, I encourage you to lower your expectations for a while and give your mind and fighting spirit a chance to rest and come back even stronger. You may find it helpful to shift your mental focus to a non-sporting activity for a number of days or weeks. Embrace this opportunity.

After *Moonshot* and *Everest* races, you may benefit from taking a major break from running or shifting your running focus significantly. After major ultra marathons, I've shifted to a season of mountain biking or cross-country skiing, a couple years of road marathon focus, and a season of adventure racing, hiking, paddling, and ad-hoc *guerrilla* races. These breaks provide an opportunity for you to find physical and mental stimulation elsewhere, which is both fulfilling and preventative for burnout in a sport you love.

On the topic of burnout, it is very common after major events for runners to experience post-race blues or other emotional high and low points. You may wish to revisit the discussion on this topic in the FAQ in Chapter 10, as I offer a series of tools to help before, during, and after.

Reviewing races and years

In the Post-Race Ritual, I encouraged you to keep your race day review and assessment brief and timely. Once you've taken some time to recover and process your thoughts and feelings about the experience, it is worth making a more detailed review. In addition, there is significant growth value in reviewing an entire season or year of racing.

For more detailed reviews, use the following prompts as a checklist to help you recall and capture what will really be the most important to you in the future.

- Funny experiences
- Moments of excitement and euphoria
- Your lowest points and toughest challenges, and what you did (positive or negative) when they occurred
- Moments of friendship and social connection, in person or virtual
- Moments of resonance and connection with your true self, when you felt alive and fulfilled

My Inner Coach can be a mean SOB

When reviewing your training and racing experiences, allow yourself once and only once to be critical. Keep your self-critiques constructive, but don't be afraid to make a brutally honest and raw assessment. Note what you will do differently in the future, and then let it go. Once you've captured the lessons learned, it is not worth revisiting your memory for another critical review. If you had a DNF or suboptimal performance, avoid launching yourself into a negativity spiral that leads into a black hole. If you tend to be extremely hard on yourself, treat yourself like a team member you value (with respect, honor, and compassion), rather than the sibling you may have quarreled with, and later regretted it. Look back once, learn from it, alter your future behavior, and move forward.

On the other hand, for positive experiences, feel free to revisit the memory as often as you wish. It is a powerful, renewable fuel to use for future events. If you did everything in a given race perfectly, then keep feeling the gratitude and commit to continuing with your momentum and reaching an even higher level of performance.

When reviewing your journey across the combination of training and one or more events, keep in mind that it is exactly that, a journey. Rather than stopping with an analysis of each event in a silo, expand your review to look at the big picture, including your patterns of behavior, stress, and emotions. Also, look for dots that you can connect over time, linking your decision points, experimentation, risk taking and growth.

Success and Failure

Ask yourself how you define success in racing. Is it a finish? A specific time or place? An object, such as an ultra marathon finisher's belt buckle, finisher's medal or t-shirt?

Some of my most valuable racing experiences would not have been considered by me as a success in the hours and days after the race. Perhaps I missed a time goal or desired place, or simply didn't feel strong, yet these races were the ones that fostered lifelong friendships, profound lessons learned, and funny stories that I hope to still laugh about in my later years of life.

My overarching guidance is to avoid attaching too strongly to a race's outcome. This means not attaching to success or failure, and not allowing either state to define you. Your potential and light as a person is much, much more expansive than the snapshot in time of a single race finish. Absolutely celebrate your high points and experience the raw emotional pain of any low points. This is the beauty of life. But, do your best to avoid attaching to either. Another beauty of life is that it is not a still image, but a moving picture.

I learned a great deal from a friend of mine who chased a goal through multiple failures. His goal was to cover a set course in mountainous southern Germany in an estimated 50 hours of solo hiking. It took him three tries and an additional 26 hours (76 hours in total), but he finally accomplished the goal. While technically two attempts were failures, he learned more about himself in those two attempts than the final "successful" attempt. Thus, in the big picture, the failures became the success, and the success was more of a celebration of the multi-attempt journey — although a rather grueling celebration!

Dare Mighty Things

Whether your race experience is that of an *Everest* attempt at first 5K or a *Moonshot* attempt at a podium place in one of the toughest ultra marathons in the world, I encourage you to dare mighty things. Believe in yourself, take risks, and push beyond your comfort zone. You have amazing potential — unleash it in your racing and in your life, and thrive in the journey.

13. RACING

14. Technology

"It's not about standing still and becoming safe.
If anybody wants to keep creating they have to be about change."
— Miles Davis

In the award-winning documentary *Personal Gold*, Olympians / Film-makers Sky Christopherson and Tamara Jenkins tell the riveting underdog story of the American Women's Track Cycling team in the 2012 London Olympics. The story focuses on a theme of *Data not Drugs* and explores not only a heartwarming story of courage and passion, but also the enormous impact and potential of *quantified self* technology in athletic performance.

Technology offers immense potential to help us better understand and connect with the full capacity and power of our minds and bodies. From biofeedback sensors to virtual coaching apps, we are seeing rapid advancement in technology that can listen to and scan our bodies, aggregate inputs from an array of sensors, correlate the data, and guide us based on this information and a vast underlying knowledge base instantly available from the Internet.

At minimum, technology has the capacity to free us from wasted brain cycles on mundane, repetitive tasks. At maximum, technology has the potential to serve as a virtual team of doctors, lab technicians, coaches, therapists, gurus, and more, all working to elevate our performance to the highest possible levels.

Technology's upside is vast. We can leverage technology to become stronger runners, quantitatively and qualitatively, as well as physically and mentally. Technology holds potential as a powerful flow enabler and quality of life enhancer.

Technology is also a double-edged sword. Its dark side is an age of distraction, disconnectedness with ourselves, superficial connections with others, and nonstop overload. In this manner, technology also stands as a flow inhibitor, blocking us from rich, effortless moments of perfection, and forcing us into a reactionary and overly stimulated mindset. It is easy to get swept up in the rush to shift to a full-on *quantified self* approach, where everything that is trackable is tracked, and a hyper-connected life, where there's an omnipresent temptation to get lured onto a hamster wheel of sharing, thinking about what to share, and reviewing what people did or did not think about what we shared.

In doing so, we risk forgetting about the benefits of a simple <u>qualified</u> self approach, driven by in-person relationships and intense moments of presence. Technology has the capacity to create significant noise, thus leading to a very small signal-to-noise ratio in our running and lives. Yet, those seeking flow state experiences are best served with much more signal than noise. Herein lies a challenging paradox.

Thriving in this rapidly evolving world does not mean shunning technology, as this would also discard a vast array of benefits. It would also be essentially impossible in a world where technology is only growing in its ubiquity. Thriving is all about taking bold control of how you will and will not leverage technology for your life and your needs! Thriving requires that you set expectations with a strong intention, know when to embrace and when to exclude gadgets, platforms and the expectations around them, and decide when you want to engage with technology and when your sole focus is you and the path at your feet.

This chapter offers insights on a Flow State Runner's behavior around technology. It also offers an exploration of key technologies that enable and support the Flow State Runner lifestyle and quality running experiences.

Aspects of Technology Utilization

As established in the opening of this chapter, technology can be both a flow enabler and a flow inhibitor. We can also evaluate technology in terms of the level of engagement and attention it requires from us, that is, how intrusive or non-intrusive it is to the experiences we are seeking. To take conscious control of your technology utilization, I encourage you to examine your technology usage patterns and consider the perspectives of how the technology enables or inhibits flow and whether engagement with the technology is intrusive or nonintrusive.

Technology as a flow inhibitor occurs in the following ways and is amplified when these technology "features" sneak into the critical moments before, during, and after runs:

- **Notifications:** news alerts, social media likes, incoming messages, app updates, friend/follow/connection requests, ads
- **Communications:** messaging overload, multiple inboxes and communications tools to track and manage
- **Expectations:** expectations over response times and availability, expectations over social media content creation and responsiveness, social media overload and superficiality
- **Gadget woes:** batteries that die during runs, user interface issues, long GPS discovery times, lost signals, tracking apps that crash mid-run, damage, loss of devices and cables
- **Dependency:** over-reliance on devices and only doing activities when they are being tracked, marketed on social media, or compared to others
- **Attention:** interfaces that require attention during your activity
- **Loss of control:** technology that takes away your control, prompting you to you shift to response mode, reacting to incoming inputs, rather than setting your own destiny. Example: you read a message or email on your smartwatch at the start of a run and your mood changes during the run, even though you can't do anything about it for a while.

- **Out-of-the-now distraction:** temptation to capture photos and videos rather than savor in-person, in-the-moment experiences, temptation to stay connected with your busy external world during a run rather than with yourself

Looking only at flow inhibitors tells a grim story and leaves one to wonder how society can accomplish anything, especially personal peace and fulfillment, given such pervasive use of technology and its associated disruptions. Fortunately, technology has a strong upside as well, and we see that for runners in the following enablers:

- **Notifications:** positive nudge to change movement patterns, alter pace, breathe more deeply, adjust intensity
- **Sensing, measuring, and monitoring:** insights into numerous biofeedback and performance metrics to increase self-awareness and ability to customize behavior to align with performance and health goals
- **Data aggregation and pattern compilation:** connecting data from an array of sources and aggregating the information to tell a story based on patterns and interrelations, such as detecting a performance pattern across the data inputs from devices tracking GPS, heart rate, routes, power output, elevation, and sleep
- **Social motivation:** positive motivation from others, or simply from the existence of others, to train, or to train at a higher intensity or duration
- **Dome of Awareness primers:** support for mindfulness training, meditation, visualization, and breath training
- **Coaching:** greater insights for your coach or for you as self-coach; automated coaching programs and recommendations based on your activities and biofeedback data

Moving on to the perspective of engagement and required attention level, technology can be active and intrusive, requiring attention to activate and interact with, or passive and nonintrusive, operating in the background to collect data and educate you when you are not in the middle of a performance activity. Some technologies are designed to be nonintrusive and passive, but become intrusive and active when they don't work as smoothly as their designers envisioned, engineers created, or marketing teams sold.

Active and intrusive technologies can quickly become a distraction if not managed with foresight, and many runners fail to realize that a series of small technology distractions combine in their totality and create a sufficient interruption to derail any potential flow experiences.

Examples of active and intrusive technology for runners include any app or device that requires interaction with it during a run, any technology that intrudes into your space to "alert" you when that alert is not fully tied to your increased focus and performance in the moment the alert arrives, and any technology that you become dependent upon and at worst, fail to perform to your highest potential without, or simply get frustrated when it isn't working as expected.

Passive, nonintrusive technologies offer their benefits without getting in the way during running experiences. Examples of passive, nonintrusive technologies include sensors that automatically collect data with no start or stop required and interface attention required only after your primary activity ends. The best of these technologies requires the least "dealing with" time before a run, as it may also become a distraction to deal with straps, sensor placement and calibration, etc.

Again, my guidance is not that you shun the inhibitors and intrusive technology. My goal is that you have awareness of the broader choices you are making with technology and consciously avoid falling into traps that are becoming all too common as technology becomes more ubiquitous by the day.

Intention

The number one question I encourage you to ask yourself before interacting with any technology around your running and other associated Flow State Runner practices is "What is my intention?" In order words, why are you using the technology in the first place?

Here is a simple example: heart rate monitors. Let's say you train with a heart rate monitor (HRM). You take time before each run to place the chest strap and ensure a good signal. You start and stop the monitor to record your run, set alarms for lower and upper zones, and stay focused on your zones during the run. When you ask yourself "Why?", my hope is that your answer relates to you following a heart rate-based training program, being interested in trends and patterns with your heart rate data, or expressing some other reason that ties to interest, needs, or motivation associated with the technology. If not, then I would find it puzzling that you would devote any energy at all to the device's use. If you did have a solid reason, what happens on a run when the battery is dead on your HRM. Are you frustrated? Do you still run?

Or, how about this example: let's say you use a social motivation app to track your performance on a hill run and you use that app and your desire to score the fastest time on the route as motivation. You are mid-run and running your best time ever. You are receiving real-time cues that your pace is ahead of the current record holder. Then you notice your phone's battery jump from less than 10% to 0%, due largely to the very cold day and that long call you got caught on right before you made it out the door to start your run. Now, that dead battery has *stolen* your run and you are suddenly very frustrated. If so, ask yourself, what the original aim was here. Was it to be in first place on the app or to have an excellent high quality running performance for yourself?

I have a personal example from an electroencephalograph headband brainwave sensing tool I use to support meditation. I love the tool, and I have responded quite positively to its insights and associated gamification. That said, I've had several occasions where I allowed myself to become frustrated with a dying battery on the device, a signal interruption, or even a method of calculating the various gamification levels. This frustration not only distracted me, but in each case also led me to initially feel that the meditation session did not "count," because of the technology "failure." That completely misses the point of my decision to use the device in the first place! So, in this case, I have allowed technology — actually, my response to technology — to interfere with the original intention, which is to have more frequent and higher quality meditation experiences.

When considering technology usage to support Flow State Running experiences, check in from time to time on your underlying intention. I'd be surprised if it is "use this device more" — it is likely more in the direction of: breathe deeply during the day, meditate regularly, be more active, sit less, train at specific programmed levels based on heart rate or power, run X kilometers per week or take Y steps per day.

With your intention kept fresh in your mind, you will be more poised to remember why you are using the technology in the first place and more poised to continue without it when it's not available.

Again, the key aim is to build greater awareness of when you are controlling technology or adopting a lifestyle where it controls you.

Technology and Behavior

You hold the sole responsibility for your behavior with and dependency on technology. Rule it or it will rule you. Embrace it wisely and thrive. This requires some conscious decision making and self-management. I encourage the following three core behaviors around technology: simplify the menu, control access to yourself, and steer your technology utilization toward enablers.

Simplify the menu
Reduce gadget distraction, frustration, and overload by taking the following actions:

- Streamline the number of gadgets and apps you use. Get rid of redundant devices, accessories, and cables. Delete unused apps.
- Make charging and remembering-to-charge easy.
- Decide what data is truly important and ignore the rest. You don't need to track everything that's possible to track.
- Limit the number of separate apps and interfaces you rely on. Use an integrator app and dashboards.
- Don't waste time with devices that require too much time calibrating, finding satellites, etc., unless that data is vital. Else, save the device for only special runs, not every run.

Control access to yourself
Always-on messaging access across multiple apps and devices does not support focus and flow. It inhibits it. It is the same with pop-up notifications on watches and phones, and the expectations around response times and demands on your attention. It is getting harder and harder to ignore a constant stream of notifications and messages, thus harder to find focus and stillness, but the following actions will make a major impact in reversing this trend:

- Be reachable only if and when you wish, and in your choice of medium, not the choice of the person or machine trying to contact you. Use the Bouncer Inner Coach concept to limit access to you.
- Use voice mail greetings and messaging auto-replies to establish your communications protocol, such as when and how you are reachable, on your terms.
- Turn off all alerts and pop-up notifications, including social media-related updates, news, weather, and messaging. Selectively turn on only what matters and is critical to your performance

and quality of life. Use do not disturb mode during times of peak focus and rest.

- Remind yourself often that someone else's lack of planning or priorities does not equate to your emergency or willingness to give them your time on their schedule. Aside from true emergencies, you decide what is important and when, not the person contacting you.

- Do not check email or messages in a critical window before any run when you seek flow and/or a mental break. The critical window is defined by you and is the amount of time you would typically need to process and deal with any inputs that likely arise.

- If you struggle with self-control, such as giving in to the temptation to engage in communications on someone else's schedule and as an inhibitor to your focus, then make it harder for yourself up front to be distracted. For example, switch your phone to airplane mode 30 minutes before your planned run time or delete distracting social media apps from whichever device you have with you during desired maximum performance and focus times.

Focus on enablers

The following actions will help you steer your attention to a higher performance, higher fulfillment lifestyle:

- Dial down technology-related flow inhibitors as much as possible and give yourself credit for every micro decision to scale down or turn off an inhibitor. It is the totality of reducing distraction that matters — even the smallest of actions contributes to the big picture, as ten micro distractions easily combine to form a major distraction.

- Employ as many enablers and nonintrusive tools as you wish. Keep in mind your checks and balances on the intention with each, as well as frequently look for opportunities to streamline and simplify as new technologies are released.

Key digital health and fitness technologies related to running and flow

In general, technology in the digital health and fitness domain takes on the following activities for us: sense, measure, test, monitor, track, record, guide, remind, motivate, teach, analyze, correlate, simplify, compare, and alter. As of 2016, we have a well-respected and passionate group of thought leaders and coaches in the digital health and fitness space, with coaches and podcast hosts such as Josh Trent and Ben Greenfield sharing helpful insights and informative interviews on emerging technologies and their potential to improve performance and quality of life. With such rapid advancement occurring, I will save specific product reviews and insights for articles and podcasts, including sharing my experiences with specific products on the *Flow State Runner* website, and focus the remainder of this chapter on a broad overview of the technology areas that I believe have the greatest impact on and potential for enhancing the quality of your running experiences, as well as your performance.

Smartwatches and fitness trackers

Think of the finish line at races and several images come to mind: a large banner, adrenaline-fueled home stretch sprints, and runners hitting stop on their watches. For decades, all that was recorded on these watches was the final time or last of the measured splits. Then, as technology evolved, heart rate data was layered on, followed by GPS location and routing data, temperature, step counts, and a host of other metrics. And now, watches are computers, capable of sharing data with social media apps, giving real time pace cues and comparisons, and providing a wide ranging data set for use in dashboard apps, virtual coaching apps, and by real-life coaches. Lastly, there is emerging technology designed to track power output, stride length, impact force, and a variety of other factors related to technique.

Breathing devices and apps

Wearable breath sensors track breathing rate, type, quality, and patterns. These devices may be clip-on, integrated into other devices, or integrated into clothing. They typically interact with an app, and some have the capability to nudge you toward desired behaviors and to guide you in a breath practice.

There are also smartphone and tablet apps designed to guide you through patterned breathing and to coach you on a variety of breathing techniques. I regularly use these apps, especially on planes and trains, when it easy to stealthily breathe stress away and find a new level of focus. There is great potential in the breathing technology space to passively and non-intrusively guide behavior in one of the most powerful tools we have, our breath.

Biofeedback

These tools track physiological functions in any given moment and over time, including heart rate, glucose, blood oxygen levels, pain perception, muscle tone, and electrodermal activity (related to sweating and arousal levels). The resulting insights can be used to steer nutrition, acclimatization, physical and mental training plans, strategy and tactics, and recovery. Related to this domain, we also consider genetic testing and its associated custom tailoring of nutrition and training.

Brain-focused, Mind-focused and Meditation

These technologies focus on brain training and brain activity sensing. Here we find the aforementioned electroencephalograph (EEG), once an expensive piece of lab equipment, now available for home use. This tool allows real-time measurement of brain wave activity and is very useful in practicing mind stillness and meditation. This domain also includes Brain Entrainment, a technology that uses sound, light, or electromagnetic fields to stimulate the brain to shift to different states. Further, we find the technology of deep brain neurofeedback, including 3D brain activity imaging, with uses in treatment and brain training for high performance.

Journals and logs

While not the flashiest of technologies, digital journals and logs serve an important role in making it much easier to track activity along with journal entries related to that activity. Included in this area is general reactive journaling (post-activity), as well as proactive journaling and a prompted mechanism to log input on mood, thoughts, perceived exertion, and other qualitative insights worthy of tracking. These tools also help with reviewing goals and priorities.

Smart clothing and shoes

Apparel technology includes embedded sensors and wireless connectivity. These tools offer the ability to provide real-time feedback on posture, breathing, movement patterns, and other biometrics. Imagine running clothes and shoes that sense muscle tension and movement patterns and provide real-time tactile input to reinforce efficient technique. Imagine smart clothes that sense your heart rate and associated increase in sweat gland activity and alert you for the optimal time to begin an interval following a rest break. That's the world this domain of emerging technology offers.

Social media and social motivation

These platforms and apps help connect suitable training partners and provide motivation by comparing performance to others, encouraging goal setting, and gamifying the stats component of running. There is excellent potential in this domain for seamless integration across devices and social platforms, and to tap further into the team training dynamic for times that runners would benefit from team energy, but must train alone.

Virtual Reality

This is an exciting technology that will have wide-ranging impacts on running. I envision that virtual reality headsets and displays will quickly evolve for use in indoor / treadmill training and for course reconnaissance. We'll also see it used to support visualization training, meditation, and relaxation, as well as for education and coaching.

Automated training plans and coaching

These tools consolidate data from a runner's various devices and draw from knowledge bases and algorithms to create customized training plans, as well as varying levels of coaching support. Available inputs for automated and real-time training plan customization include weather, location, availability of training partners, recent race performance, bio-feedback data on health-fitness-recovery, preferences, events, seasons, locations, and more.

Hub / integrator apps

Of increasing importance over time is technology that makes sense of an overwhelming array of sensors and metrics, and helps us live higher performing, more fulfilling, happier lives. Technology in this domain simplifies a huge amount of data, focuses the user on what is truly important for them, and guides activity and behavior in a nonintrusive manner. This technology also provides access for coaches and health professionals, thus expanding the support team in a streamlined, efficient manner.

Recovery and Sleep

Recovery technology includes sensory deprivation tanks and floating, electric muscle stimulation devices, and a host of products designed to track and improve sleep. Sleep technology offers great promise for one of the most critical and most abused aspects of leading a healthy life. This technology includes light therapy for jet lag, seasonal affective disorder, and establishing sleep times; blue light reduction in the evening to foster sleep; and integrated and controlled home lighting to support desired focus and rest.

Other Gear

This broad *other* category includes zero gravity treadmills, hyperbaric tents, elevation masks, *smartglasses*, and a constant stream of emerging technologies and ideas that fill the pages of crowd-funding sites. For arguably the most primal of primal activities, running has no shortage of high-tech gadgets in its domain!

These technologies will have far-reaching effects into not only our daily decisions and actions at even a micro-level, but also into what we share with others about our behavior patterns and lifestyle. Both are of keen interest in business, as the related data provides vast insights to interested parties ranging from insurance underwriters to marketers.

Closing Thoughts

Technology can be fascinating and exciting to incorporate into your running and daily life at an ever increasing rate. In all the areas where technology helps you perform as desired and live a more fulfilling life, by all means, use it. Please remember though to ensure that you take control of your technology, rather than let it take control of you. And at the end of the day, remember to savor the view, savor the real conversation and in-person connection with others, and hear the sounds of real people and nature. These authentic moments of presence will provide more long-term value to you than the data points of your max heart rate and power output, temporary ranking on the hill climb, or number of likes for a photo of yesterday's run that you shared.

15. *Your Evolution as a Flow State Runner*

"You can't connect the dots looking forward;
you can only connect them looking backwards. So you have to trust
that the dots will somehow connect in your future."
— Steve Jobs

This final chapter brings us into the finisher's chute of *Flow State Runner*, thus on to many more start lines with enhanced perspectives and new paradigms. I encourage you to view your experience with this book and its associated exercises as one step in your evolution as a runner. There are more steps to come, as you continue to explore, learn more about yourself, experiment and integrate new experiences in life. There are six key overarching themes I ask you to consider over time, as your journey continues to unfold in the years and decades to come. How you approach these themes will impact not only your daily experience running, but more importantly, the long-term role of running in your life, as well as your overall fulfillment.

These key themes are:

- Commit to a growth mindset
- Seek perspective and authenticity
- Be of service to others
- Get out of your comfort zone
- Regularly express gratitude and compassion
- Create high quality experiences

Growth mindset

A growth mindset is one that embraces opportunities to learn, considers different perspectives, and evolves, especially when it is not easy or comfortable to do so. I encourage you to hold yourself to a high standard of lifelong learning and continuous improvement. Much awaits when you are open to growth. I suggest reviewing this book over the years as your life and experiences evolve. You may see some concepts differently and you will have new life experiences to layer on top, which may open an entirely different perspective on some topics.

Perspective and Authenticity

Zoom out of daily life from time to time and consider the big picture, your life over years and decades, rather than zoomed in to worrisome social media exchanges, your performance metrics, and your place or time in your last race. Too often we give our maximum attention to ultimately meaningless activities and worries, at the expense of universal long-term measures of happiness, including flow, relationships, sense of meaning, health, and authenticity.

Service to others

Great fulfillment and education lies in the experience of being of service to others. Opportunities for service are unlimited and need not be complex or time consuming. This includes mentoring a new runner, coaching or teaching, volunteering at a race, organizing a kids run, or simply offering some words of encouragement. Consider the Steve Jobs quote in this chapter's opening. If you trace the dots back related to your introduction to running and key running moments, you will likely find some notable people who inspired you, and sometimes with only the slightest of interactions. You have the power to be that person for anyone you interact with — young and old, from all walks of life. Someday decades from now they will look back and connect the dots of their fulfillment as a runner to you.

Get out of your comfort zone

Your comfort zone is simply a paradigm — a way of viewing the world based on your experiences, impressions from childhood, knowledge, skills and preconceived notions. Fear and your Inner Critic work together in an attempt to keep you in the familiar, in your comfort zone. Growth however, only occurs when comfort zone paradigms are challenged, shattered and newly assembled. This a constant process though, as you will get comfortable in the uncomfortable and need a new *uncomfortable* to seek out. It is a beautiful process of evolution in life, involving struggle, failure, and victory. Embrace the discomfort and the struggle, as these are the keys to growth.

Gratitude and Compassion

The practice of gratitude extends beyond mere social pleasantries and politeness and at its essence involves how you treat yourself. A gratitude mindset is one that encourages pausing to be thankful for that which is so easy to take for granted: life, health, air, water, food, relationships, love, the ability and place to run, a friendly wave, nature, and more. Along with gratitude is compassion, for yourself and others. We need self-drive and motivation to move forward in life, but at the same time, we also need compassion, as it reminds us that life can be brutally hard at times, and there is a tragic story or gut-wrenching situation in the lives of nearly everyone we meet. Just like with the connecting the dots example, you never know what someone is struggling with and how your brief moment of compassion may alter their path in a positive direction. Likewise, a moment of self-compassion may also allow you to alter your life, perhaps keeping you engaged in running through any low points and helping you transition to new phases in life.

High Quality Experiences

I encourage you above all other running aims to create high quality, meaningful running experiences. These experiences may sometimes include profound and memorable times of flow, while other times simply exist as intense moments of awareness and presence. Consider viewing a high quality run as a run that is in alignment with your goals and what you identified as your motivator for running. A high quality run is a run that taught you something, that opened a new door or relationship, and that left you feeling happy. It doesn't need to be any more complicated than that.

In addition, you may wish to expand your definition of a high quality running experience to the period of time before and after your runs, and all the flow and energy your bridge across elements of your life because of running's role in it.

Closing Thoughts

My overwhelming thought at the end of this book is one of gratitude. I am grateful for your energy and time. My hope is that you found *Flow State Runner* a source of helpful ideas, tools, and new perspectives. My dream is that you experience more high quality running experiences and that some of the concepts from the book will carry over into other areas of your life.

There are few greater joys than living an authentic and fulfilling life, pursuing what you love, and being of service to others. One of those few joys is inspiring others to do the same. All of these joys I wish for you.

Thank you for reading *Flow State Runner*. I hope we see each other out on a run and share a smile one day. I'll be the guy with the Alphorn on my shoulder and a grin on my face — you can't miss me.

> *"Plenty of people miss their share of happiness, not because they never found it, but because they didn't stop to enjoy it."*
> —*William Feather*

15. YOUR EVOLUTION AS A FLOW STATE RUNNER

Appendix

Appendix A - Resources & Further Reading

Please visit http://flowstaterunner.com/resources/ for the most recent version of all reference items, including live links for book shopping and quick links to all referenced online programs.

Breathing & Autonomic Nervous System
Books

- Benson, Herbert. The Relaxation Response. HarperTorch, 2000
- Coates, Budd. Runner's World Running on Air: The Revolutionary Way to Run Better by Breathing Smarter. Rodale Books, 2013
- Satchidananda, Sri Swami. Yoga Sutras of Patanjali. Integral Yoga Publications, 2012

Online Resources

- https://en.wikipedia.org/wiki/Parasympathetic_nervous_system
- http://mentalfloss.com/article/65710/9-nervy-facts-about-vagus-nerve
- http://mcat-review.org/respiratory-system.php
- http://www.diffen.com/difference/Parasympathetic_nervous_system_vs_Sympathetic_nervous_system
- http://www.kundaliniyoga.org/pranayam.html

Flow, Human Performance, Mind Training
<u>**Books**</u>

- Csikszentmihalyi, Mihaly. Finding Flow: The Psychology Of Engagement With Everyday Life. Basic Books, 1998
- Csikszentmihalyi, Mihaly. Flow: The Psychology of Optimal Experience. Harper Perennial Modern Classics, 2008
- Divine, Mark. Unbeatable Mind. 2015
- Divine, Mark. Way of the SEAL. Readers Digest, 2016
- Jackson, Susan A. Flow in Sports: The keys to optimal experiences and performance. Human Kinetics, 1999
- Kotler, Steven. The Rise of Superman: Decoding the Science of Ultimate Human Performance. New Harvest, 2014
- Ratey, John J. Spark: The Revolutionary New Science of Exercise and the Brain. Little, Brown and Company, 2008

<u>Online Resources</u>

General:
- Flow Genome Project: http://www.flowgenomeproject.com
- Unbeatable Mind Academy: http://unbeatablemind.com/
- SEALFIT: http://sealfit.com

Neurochemistry:
- http://www.humanillnesses.com/Behavioral-Health-A-Br/Brain-Chemistry-Neurochemistry.html
- http://www.chemistryexplained.com/Ne-Nu/Neurochemistry.html

Runner's High
Research

- Kotler, Steven. Runner's High Revisited--Runner's high: scientists come closer to unraveling the mystery. Psychology Today, May 20, 2008.
- Boecker, H.; Sprenger, T.; Spilker, M. E.; Henriksen, G.; Koppenhoefer, M.; Wagner, K. J.; Valet, M.; Berthele, A.; Tolle, T. R., The Runner's High: Opioidergic Mechanisms in the Human Brain. Cerebral Cortex 2008, 18 (11), 2523-2531.
- Sparling, P.; Giuffrida, A.; Piomelli, D.; Rosskopf, L. B.; Dietrich, A., Exercise activates the endocannabinoid system. Cognitive Neuroscience 2003, 14 (15), 1-3.
- Blumenthal, J. A.; Babyak, M. A.; Doraiswamy, P. M.; Watkins, L.; Hoffman, B. M.; Barbour, K. A.; Herman, S.; Craighead, W. E.; Brosse, A. L.; Waugh, R.; Hinderliter, A.; Sherwood, A., Exercise and Pharmacotherapy in the Treatment of Major Depressive Disorder. Psychosomatic Medicine 2007, 69 (7), 587-596.
- Fernandes, Maria Fernanda A. et al., Leptin Suppresses the Rewarding Effects of Running via STAT3 Signaling in Dopamine Neurons. Cell Metabolism, Volume 22, Issue 4, 741 - 749

Online Resources

- http://runnersconnect.net/running-tips/why-runners-high/
- https://www.psychologytoday.com/blog/the-playing-field/200805/runners-high-revisited

Running Technique & Training
<u>Books</u>

- Romanov, Nicholas. The Running Revolution: How to Run Faster, Farther, and Injury-Free--for Life. Penguin Books, 2014
- Romanov, Nicholas. Pose Method of Triathlon Techniques. Pose Tech Press, 2008
- Dreyer, Danny. ChiRunning: A Revolutionary Approach to Effortless, Injury-Free Running, Touchstone, 2009
- MacKenzie, Brian. Power Speed ENDURANCE: A Skill-Based Approach to Endurance Training. Victory Belt Publishing, 2012
- Murphy, T.J. and MacKenzie, Brian. Unbreakable Runner: Unleash the Power of Strength & Conditioning for a Lifetime of Running Strong. VeloPress, 2014
- Abshire, Danny and Brian Metzler. Natural Running. VeloPress, 2010

<u>Online Resources</u>

- The Pose Method: http://posemethod.com/pose-method/

Mobility
<u>Books</u>

- Starrett, Kelly. Becoming a Supple Leopard 2nd Edition: The Ultimate Guide to Resolving Pain, Preventing Injury, and Optimizing Athletic Performance. Victory Belt Publishing, 2015
- Starrett, Kelly. Ready to Run: Unlocking Your Potential to Run Naturally. Victory Belt Publishing, 2014

Web Resources

- Mobilitywod.com by Kelly Starrett http://mobilitywod.com
- Stretch Therapy by Kit Laughlin www.kitlaughlin.com
- Fluid Stance http://www.fluidstance.com/

Sleep
Online Resources

- Sleep Expert Doc Parsley's website by Kirk Parsley, M.D. http://www.docparsley.com/
- http://www.health.harvard.edu/staying-healthy/blue-light-has-a-dark-side
- http://www.scientificamerican.com/article/q-a-why-is-blue-light-before-bedtime-bad-for-sleep/

Ultra Running
Books

- Jurek, Scott. Eat and Run: My Unlikely Journey to Ultramarathon Greatness. Mariner Books, 2013
- Karnazes, Dean. Ultramarathon Man: Confessions of an All-Night Runner. TarcherPerigee, 2006
- McDougall, Christopher. Born to Run: A Hidden Tribe, Superathletes, and the Greatest Race the World Has Never Seen. Vintage, 2011
- Powell, Bryon. Relentless Forward Progress: A Guide to Running Ultramarathons. Breakaway Books, 2011

Yoga
Books

- Divine, Mark and Divine, Catherine. Kokoro Yoga: Maximize Your Human Potential and Develop the Spirit of a Warrior--the SEALfit Way. St. Martin's Griffin, 2016
- Satchidananda, Sri Swami. Yoga Sutras of Patanjali. Integral Yoga Publications, 2012
- Long, Raymond A, MD. The Key Poses of Yoga. Raymond A. Long, MD, FRSC, 2008

Online Resources

- Vipassana Meditation Retreats: https://www.dhamma.org/en-US/index

Appendix B - Jeff's Transformation Story

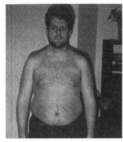

Image: Jeff 1996 at 24

Image: Jeff 2016 at 44

I struggled with my weight through childhood, trimmed up in my teen years, and then started gaining a lot of weight each year for five years starting from age 18. I was headed down a dangerous path, transitioning from college to a sedentary job with a very low activity level and very poor choices in nutrition.

At 24-years old, I was seventy pounds (32kg) overweight and had been gaining weight steadily with each passing year. I led a sedentary lifestyle, firmly entrenched behind a desk in an IT job and on the sofa at home. My standard January ritual was to buy a new pair of running shoes with a commitment to "finally" start running. By the end of each year, those shoes were more at home in a fast food restaurant than on a running path. My wife would drag me out to the park with our spirited Cocker Spaniel puppy, and do her best to coax me into running just 400 meters. I never made it.

That all changed in 1996, when I tuned in to the universe and got a message to transform myself. And by tuning in to the universe, I mean I finally listened to my wife Becky and to Mama Lance, Becky's grandmother. My prior conversations with Mama Lance had revolved essentially around Becky, the weather, and food. She was always soft-spoken with me and I don't recall many personal conversations. One day she approached me, and quite directly but in her gentle, soft-spoken voice, told me I was gaining too much weight and needed to do something about it before it was too late. There's a saying, "when the student is ready, the teacher will appear." I was finally ready and her message resonated.

Persuaded that I needed to make a change, I started looking for a "how" that would work for me. I did not find it in books or from respected mentors, but on TV. Channel-surfing one day while thinking maybe I'd get fit through golf, I watched the Ironman Triathlon World Championship in Hawaii and I was instantly mesmerized. These triathletes were so fit! My rather naive thought process went like this: "Ironman triathletes look fit. I want to look fit. I will become an Ironman triathlete."

I signed up for the nearest and soonest race I could find. It was in Florida in 9 months. I had no concept of the distances, how to train, how to eat, or anything else. I started reading, interviewing people, training and racing.

I lost seventy pounds in nine months and finished that first Ironman, albeit with excruciating knee pain and a very ugly 6-hour limping marathon. I cried when I crossed the finish line, from the joy of making a dream a reality and also of finally wearing out a pair of New Year's resolution running shoes by actually <u>running</u> in them!

Twenty years later and I've maintained a healthy approach to nutrition and body composition, despite many life changes, international moves, and extensive travel. Sometimes it's harder than others, and I'm still learning how my body's needs fluctuate with age, my approach to work, play, training, and more.

Appendix C - FSR LUNP Evaluator Tool

Flow State Runner LUNP Evaluator

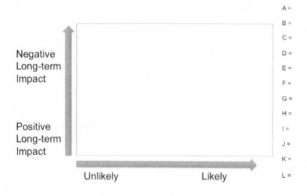

Appendix D - Colors Mind Tool

GREEN	Red / Orange
• Energy that pulls you forward and supercharges your system • Plants / trees giving off oxygen - Visualize breathing 100% pure O2 • Wide scan focus • With each inhale, allow eyes to relax and see WIDE angle • Allow the green to enter and charge the body.	• Energy that PUSHES you forward like solar waves arriving on your back • Warm energy • With each exhale, allow eyes to focus on a single point and feel the red energy push you forward)
Blue	**White**
• Energy like a blue laser or refreshingly cool blue lake • Cooling energy with wide scan focus • Warming energy with narrow, laser beam focus • With each inhale, the blue intensifies, along with its associated concepts	• Energy that envelopes and calms you • Peace, Stillness, Cerebral • Inhale: white energy descends from clouds and wraps you up in peace and calm
Brown	**Mixed Colors**
• Energy that pulls you forward and faster • Earth – Gravity • Falling toward the earth, as it spins • Exhale: surrender and gravity does the work for you	• Energy pulsations, waves or sparks • Like wildflowers or twinkling stars • Runs up and down the spine, as a quick charge or boost, tapping into each color briefly and making you instantly more alert

Appendix E - FSR Run Template

Objective	
Theme	
Stats	
Setting	
Yin - yang	
Guide focus	

Pre-run ritual	
Warm-up focus	
Micro Challenge	
Release trigger	
Workout Plan	
Post-run ritual	

Visit **www.flowstatecoaching.com** for
inspiring videos and other resources to help you
continually improve and stay motivated.

About the Author

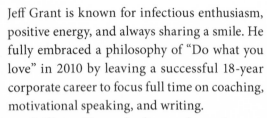

Jeff Grant is known for infectious enthusiasm, positive energy, and always sharing a smile. He fully embraced a philosophy of "Do what you love" in 2010 by leaving a successful 18-year corporate career to focus full time on coaching, motivational speaking, and writing.

Jeff has a 20-year background in endurance and adventure sports. He has finished some of the toughest events on the planet, including the Marathon des Sables (a weeklong stage race through the Moroccan Sahara), the Ultra Trail du Mont Blanc (a 166KM extremely mountainous run in the Alps), numerous ultra marathons, Ironman Hawaii and other long distance triathlons, mountaineering expeditions, and even some shark diving.

In 2010, Jeff branched out from traditional endurance sports to complete the grueling SEALFIT Kokoro Camp, a 50-hour non-stop, no-sleep crucible modeled after the US Navy SEAL's *Hell Week* and designed to teach mental toughness and test participant's limits across many spectrums. After several years of hard work, Jeff earned a unique civilian instructor position in the cadre for this grueling and transformational mental and physical challenge.

Jeff is a qualified yoga teacher, with over 600 hours of training courses and 20+ years of practice. He also completed numerous CrossFit and other movement-related certifications, ran a CrossFit gym and functional training center for 5+ years, and studied the Pose Method® directly from Dr. Nicolas Romanov.

Jeff has coached thousands of runners in workshops in Switzerland and the US, runs the Hillseeker® online coaching business, and enjoys

348

tapping into his corporate experience as a motivational speaker for businesses and teams. He also enjoys playing jazz trombone, blues harmonica, and African drums, as well as dancing Lindy Hopp.

Jeff lives in Zurich, Switzerland with his wife Becky and a large collection of musical instruments, yoga mats, running shoes, and adventure gear.

Endnotes

1. Extended version in the Appendix
2. May 1, 2008 http://www.chattanoogan.com/2008/5/1/127019/Local-Senior-Olympic-Participants-Get.aspx
3. *A runner's high depends on cannabinoid receptors in mice* PNAS 2015 112 (42) 13105-13108; published ahead of print October 5, 2015, doi:10.1073/pnas.1514996112
4. *Leptin Suppresses the Rewarding Effects of Running via STAT3 Signaling in Dopamine Neurons*, Fernandes, Maria Fernanda A. et al., Cell Metabolism, Volume 22, Issue 4, 741 - 749
5. https://en.wikipedia.org/wiki/Leptin
6. https://www.psychologytoday.com/blog/feeling-it/201309/20-scientific-reasons-start-meditating-today
7. Wikipedia https://en.wikipedia.org/wiki/Yin_and_yang
8. http://facetoface.org/
9. http://bit.ly/hillwods
10. https://en.wikipedia.org/wiki/Racewalking
11. http://www.runningusa.org/index.cfm?fuseaction=news.details&ArticleId=333

Made in the USA
Middletown, DE
02 August 2020

14142403R00220